INTERIOR DESIGN
MASTER CLASS

INTERIOR DESIGN
MASTER CLASS

100 LESSONS FROM AMERICA'S FINEST DESIGNERS ON THE ART OF DECORATION

Edited by

CARL DELLATORE

Rizzoli
NEW YORK

New York Paris London Milan

Contents

INTRODUCTION | Carl Dellatore   6

Theory   9

RESTRAINT | Steven Volpe   10
AUTHENTICITY | Steven Gambrel   12
NEGATIVE SPACE | Katie Eastridge   16
AWARENESS | Barbara Barry   18
HISTORY | Arthur Dunnam   22
INTUITION | Amanda Nisbet   26
EVOLUTION | David Easton   28
INTEGRATION | S. Russell Groves   32
CONFIDENCE | Robert Stilin   36
RESPECT AND TRANSGRESSION | William T. Georgis   40
PSYCHOLOGY | Barry Goralnick   42
PERSONALIZATION | David Mann   46
ARCHAEOLOGY | Suzanne Tucker   50
VALUE | Scott Salvator   54
INTEGRITY | Shawn Henderson   56
TEACHERS | Vicente Wolf   60
TASTE | David Kleinberg   62
PASSION | Robert Passal   66
ASPIRATION | Stephen Sills   68
PERSPECTIVE | Benjamin Noriega Ortiz   72

Structure   75

SYMMETRY | Mark Cunningham   76
FLOOR PLANS | Etienne Coffinier and Ed Ku   80
PORTALS | Richard Mishaan   82
PROPORTION | Campion Platt   86

SILHOUETTE | Jayne and Joan Michaels   90
SCALE | Juan Montoya   92
COMMUNICATION | Windsor Smith   96
FRAMING | Salvatore LaRosa   98
DEFINITIONS | Mary Douglas Drysdale   102
JUXTAPOSITION | Matthew White and Frank Webb 106
INTIMACY | Bobby McAlpine   108
PLANES | Daniel Sachs and Kevin Lindores   112
DESTINATIONS | Alan Tanksley   114
GEOMETRY | Eric Cohler   118

Style   121

STYLE | Suzanne Kasler   122
VINTAGE MODERN | Thomas O'Brien   126
MODERNITY | Alan Wanzenberg   130
TRADITION | Alexa Hampton   132
GLAMOUR | Kelly Wearstler   136
SIMPLICITY | Jesse Carrier and Mara Miller   140
EXUBERANCE | Anthony Baratta   144
FAMILY | Eve Robinson   148
NUANCE | Suzanne Rheinstein   152
WELCOMING SPACES | Timothy Corrigan   156
LUXURY | Tom Scheerer   160
TRENDS | Madeline Stuart   164
COMFORT | Bunny Williams   168
HUMOR | Harry Heissmann   172
REINVENTION | Miles Redd   176
SEX | Martyn Lawrence Bullard   180
SCANDINAVIA | Rhonda Eleish and Edie van Breems   184
FANTASY | Raji Radhakrishnan   188

Process   191

TRUST | Meredith Harrington   192

PROBLEM SOLVING | Celeste Cooper   194

TEXTURE | Timothy Brown   196

MATERIALS | Terry Hunziker   198

LIGHT | Victoria Hagan   202

RELATIONSHIPS | Barry Dixon   204

THE REVEAL | Anthony Cochran   208

PATTERN | Markham Roberts   210

EXPECTATIONS | Paul Siskin   214

COMMISSIONS | Amy Lau   216

QUALITY | Thad Hayes   218

EDITING | Jane Schwab and Cindy Smith   222

LAYERING | Alex Papachristidis   224

Elements   227

COLLECTING | Nancy Braithwaite   228

PATINA | Kathryn Scott   230

ANTIQUES | Timothy Whealon   232

CURATION | Martha Angus   236

LIGHTING | Jan Showers   238

TEXTILES | Kathryn M. Ireland   242

BOOKS | Rose Tarlow   244

PROVENANCE | Thomas Jayne   248

CRAFT | Brad Ford   252

ALCHEMY | Glenn Gissler   256

ART | Brian J. McCarthy   260

SOURCING | Emily Summers   264

COLOR | Mario Buatta   268

GRAY | Laura Bohn   272

WHITE | Darryl Carter   276

RED | Alessandra Branca   280

NEUTRALS | Mariette Himes Gomez and Brooke Gomez   282

BLACK | Kara Mann   286

RARITY | Ernest de la Torre   288

Inspiration   291

INSPIRATION | Thomas Pheasant   292

JAZZ | Sandra Nunnerley   296

CLASSICAL MUSIC | Michael Simon   298

PARIS | Penny Drue Baird   302

AMERICA | Jeffrey Bilhuber   306

AUTOMOBILES | Joe Nahem   310

FASHION | Robert Couturier   314

FOOD | Carl D'Aquino and Francine Monaco   318

POETRY | Ann Pyne, McMillen, Inc.   320

JAPONISME | Ellie Cullman   324

LITERATURE | Maureen Footer   328

TRAVEL | Matthew Patrick Smyth   330

COUTURE | Charlotte Moss   334

FENG SHUI | Bruce Bierman   338

CROSS-CULTURALISM | Jiun Ho   342

FILM | Stephen Shadley   344

INDEX   348

PHOTOGRAPHY CREDITS   351

ACKNOWLEDGMENTS   352

Introduction

CARL DELLATORE

In 1897, when the great novelist Edith Wharton and her friend, architect Ogden Codman Jr., published *The Decoration of Houses*, the world hovered on the brink of new movements, technologies, and modes of production that would radically transform the built world. Wharton and Codman sought to make sense of both this ferment and the past—recent and distant—for the lay reader, purporting to set forth the rational relationship between structure and surface, architecture and ornament. Wharton proclaimed, "It is with the decorator's work alone that these pages are concerned," and in so doing, she established her book as the springboard from which any informed knowledge of interior decoration began.

The twentieth century saw a great many interior decorators who carried Wharton's precepts forward through their own aesthetic lens: Elsie de Wolfe, Rose Cumming, Eleanor Brown, Frances Elkins, Dorothy Draper, Sister Parish, Albert Hadley, Joe D'Urso, Angelo Donghia, Ward Bennett, Michael Taylor, Billy Baldwin, and Mark Hampton, among others. Some of these designers wrote landmark books setting forth their own conception of interior design, such as *Billy Baldwin Decorates*, *Mark Hampton on Decorating*, and Elsie de Wolfe's *The House in Good Taste*.

By the late 1980s, interior design had hit its stride, bringing with it an outpouring of monographs, as the design of one's own space had become a national, if not a global, obsession. Yet there have been few attempts to provide, in the manner of Wharton and Codman, a comprehensive account of what the industry's finest practitioners believe works in interior design today, and why.

While I would not attempt to draw a direct comparison to *The Decoration of Houses*, I have always envisioned *Interior Design Master Class* as a modern-day answer to Wharton and Codman's accomplishment by applying their room-by-room and element-by-element organization of the subject of decoration to its contemporary creators. In the voices of more than one hundred preeminent American designers, this is a comprehensive guide to the elements of interiors, including planes, portals, furniture, and color, to name a very few, as well as a meditation on related subjects such as archaeology, psychology, and literature.

Today, the welcome democratization of decoration that has taken place since the advent of the internet continues to expand, and more people than ever are interested in the design of their home. *Interior Design Master Class* offers a view into the world of the finest practitioners in the decorative arts, uncovering the intellectual and philosophic roots of this most ancient and necessary of arts. My hope is that it will instruct and inspire a wide audience, from the curious layperson to students of design as well as practicing professionals.

We all inhabit dwellings of some kind; the more thoughtful the attention we exert upon them, the more our infrastructure—our whole built world—is beautified.

A soaring eighteen-foot ceiling presented a particular challenge in how to bring the volume of this Madeline Stuart-designed living room in Los Angeles down to a human scale. An equally expansive chandelier, six feet in diameter and hung low on a long chain, accomplishes the task by lowering the center of gravity.

THEORY

Restraint

STEVEN VOLPE

Restraint, to me, is an ideal. I see it as an ongoing effort to pare back to the essence of an idea, so as to arrive at a design strategy that confers authenticity. My aspiration, no matter what the project is, remains the same: to give full expression to my clients' way of being in the world and to marshal resources efficiently in order to produce an interior that reflects their own lives—and what they wish for most passionately.

Restraint, as I think about it, is an ethos. I surrender to this obligation as I work to make a scaffold for living that not only functions well, but also *represents* a client to themselves and to others. I discovered this way of working as a child, struggling to give voice to an emerging sense of self. I found that I could say things with objects, their selection, and their arrangement. Objects became my words, and that is how I became a designer.

So much of what we see in design these days reveals another way of thinking. Designers establish their own language and their own sensibilities and preferences, and clients go to them specifically for that. I am more interested in the process and dialogue, a deep and sustained conversation that, like a good dinner party, does not know where it will go until it finds its way. I like to learn about my clients and discover together what we might do to make their home come to life.

One thing I do insist on is the value of authenticity and the need to parse resources to achieve the greatest degree of authenticity possible. We avoid the generic, the expected, and the sought after in favor of the lesser-known, the peculiar, and the extraordinary. This is how we approach not only the selection of objects, fabrics, lighting, and so on, but also—and very much so—their commingling. Objects, like people, accrue meaning as they meet others, and this is a process that takes place in real time. Of course, we ultimately settle on an arrangement that is more or less fixed, at least for the life of the interior. But a dynamic tension remains, however ineffable, because the elements have not been selected and composed with stable meanings in mind. We orchestrate major and minor elements as delicately as we can, certain that the sum of the parts—their polyphony, if you will—is greater than the accumulation of individual characteristics.

Intelligence about quality is essential to a design process steeped in restraint. So is a keen sense of value. The measure of value, whether of an object or an ensemble, has nothing to do with cost. We work to counter habits and norms that demand we produce the tried and true. That means we are constantly looking, studying, and searching, and we encourage those who choose to work with us to join a journey to the unknown. Steering clear of the obvious somehow yields elegance again and again, so long as it is governed by a sense of restraint. A potent sofa demands a humble fabric; they engage and speak thoughtfully to each other and are then prepared to meet whatever other objects surround them. Individual elements should never shout or demand attention; they should reveal their meanings slowly, often over a long duration, to sustain a passionate engagement for our clients.

Perhaps the best way I can say this is to offer an analogy: making an interior is like preparing a stew. You don't take everything you like and throw it in a pot, hoping for the best. Instead, you make selections, edit and edit again, and determine the overall intention. Choosing ingredients, settling on their proportions, attending to the nuances of color and texture are all things vital to a good stew *and* a good room. Design is about life being lived—it's as simple as that. There is no need to oversalt.

Authenticity

STEVEN GAMBREL

Authenticity in interior design is best defined by example and by experiencing programmed spaces filled with life.

I travel extensively, searching for expressions of authentic lifestyles. I have visited grand Irish Georgian manor houses, Belgian castles, and Italian villas and palaces. The private houses I visit are often teeming with life, which is revealed through layers of alterations that make the rooms rich with meaning and complexity. I see these structures as extensions of the inhabitants and a mechanism for delivering emotional experiences to the occupants and visitors of the rooms. The architecture of these houses varies considerably, from Gothic to Georgian, but the true "style" of the houses comes from the lifestyle of the occupants within the walls.

The characters I have met have been mostly witty, kind, eccentric family types, dressed in well-made but slightly worn outfits, gently aged from years of walks in gardens and stone halls. Typically, there were dogs and piles of boots in baskets lined up on chipped stone floors. There were large, charred chimney breasts with firewood stacked in corners, resting casually next to refined tapestries and polished wooden tables. The alchemy of rough and refined elements combines seamlessly. I took visual note of the way that lunch was served, for example, and the simple materials and casual approach to daily routine. This search for the authentic, as interpreted by someone living within generations of collected environments, helped me better understand the continuum of the creative process as an ever-evolving interpretation of one's environment.

Although I have photographed endless historic details, observing living environments has influenced my design ideas most and heightened my understanding of

The large public room of a loft in Lower Manhattan features walls clad in Mexican bark paper, while the custom-designed steel cabinets, which emulate safes found in the building when it was a manufacturing facility, flank a painting by Mark Francis. The contrasting textures pay homage to the industrial nature of the original space.

authenticity in design. The occupants have their own personal taste, no doubt, but they also bear the influences derived from generations of collectors and the decorators and architects who preceded them. The variety of architectural styles and decorative periods within a collection of local house tours has aided in my education of what parts of the decoration were textbook examples and what parts were the works of an "eccentric" with style beyond the norm. The moments of finding examples of the unusual have been the moments when I truly felt inspired to return and propose something unique to my clients. In one gray, secluded castle in Ireland, the extravagant colors and decorations of the public rooms had such spirit and uncharacteristic wit that I needed the backstory: designer Oliver Messel had been a distant relative of the castle's owner and had spent a summer there in the 1930s elaborating on period rooms until they reflected the deeply unique personality of his patron and the dynamic period of the time, while remaining historic and relevant to the fabric of the house.

When trying to fully visualize the essence of a particular region or decorative period, I look for the house or garden altered or created by an expatriate who came and adopted the region as his own, filtering the best of what he saw while building an edited version of the local vernacular. The expat's twentieth-century interpretation reveals just as much about his generation and values as it does about the values of the previous generations and region of his adopted country. It seems to be a basic human desire to contribute to the social and physical vision of the time in which we live.

On a memorable trip to Italy, several academics suggested I visit La Foce in the Val d'Orcia region to truly understand the essence of a typical Renaissance-style Italian garden. The lasting irony was that the garden was entirely created by an English architect named Cecil Pinsent for an American heiress, and together they discovered what it meant to be authentic through their vision—circa 1927—of a

timeless landscape. I left inspired to produce work layered in meaning, as my personal contribution to the brief time we have to learn and create.

On a trip to Ireland, upon first viewing Russborough House, an enormous eighteenth-century Irish Palladian manor house, I stood speechless in front of the massive edifice. Soft, quiet, humble, and effortless, it summoned the memory of a youthful moment when I was a student of architecture at the University of Virginia, off for a summer sketching in the Veneto and measuring the villas of Palladio. Palladio's proportions have influenced centuries of designers in multiple regions, including my university's grounds. They provided a connecting thread through time, with structures that seem familiar yet are entirely characteristic of their place and period.

At Russborough House, I explored every room, searching for a relic of authenticity to take home in the form of a shape or color. Upon entering a particularly extraordinary room, I gasped at the wicked use of color, modern beyond modern, only centuries old. I did not need to understand the origin or reference; I only wanted to absorb the color so I could release it on some unsuspecting client, probably in lacquer and most likely on upper Fifth or Park Avenues.

Weeks later, on a long worktable in New York, I gathered samples of waxed, wired oak, raw plaster, and glowing ebonized trim pieces modeled on my travel sketches and placed them next to layered scraps of rugged Belgium linen and finely woven silk velvet in chartreuse and salmon. I settled on a scheme that seemed irreverent, oddly familiar, timeless, and somehow relevant to today.

Recently, a friend suggested that the central tension in my work is "evolution versus creationism." There are houses and environments that have evolved over centuries, adapting to changing conditions and new generations, and there are houses that take two years to design and build, yet still are evolved, fully developed, and entirely relevant.

Both are authentic.

In an eighteenth-century sea captain's house in Sag Harbor, New York, owned by Gambrel, this room is in the oldest part of the structure. Found antique wood paneling, an ode to the flotsam that early settlers used to build and decorate, was installed and painted royal purple. The painting, by Belgian artist Louis Van Lint, is from 1954.

Negative Space

KATIE EASTRIDGE

In visual art, negative space is the blank or empty space between positive forms. In studying the wood reliefs of Dada artist Jean Arp, I discovered how to look at blank spaces and how to envision and create newly enlivened forms out of the nothingness. In interior design, the negative space exists between the furnishings in a room. When the negative spaces are well considered, the room becomes an active and enveloping experience; the eye is engaged and finds relationships and juxtapositions. When negative space is handled ingeniously, the sum total of the parts in a room becomes indelible.

Negative space takes the superficial and makes powerful connections between artfully positioned objects, possessions, and furniture. When a space and its contents beckon, there is a buzz, an atmosphere for living; there is also a desire to enter, to be sheltered and inspired, and to be comfortable.

I first learned about negative space in a life-drawing class as a very young artist. Sitting at a drawing board looking carefully at the negative spaces in between the torso and limbs, I learned to transcribe the three-dimensional human form before me into a two-dimensional pencil drawing. The negative spaces revealed how to fit the puzzle pieces of the body together. The satisfaction I got from this kind of problem solving engaged me as a child and became a lifelong habit.

Later, in graduate school, I found a mentor, Henry Holmes Smith, a philosopher and photographer who taught me the necessity of another kind of negative space. From him, I learned the value of patience, timing, and silence in the stillness and blackness of the darkroom. In life, it is imperative to make room for quietude amid all the activity.

My creative soul also depends on the negative space provided by sleep. During the day, I move at a breakneck pace to accommodate and solve the questions and problems that arise in a busy interior design studio. By the end of every day, I try to move each design to the best possible place. Some decisions feel good, others uncertain, but I never worry. In my mind's eye while asleep, there is a tiny camera roving over every room in progress. The camera rolls around looking at each relationship; it goes high and low and shows views from all vantage points. Through this visualization, I see interiors more clearly than any drawing can demonstrate. I see the successes, but mostly I see what doesn't work, and the next morning I can adjust the forms accordingly. The clearing of the mind in deep repose anchors the root of my creativity.

Making room for negative space in our busy lives is as important as harnessing visual or energetic negative space in design. Whatever you are creating, it cannot be brilliantly achieved with the constant presence of phone alerts or the demands of work and home. It is a necessary and responsible discipline to work without distraction some of the time every day. Nurturing and protecting the negative space in your life is a requirement for inspiration and creativity. It is good for you and good for your work.

Take a walk in a new place. Go to a museum you've never seen before. Visit World Heritage Sites—my personal goal is to visit them all—and marvel at the natural and built wonders on our planet. Read a new poem each week. Then read it again and let it resonate. Look at the sky. Watch the sun come up. These experiences great and small add to who you are and affect how you relate to others and the home you inhabit. Take care of your negative space.

A canvas by American artist Rockwell Kent hangs above the fireplace in this room decorated in subtle shades. Textures abound and include a nubby check, a taupe stripe, and mohair in the seating area in the foreground. A work by contemporary American painter Joan Snyder hangs on the rear wall.

Awareness

 BARBARA BARRY

I'm listening, but while I'm listening, I'm also having a silent and parallel conversation with myself analyzing, comparing, and cataloging everything about you and around you. I'm taking it all in, and as you are speaking, *I* am taken in.

Perhaps it's the shape of your head and how it's framed by the window, or maybe it's that wave of your hair and how it mirrors the ruffle on your blouse's neckline. It could be the round cup sitting on its perfectly round saucer and how it is placed on the square place mat in front of you.

The whole composition vies for my attention and it is equally, if not more, compelling than what is being spoken.

I can't seem to escape these compositions; they are important to me and always have been. I adjust the crooked painting when entering a room; straighten the book to parallel the table. I have done so without even knowing it my whole life and to the extent that if I am unable to correct what's in my prevue I am hard pressed to pay attention.

Am I proud of this peculiarity?

Yes, I am. Because over time, I have come to realize it is *who I am*, and I see how it has led to a life in design. I find it magical (and fortunate) that you can use what drives you crazy and make it your work—or rather, make it work for you. So while you can't escape it, you *can* learn to embrace it and cultivate it as you go.

I cannot escape looking at the '*everyday beauty*' of my world. Noticing how the color of my morning coffee changes as it mixes with the milk in my pristine white porcelain cup . . . always subtly different and always altogether mesmerizing. When outside I glance up to see the fuzzy white arc of a jet contrail and it becomes a minimalist modern painting in a clear blue sky.

For me, life is a series of beautiful compositions, little ones and big ones alike, each a balance of form, color, and light.

A symphony of soft celadon pays homage to the cool Northern California light in this luxurious living room. When restoring this landmark residence everything from the plaster moldings to the Belgian black-and-nickel fireplace to the furnishings was custom designed to create a tonal painting and a feeling of harmony.

OVERLEAF: The golden afternoon light of Southern California sets this dining room aglow. Custom sideboards, mirrors, and lamps are repeated on all four sides of the room anchoring the wood-grained table and vintage T. H. Robsjohn-Gibbings dining chairs. A Danielle Mourning photograph serves as a window to a garden beyond.

Noticing the color of the sky in the early morning and comparing it to the color of the midday sky and then to the deepening sky in the evening is a dialogue of nuance, variation and mood. The awareness of these subtle differences helps me when I'm working with color to create the mood for a room.

For me, this is where design lives—in the differences between things large or small, textured or smooth, geometric or organic.

Observing the shapes of leaves in a tree to the shape of the tree itself, and then to see the shape of that tree on the hill teaches me about scale and proportion. It teaches me that each piece is part of a larger whole, and how nothing stands alone. Understanding this helps me understand the importance of the interplay between each component when creating a room. What shape the pillow on the sofa might be or the shape of the lampshade sitting next to that sofa and how all these things, including the shape of the sofa itself sit in the room; how they work together to create the larger composition of the room as a whole.

The *daily* observation of my surroundings has built in me the capacity to discern and, hopefully, be a better designer. And good design, for me, is anything that is resolved . . . the extraneous stripped away. Think back to that hillside with the shape of that tree on the hillside, a perfect and timeless composition and how you never tire of it. Not unlike the simple black dress, worn year after year.

Or Rockefeller Center in New York City, the epitome of the modern age then and now.

Each has a critical proportion, a balanced composition.

Looking closely at the things that endure, man-made or natural, heightens my awareness and aids in my own critical process of design.

So the next time someone is speaking and you find yourself unable to pay attention because the sky is turning the color of ripe peaches, don't worry. When something is said and you can't remember what it was because you were busy arranging the salt to line up with the pepper, don't be alarmed. You were working. You were taking note. It is who you are.

And that understanding of yourself is the privilege of *your* lifetime.

History

Wall paneling upholstered in grass cloth, custom-designed carpeting, a 1970s brass ceiling pendant, and a custom iron-and-quartzite coffee table harmonize to create a welcoming sitting area in this house on New York's Long Island. The painting is by Santi Moix.

OVERLEAF: The original Louis XVI boiserie paneling on the walls of this dining room in a 1920s residence in Connecticut mirrors the tones of an Amritsar carpet from the late nineteenth century. A 1940s Venetian chandelier, a canvas by David Hockney, and a sculpture by Alexander Calder complete the tableau.

The role of history in design, for me, consists of three aspects: design and how it manifested throughout history; the history of design, which focuses on how the practice developed and noteworthy individuals who have distinguished themselves as designers; and our own personal histories, which establish a filter and framework for how we process the elements of design that we are exposed to.

What we know about ancient civilizations comes from the physical evidence left behind. Aside from human remains—which tell a story unlocked by advancing technology—the most startling and informative clues to what life was like in the early days of civilization come from objects of beauty. The lines, color, and form of humble shards of pottery convey that while man was satisfying his most basic needs, he also found time to incorporate decorative embellishments into everyday objects. These decorations went above and beyond the mere utilitarian; they exhibited design. In every ancient civilization we have discovered, again and again we find this obsession with embellishment. And it occurs not just in the tombs of the exalted and powerful or the magnificent ruins of ancient cities, but also in the everyday objects used by the masses.

Venice remains one of the world's most richly preserved examples of man's historical obsession with design. At a time when much of the world was still surviving in rather primitive conditions, in Venice there blossomed a civilization that devoted immense amounts of wealth, manpower, and time to pushing the boundaries of beauty. The result was a concentration of fifteenth-century structures—some even earlier—so opulent and beyond anything that the world had produced to date that experiencing them today still brings chills to the spine.

From the remnants of ancient history cataloged in countless books and museums to the still-living treasures of recent history, proof abounds that humans are innately fascinated with design and have a strong desire to incorporate beauty into their lives.

Much has been written about the individuals who feature in the history of design, and I don't plan to linger on them here. While countless lesser-known talents certainly preceded them, perhaps some of the earliest household names associated with the elevation of interior design might be considered architect-designers. In the sixteenth century, Andrea Palladio's classical structures influenced by his study of ancient Rome brought architectural references from the exterior in. Frescoes developed in tandem with the ordered architectural envelope added further enrichment. This kind of attention to detail in a residential interior—rather than a cathedral or palace—was a new direction, and in hindsight it certainly foreshadowed where the residential interior was headed. William Kent and Robert Adam had flourishing practices that seamlessly brought together architecture and interior design, creating environments of rich detail fashioned by the greatest artists and artisans of the day. These spaces were designed to impress the visitor and establish the wealth, power, and superiority of the owner.

With the rise of the merchant class in the nineteenth century, the segment of society that could afford to indulge in the embellishment of residential interiors ballooned dramatically. Furthermore, the romanticism of the age emphasized mood and atmosphere: the home was becoming a cocoon of safety where one would seek private time with family and friends. And for the first time, rooms of real comfort began to rank equally with chambers designed to impress.

As design progressed into the twentieth century, England boasted the Institute of British Decorators with more than two hundred members; in America at the same

time, Edith Wharton and Ogden Codman published *The Decoration of Houses*, which proved to be a true turning point aesthetically. By advocating the elimination of "Victorian clutter," the book paved the way for cleaner, more edited styles that were beginning to emerge. By the time of the 1920s and '30s, the masterful practitioners of interior design, interior architecture, and furniture design became numerous. These visionaries studied what came before them and distilled it into a new aesthetic tone that rang true for the time.

Today, as in fashion, interiors exhibit an anything-goes attitude. More than ever, we can forge our own aesthetic path independent of the mainstream. We draw upon both the innovative materials and technological advancements of modern times to achieve this, as well as the elements of the past that still speak to us. Studying, appreciating, and understanding its history furthers our ability to put design today in its proper context and perspective.

Finally, I want to speak to our personal histories and how they affect our perception of and reaction to design. Each of us is not only the product of our genetic makeup, but also the product of our personal history and experiences. If we grew up in modest circumstances, for example, we may long for the opulence we feel was denied us or perceive all things opulent as ostentatious or showy.

From what I have observed, it is a rare individual who has an utterly innate sense of taste. Far more common is the "inner eye" that has evolved through the experiences of life. And while there are more significant aspects of our personalities that define us, don't discount the personal aesthetic filter: it likely weighs more heavily on how we behave, what we desire, and the things that we avoid than any of us even realize.

In our quest to be current, it can be easy to overlook history. But I would argue that we owe all we have today, both good and bad, to what came before. Even for those who might feel immune to aesthetics, I propose that design in one form or another resonates with the core of the human condition and has done so since civilized man came to be.

Intuition

AMANDA NISBET

I confess that I have never been good at clearly articulating my design process, and for good reason. While the aesthetic of many decorators that I admire draws on balance and symmetry and the pursuit of a series of rules, that has never been my way. Rather, I tend to favor intuition.

I can trace my intuitive approach to two influences. The first is my experience of Italy as an art history student—not Italian design, but what I call the Italian ethos. Living in the land of grand gestures proved immensely liberating. You'd see a woman who wasn't conventionally attractive, yet she'd throw on a purple corduroy blazer, wrap an orange scarf around her neck, and take off on a chartreuse Vespa, and she'd be stunning. That belief in trusting your taste and following your nose made a great impression on me.

No less an influence was my life as an actress, which preceded my design career. I found it easy to become someone else when handed a script. What came harder was improvisation. You inhabit a character's persona when you do improv, but who that person is, what she thinks, and how she responds has to spring entirely from one's own imagination moment by moment. From a design standpoint, this technique taught me to respond intuitively to a space—I have an immediate sense of how a room should be the moment I walk into it—and, once I've absorbed a client's needs, to let my imagination build on that intuition to create a design.

Let me add, however, that there is a critical difference between trusting your instincts and winging it. It's true that some people have better instincts than others, but intuition can nonetheless be trained and strengthened like a muscle. The key lies in connecting your instinctive-response mechanism to memory—emotional memory in particular. The nose that I follow is informed by a lifetime of indelible tableaux, like the Italian woman on her Vespa. Countless such experiences have informed and enriched my design sensibility, and they collectively comprise the core of my working method. And anyone, whatever his or her philosophy, can benefit from strengthening the instinct muscle.

The living room of a townhouse I designed on Manhattan's Upper East Side exemplifies this approach. The space featured a bay window overlooking a sunlit rear garden, and the moment I saw it, I knew I wanted to draw in that delightful sunshine with bright yellow curtains. While the rest of the decor remains more subdued, toward the project's conclusion, I found a pair of metal palm-leaf pendant fixtures that bordered on gauche, yet I knew instinctively that they'd perfectly complete the room. Rather than more proper, predictable lanterns or chandeliers, these outré characters gave the room a bit of edge—a whimsical kick— and brought it to life.

In another Manhattan apartment, this one for a glamorous couple that loved to entertain, I believed the living room should be a romantic one in which guests would linger; remembering my clients' love of the water, my instinct was to create a "midnight swim" room—an Upper East Side take on Capri's Blue Grotto. Both the blue silk wallcovering and the carpet shimmer with movement, and the fourteen-foot-long box-tufted blue sofa counters the ethereal, liquid quality with a clubby elegance. It was a counterintuitive impulse that proved just right.

Trusting your intuition can produce design magic. The great Paul Sills, who taught improvisation for the stage and was a founder of Chicago's legendary Second City theater, put it perfectly: "There is no technique," he said. "You just need a little respect for the invisible."

In a bold gesture embracing a pink palette, this Manhattan dining room is sheathed in a magenta silk wallpaper. The custom black carpet with subtle silver abstract motif adds to the drama, as does the black-glass tabletop.

Evolution

DAVID EASTON

Times of social and political turmoil always seem to be followed by the simplification, often radically, of design. One need only note that after the French Revolution, the rococo gave way to strict, spare neoclassicism; World War I, it might be said, engendered the Bauhaus.

Interior design today is a case in point.

Looking back on my career, I've seen several changes in the zeitgeist of design. After studying at Parsons, I received a traveling scholarship. One of the judges was Edward Wormley, the modernist furniture designer, and he told me, "When you return, give me a call." I did, and I stayed with him for several years. I was very lucky to work for him; his work gave me, in a sense, a preview of the future. Later, when I worked for Parish-Hadley, things were yet again different. It was all curtains—curtains, curtains, curtains! Sister Parish was very decorative; Albert Hadley, more architectural. And then when I began my own design practice in New York, there was a sense of abundance: tables, lamps, lampshades, trims, and multiple seating areas. Now things are much more edited, and people don't want as much fuss.

The bulk of my career's work has been for affluent people who have taken pleasure and time in decorating. Today, more and more, clients want everything yesterday, which I believe is in response to the speed at which society is evolving in this, the information age. I grew up with a settled-ness that now seems to speak of the twentieth century. In my grandmother's house in Oak Park, Illinois, there was a vast dining table. We had our meals there and enjoyed our lives together. My grandparents were very happy sitting on the front porch, playing cards. It was a wonderful way of living, but it seems lost today.

Everyone is in flux, often living in more than one place. The meaning of home and office are changing rapidly. Public spaces such as cafés, hotels, and restaurants have subsumed the former functions of the living room, the dining room, and even the boardroom. It is not uncommon at 8:00 a.m. or 8:00 p.m., or even on the weekend, for that matter, to see men and women around a table in a restaurant discussing business. And as the lines between home and work are blurred, so, too, are dress codes: casual Friday was the norm a decade ago as a break from a suit and tie, and now casual is the everyday norm.

Another important social change is the proliferation of visual information available on the Internet, which promotes multicultural influences in interior design. That access to information is causing a decline in culturally monocular aesthetics, in purely French or English rooms, for example. We now have interior design without national frontiers, which, in part, has caused the rapidly advancing move toward eclecticism.

The only thing certain about the future of design is that interiors will change again in the decades to come, in ways we cannot conceive, as society continues to evolve.

I believe decoration for the sake of decoration is over, and that the design of homes must be more direct in terms of function. That is, *if* we live at home. I don't mean that facetiously, but who knows what life is going to be? Will we take time to shop and cook? How will we feed and educate our families? These questions (and more like them) are yet to be answered, but one thing is certain: evolution will impact the home and, in turn, the way the home is designed.

Speaking personally, I look to Charles Darwin, author of *On the Origin of Species*, as the prophet of many of the changes we are experiencing today. When Darwin set out in 1831 on the *H. M. S. Beagle* to make his historic five-year circumnavigation of

In Easton's own home, this corner banquette was designed in a Louis XVI style and is juxtaposed by a brick-red lacquered oval table. The fireplace mantel is a copy of one that Easton saw in a villa in Tuscany, and the four pieces of art are nineteenth-century colored engravings of Naples and the Italian countryside.

the globe, he took a heroic chance in order to broadly scope the world; to understand what the world *was* was the first goal of his voyage. His observation was that the world evolves according to survival of the fittest.

Designers create environments for their clients, who have made their own voyage out into the world and found a house—an environment where they can love their families, enjoy their gardens, and, within a world of constant unknowable change, find peace and beauty in the long odyssey of life. But today that house—that home—is likely to be smaller, simpler in terms of furnishings, and inflected with both informality and a multicultural diversity of stylistic elements. To be an interior designer with longevity, I believe one must be aware of the present and future social context, which appears to be evolving at the speed of light.

Designers who do not heed society's evolutionary changes will go the way of the dodo. In design, as in life, there is survival of the fittest; designers who can respond to contemporary clients' demands are most likely to succeed.

An open floor plan in one of the Richard Meier buildings overlooking the Hudson River in New York City is ingeniously "divided" by a mahogany-and-glass folding screen, which separates a studied dining room from the rest of the space while maintaining spectacular views throughout.

Integration

S. RUSSELL GROVES

In his 1919 *Bauhaus Manifesto*, Walter Gropius said "The ultimate aim of all visual arts is the complete building." As an interior designer and architect, I can attest—passionately—to the truth of this sentence. During my education at the Rhode Island School of Design, I was fortunate to be exposed to a variety of artistic disciplines. I was drawn to many of them: photography, sculpture, filmmaking, and fashion, to name a few. I obtained a rather broad education in both the fine and applied arts and was ultimately proud to graduate as an architect.

What excited me about architecture was that it combined philosophy, math, science, and literature into a highly complicated, interrelated, and complex art form. In school, I learned a German word, *gesamtwerk*, used to describe my favorite works by Mies van der Rohe, Frank Lloyd Wright, and Le Corbusier. *Gesamtwerk* signifies a totalized work of art and architecture, in which both grand conception and minute details are unified into a consummate whole.

Wright designed not only the structure and layout of the Robie House in Chicago (and all his projects, for that matter), but also the furniture, the light fixtures, the faucets, the fabrics, and the silverware—even the wife's dress. He knew that a successful design exuded a harmony founded upon a deliberately holistic approach: "[Inside and outside] are of each other," Wright wrote. "Form and function thus become one in design and execution if the nature of materials and method and purpose are all in unison."

Great design begins with an overall concept of the entire space. Design mistakes are made when the space is laid out without considering the function from the start. A living room, for example, may have beautiful proportions, but if furniture cannot be properly arranged to promote an intimate exchange among its inhabitants, all is lost.

This generous living room incorporates a landscaped wraparound terrace with striking views of Park Avenue. Luxurious with a high level of craftsmanship, the expansive space allows for formal entertaining and also exudes a quiet, open feeling.

As a designer, one must consider all elements as integral to one another. Similarly, how one room relates to the next is essential. Rooms are like performers in a play; they must work together for the production to be a success. The design process involves the designer's aesthetic vision, the clients' goals, and the specifics or limitations of the actual space itself (which the designer is to mold), for a cohesive realization to be obtained.

In my process, I lay out the floor plan, while at the same time selecting and orchestrating the furniture and other appointments to complete the ensemble. I think about art and where it should be located. Art has its own voice and resonance, and is as important, if not more so, than any other element in the overall creation. In all of my projects, architecture, interior design, and art are inextricably intertwined.

Architects, interior designers, and decorators are involved in an innovative dialogue that traverses borders. One discipline is not more important than another when working on a design solution; what is important is the integrated solution itself.

The great advantage of a single architect-interior designer orchestrating all aspects of a project is that a holistic vision will prevail. Often, when working together, two separate firms (one architecture, and the other, interior-design) do not share a mutual vision, and the result is diluted or muddied. Commissioning a single designer who has the appropriate qualifications and skill set simplifies the process for the client because it means fewer meetings, less coordination, and less probability of something getting lost in translation.

The *Bauhaus Manifesto* provides the definitive exhortation to the architect-designer to marshal, in one grand scheme, both the functional and artistic elements of buildings and their interiors: "Architects, painters, and sculptors must recognize anew and learn to grasp the composite character of a building both as an entity and in its separate parts."

Almost a century later, this unity remains the seamless dream of every designer: to shape the envelope *and* its contents.

This dramatic open bathroom, with his-and-hers travertine-and-walnut vanities, is accentuated by abundant natural light.

OPPOSITE: Nestled in rural Connecticut, this converted barn retains the original distressed-wood beams and wide-plank flooring. Filled with a combination of custom and vintage furniture, including Shaker pieces, this bedroom is light, airy, and relaxed—the perfect retreat for a busy New York City couple and their children.

Confidence

 ROBERT STILIN

Some years ago, I took up bicycling. Four months after I started, I agreed to a high-intensity five-day ride in Colorado, which turned out to be one of the most challenging experiences of my life.

During the 500-mile ride, which included climbs up to 5,000 feet, I came close to giving up more than once. Each time, my mentor, who was also riding, helped me continue by encouraging me to focus only on the immediate next step: "Let's get through the first twenty-two miles, and we'll re-assess." Using this strategy, I was able to achieve something I had previously considered impossible. After completing the ride, I was overcome with joy, exhilaration, exhaustion, and an overwhelming sense of confidence and accomplishment. Taking that ride one step at a time is a metaphor for how I lead my life and my career. I use the same strategy when designing a 12,000-square-foot house, putting it together piece by piece and one room at a time. The range of experiences that each new day offers, be it through relationships, projects, or life challenges, reinforces my confidence and who I am as a designer.

When you live your life with self-assuredness and you know what you want and what you like, it allows you to continuously move forward and avoid getting stuck. Being empowered to make a choice, whether on a chair, a house, or an investment, is pivotal.

I am a decisive person by nature. That doesn't always mean I make the right decision, but by allowing myself the freedom to make mistakes, I have the invaluable opportunity to learn from them. Ironically, this freedom also results in fewer mistakes. There is nothing to fear in failure; it teaches us that there is always a solution to every problem. This philosophy has exponentially increased my self-confidence not only as a

A 1970s slipper chair by Kappa covered in boiled wool stands in front of cabinets by Ico Parisi. The work above the cabinets is Richard Prince's *Untitled*, 2009. Above the mantel is a 2007 Damien Hirst painting.

OVERLEAF: In the dining room of the designer's home in East Hampton, New York, a set of 1940s vintage oak dining chairs by Charles Dudouyt sidle up to a custom oak-and-bronze table. A grand-scaled photograph by Frank Thiel anchors one wall; to the right of it is a vintage English tubular steel–framed chair in its original leather.

designer, but also as a father, a brother, a friend, and a person in this world.

Learn by example from the people in your life—those who are fearless make the best teachers. Observe their process and apply it to yourself and your own story. You'll notice that self-actualized people are consistently open, adaptable, and resourceful. Fear and inflexibility can result in disaster. Designers need to be open to the inevitable organic evolution of a project, allowing every decision to inform and reinforce the next one. This openness provides opportunities for new ideas and innovative solutions that might never have come to light if one had rigidly stuck to a plan. In design as in life, there are an infinite number of good choices and successful outcomes for every situation, and it's your job to discover them.

As a designer, confidence means accepting that you don't know everything and recognizing the opportunity for self-discovery, growth, and evolution in that knowledge. It's OK to not have all the answers, but it's vital to constantly expose yourself to new ideas. Go to places you might not normally visit and explore. Embrace new environments. Touch, feel, and smell; fully immerse yourself and experience the elements. Stand barefoot on the rug, rub the towel on your body, demystify the objects, and enter the picture frame. Absorb, absorb, absorb.

Most importantly, never keep anything you don't like, and always strive to be honest with yourself. Realizing what you want, and what you are comfortable with, results in a more successful project.

In the end, confidence in design, as in life, comes down to the answers to a few core questions: Does it make sense? Is it going to be comfortable? Are you going to enjoy it? Does it feel good? And, most importantly, does it make you happy?

Respect and Transgression

WILLIAM T. GEORGIS

Rather than address a single topic, I'd like to explore two opposing yet related topics: respect and transgression. To respect something is to consider it worthy, valuable, and dear, something you refrain from interfering with. To transgress is to go beyond a limit, to violate a law. I have always been intrigued by both and endeavor to incorporate them in my practice.

These themes can come into play in the context of a design or architectural project. Whether in an urban, suburban, or rural setting, projects have a physical context that consists of the existing interior and exterior architecture, the adjacent buildings, and the topography or surrounding landscape. With some projects, I inherit an extraordinary context worthy of respect and restoration. It could be an amazing neoclassical or modernist interior. I employ one of two strategies; one is to respect the context and work within the language of the space, as I did with the restoration of the interiors of the landmark Lever House in New York, where the interior design is at peace with the interior architecture.

The other approach is to reinforce the interior architecture but work against the context in furnishings, which is my usual strategy. In a remarkable Beaux-Arts Manhattan townhouse, I restored the existing interior architecture and opted for a decidedly nontraditional furniture plan. A conventional plan with multiple seating arrangements was eschewed for a single arrangement consisting of a large, round, custom-designed sofa surrounded by a variety of baroque and neoclassical antiques and contemporary art on the periphery. I'm not always fortunate enough to inherit significant settings, but the same principles can work regardless. In the case of new construction or gut renovations, I have the luxury of creating my own interior context, generated from my response to program and client.

Patronage also brings into play the concepts of respect and transgression. Design is an extremely intimate affair, and clients are not always able to articulate their dreams or willing to share their deepest desires. It is the task of the designer to intuit what it is they need, to make a place in the world for them. For instance, with one client I sensed an unconventional, prurient interest in the affairs of others. The design of his loft was inspired by Greek temples, with the cella—the area that housed sacred cult sculptures—made of black steel; containing a gym, kitchen, and bath; and built between a double row of columns. I introduced a transparent glass bubble to be used as a guest room; a movable sheer curtain provided the only means of privacy. The client was thrilled. For another seemingly conventional client, I designed a bullet-riddled mirrored powder room after a more decorous proposal was deemed "too tasteful." Clients never cease to amaze and inspire me.

Herman Melville said, "There are times when even the most potent governor must wink at transgression in order to preserve the laws inviolate for the future." I couldn't agree more.

A mirrored disco ball conjuring the 1970s, two slipper chairs in a bold zebra pattern, and a monumentally scaled painting by Julian Schnabel, himself a famous transgressor, animate this provocative room on Manhattan's Upper East Side.

Psychology

BARRY GORALNICK

I started my undergraduate studies as a premed student who wanted to be a psychiatrist before switching to architecture. Little did I know, psychology is a major part of a designer's work.

Each project brings the designer into contact with a new set of clients (also known as patients). The designer comes prepared with formal architecture and design training, an experienced eye, and a practical knowledge of how people live, honed through years of working with a diverse group of clients. In school, one studies the psychology of design, a science about how people use space, how to move people through space, and the effects of living in different environments. Scientific studies show that good design can increase productivity, reduce stress, improve family relationships, and even lead to a longer life.

Clients arrive complete with their personal tastes, relationships, family history, memories of past homes, and perceptions of their place in the social structure. There are emotional attachments to, and reactions against, objects and places, colors and textures.

The designer/client relationship is an intimate one. Designers must learn how clients live, how they entertain, how (or if) they cook. After all, when designing their bath and bedroom, there is a need to learn everything, down to where they want their Waterpik.

As in any doctor-patient scenario, there is an initial consultation. Both parties have to decide if they want to embark on this long journey together. I've had extremely personal conversations with clients before they even engage me: "I need a gorgeous bedroom. Maybe it will rekindle my romance." (I didn't take that job—way beyond my powers.) "I have twin boys, one masculine and one feminine. Can you create a room that will make them both happy?" (The solution was to do a

neutral room with accessories featuring each personality.) "We are merging households. We each need to keep our identity and forge a new one together." (The Brady Bunch did it, and so can you. Careful editing and rethinking are required.) Some people use home design to sublimate other problems. "If we have the perfect home, everything will be alright." (Stop, and get another kind of professional help immediately.) The designer and the client need to determine if expectations are realistic.

A good designer draws people out. To create a new home completely custom designed to meet their needs and desires, clients must share all relevant (and sometimes seemingly irrelevant) information with their designer. This is not the time to hold back. Communications should be verbal and visual. Learning what a client does not like and why is as important as what he or she does like. The more open the client is, the stronger the outcome.

Real skill and talent lie in the ability to analyze what clients are saying (and not saying) and synthesize that information. Simply telling someone what his or her home should look like is not nearly enough. It is critical to explain the "what" (design solutions) and the "how" (the process of getting it done), but even more important, the "why" (why this is the best solution for them). If the client is not getting what he or she needs, it's important for him or her to feel comfortable speaking up.

Like an analyst, a designer earns trust and assumes a role of authority over time. Sometimes the most basic advice from an authority figure leads to a moment of true insight. People often repeat their "baggage" by rote: "I hate blue. My mother never let me wear blue." Well, they may look great in a room with blue hues, and it is a designer's job to point that out, open minds, and find unexpected solutions. In the process, clients

will learn a lot about themselves and create a world that is happier for them and their family.

In my professional experience, every time we get pushback initially, when the final project is revealed, clients are extremely happy: "It's exactly how I want to live, and I didn't even know it. How did you know?" My answer: It's all in the analysis.

A Los Angeles-based couple purchased this Central Park West apartment; a gut renovation, fresh furnishings, and a newly curated art collection helped them find their inner New Yorker and revealed their Manhattan psyche.

Personalization

 DAVID MANN

One cannot overestimate the reward or power of a personalized home. Indeed, I have always found that the homes I visit and enjoy reading about most are the ones that seem strongly related to the character and demeanor of the owners. As a culture, we enjoy learning about others, how well they live, and how enriched their lives are by the art, architecture, and design with which they surround themselves.

When one mentions personalization in relation to interior design, most people assume that means the accessorizing done during the final stages of a project. Many people leave personalization, if you can call it that, to the styling of coffee tables and shelving. What I want to emphasize here is personalizing the project as a whole, including lighting, hardware, doors, trim, millwork, finishes, and fixtures, as well as decor, art, and accessories.

When I begin discussions with a potential client, I set forth my basic approach to residential work—that I am creating a home that is a true reflection of who the clients are and how they want to live. The home should not be a rehash of formulaic design responses; it should be specifically for the owners and not a marketing tool for the designer.

The first thing to do is a complete survey of the site to understand the life of the location, the play of light at different times of the day or in certain weather conditions, and unique features and details. Next, I begin a visual dialogue with the client. I assemble a large notebook of inspirational images that serve as rough ideas and act as a starting point, showing the direction the project will head. In reviewing these images with the client, I encourage comments, both

positive and negative, in order to generate a fully rounded understanding of the client's proclivities. This first conversation usually leads to further discussions and visual exchanges that increasingly focus on results that marry the firm's sensibilities with what is right for the client and his or her project.

Although interior design is a collaborative process, a designer cannot simply do what the client wants. Rather, it is important to listen and observe carefully and then respond in a sympathetic way that filters the client's aspirations through the best of the designer's aesthetic and practical experience. A designer takes on a project much in the same way a great actor takes on a role; the actor must fully research his character until he feels at one with the person he is portraying. An interior designer does the same. Once he or she understands a client, it becomes possible to make design choices "in character." This is not to say that the client is then out of the picture. The designer must review each decision and selection with the client and treat these reviews as a continuation of the collaborative visual dialogue. Sometimes this is very fluid and the project evolves seamlessly, with both parties in unison. Other times, it can take several passes. In addition, a designer must always keep an open mind and allow for the unexpected to happen.

When I began my career in design, I thought it was going to be all about creating beautiful spaces. This is still a primary goal, but what has delighted me as much, if not more, is getting to know the people who inhabit them. The more a designer is able to translate who a person is into the visual language of interiors, the more the client will come to see that home as a beautiful emblem of his or her identity.

Walls flecked with mica-infused paint, an Hervé Van der Straeten pendant, a custom antiqued brass-and–silver leaf stair rail, and meticulously placed sheets of griege onyx marble unite to create a memorable entry foyer.

A pair of artworks, *Untitled*, by Paul Sunday, set the rhythm for matched furnishings in this luxurious living room, which features two angular shagreen armchairs and two club chairs. Gold-leafed glass tiles surround the firebox.

Archaeology

SUZANNE TUCKER

When embarking upon a new project and getting to know clients, there are hundreds of questions to ask up front and thousands more to be explored along the way in order to design a unique and lasting home for them. Some of the initial research is about lifestyle: How do they live? How do they *want* to live? What are their routines? From there, the queries progress to the more practical: Do they cook? Do they need blackout shades for sleeping? Do we need to consider pets? Do they have a grand piano? Inevitably, the questions evolve into those of a more esoteric nature: What do their memories evoke? Is there a particular style reminiscent of their family home? Do certain colors have associations? What resonates from their past, and what do they want to bring forward into this next home?

Beyond wearing my hat as decorator, consultant, or designer, I have acted at times as detective, psychologist, marriage counselor, and confidant. But I find one of the most important roles a designer can explore to the fullest is that of the archaeologist, understanding who the clients are, excavating what echoes from their past, and unearthing what has made them who they are.

Equally important and undoubtedly of deeper value is a designer's own internal archaeology—the excavation and understanding of ourselves, our own historical and cultural influences, and that of our individual visual memory banks. Freud theorized how early childhood experiences impact our behavior later in life. I believe the same principle applies to the way our visual and sensory recollections impact us as creative individuals. From spatial thinking to tactile preference, from a sense of color to evocative fragrances, from an affinity for to an aversion of antiques, and from an identity deeply rooted in the past to one firmly planted in the present, they all can be traced back to our childhood recollections.

Where we grow up is a critical part of this. My personal experience growing up in California deeply influenced my sense of design. I have discovered time and again how subliminally and profoundly my Montecito surroundings molded and informed my understanding of home: the commanding architecture, significant gardens, and even the seductive scents in the air and rather magical quality of light. The imagery is embedded in my psyche, like the quatrefoil window that I passed on my way to school, the Palladian arches at the teahouse where we had lunch, the floor-to-ceiling artwork in a friend's living room hung salon-style, the texture of an iron gate and how it felt in my hand. I can conjure colors, such as the mixture of ocean foam and sand as a wave retreats from the beach or a particular shade of muted purple that the mountains take on only when the sun is setting at a specific time of year and the California lilac is in bloom. These remembrances are specific and personal.

A sense of style also develops because of or in spite of one's family. I know from my own upbringing that I was influenced by my mother's love of gardens, the daily fresh flowers in the house, the black-and-white checkerboard floors, the way my parents entertained, how the table was set, and which dishes were used. All these influences and more are there to be accessed deep within my visual bank and used as needed in my toolbox.

The designer as archaeologist, uncovering and understanding all those childhood experiences and associations, will invariably inform us about our true design identity more than any school, textbook, or internship can ever teach. A well-informed designer is a visual translator, and his or her work should be rooted in that knowledge of self. Together with many years of learning and experience, this elevates one's work from

The painting, *Visca*, by Gustavo Ramos Rivera, adds a playful, contemporary note of strong color in an otherwise tranquil end of the living room. A pair of Regency chairs from an Albert Hadley auction are joined by two reproductions to complete the suite, which surrounds a marble octagon table designed for Nancy Dollar by the late Michael Taylor.

merely decorative to deeply meaningful and personalized. Developing a well-rounded and full-bodied design vocabulary takes years, but by mining one's heart and one's mind for those essential, soulful recollections that have contributed to a designer persona, one can bring a unique approach to his or her work and creativity. All the top successful designers that I am fortunate to call my colleagues and friends may not share the same stylistic approach or sensibilities, but we all share the archaeologist's trait of endless exploration and passionate curiosity. That inquisitiveness must be a lifelong, never-ending education nurturing our creativity as designers. The past is what we bring to the present to design the future.

With spectacular views of San Francisco from the East Bay to the Golden Gate Bridge, this living room has a color palette inspired by the abundant water and sky. Creamy tones balance the space by referencing the inevitably foggy days of the area.

Value

 SCOTT SALVATOR

A well-designed home is full of stories, but at the same time it needs no explanation. It is evidence of one's life. As with couture fashion, it fits only the people who live there and would be ill-suited to anyone else.

Something so incredibly personal, so comforting, and so reflective of a client is invaluable. To sit in a chair made to fit one's frame, surrounded by collections from one's travels, books one has read, fabulous art, and one's favorite color on the walls—this is as good as it gets.

Value is the result of the highest level of interior design, where everything is custom, but to achieve such results, the designer must have intimate knowledge of every trade, art, and craft. Details on rugs, carpets, antiques, reproductions, upholstery, curtains, lighting, and painting constitute only a small part of the knowledge a designer must possess.

Interior design may be compared to a composition or work of art that should reflect the client's personality and style as well as that of the designer. The best rooms result when the client and designer have collaborated over the years and developed a personal language. The more yin-yang between the client and designer, the better the result. However, make no mistake, the designer must be in control, anticipating the needs and likes of his client and implementing them.

A designer's relationship with his client is much like a Renaissance artist and his patron; one produces the work, under the sponsorship and guidance of the other. As with a painting, only one person holds the brush—a collaboration doesn't mean one person paints the mouth and another, the ears. The value in the composition arises from the designer's skillful interpretation of the client's likes and dislikes, his or her wants and needs.

There is value—great value—in the many technical components of interior design that are learned, not innate. While design school provides an important background in the decorative arts, as well as many other areas of design, most of the valuable technical requirements of interior design aren't taught in school, and they must be learned while working as an apprentice to a seasoned designer. The right proportion or height of a chandelier over a table is mastered; correct table heights, seat heights, and proper sofa proportions are all acquired. The great fashion designer Halston may have been able to make a dress with a single cut, but no one has an inborn flair for cutting a jabot—it is learned, as is the construction of upholstered furniture, the proper way to stencil a floor, and the formulation of a glaze for a wall.

Years of experience are required for the design professional to acquire the technical and practical knowledge necessary to decorate a house as a consistent whole. The last thing a designer wants to hear are comments such as "approachable," "understated," or "livable"; all we really want is a *wow*. When it all comes together, usually over months or years, the result is seamless, whether the room is minimal, cluttered, casual, or eclectic. That is of priceless value to a client.

In a historic thirty-eight-room mansion in Peapack-Gladstone, New Jersey, completed around 1900, the Belvedere Room faces Ravine Lake. Sumptuous red curtains are made less formal by the bistro-style wicker furniture.

Integrity

I am in awe of my clients. They are movers and shakers. Because clients' lives are busier than ever before, I create homes whose balance and order elicit a sense of peace. And as sensory overload becomes standard, the design profession as a whole is taking a less baroque approach to interiors in response.

You could measure this shift to calmness in the amount of furniture filling an interior. Fewer items presumably equal a more contemplative atmosphere. In fact, creating a haven is more trigonometry than simple subtraction, because every remaining object has to convey that much more meaning.

Which is perhaps why, to this day, I am haunted by a side table. In a project that shall remain nameless, this derivative, anonymously made table presented a good-enough solution for a deadline. What would have been the better solution? I could have found one of the two pieces on which the side table was based, or a trusted artisan could have realized a custom design inspired by those originals, tailor-made for my client's situation.

I liken integrity to hearing voices. When I ask whether an object channels them, I recall launching my career in New York at the dawn of the Internet. Whereas a designer can source a world of goods without ever leaving the studio today, back then, beating a path to showrooms was the norm. Yet the best dealers repaid the effort in knowledge. I remember their enthusiasm for a collectible's design precedents and production challenges, and the humility with which they tended these antiques' legacies. Integrity inspired that passionate storytelling and their stewardship of material culture overall.

In a similar vein, my artisan collaborators' attention to craftsmanship is palpable, and their respect for raw materials is a reminder of the larger world we occupy. History hasn't cornered the market on narrative.

Cost or provenance is no indicator of integrity, either. Design—whether of interiors or furniture—is a process of improving lives, and people of all stripes should have access to this intelligence. I am consistently surprised by new, affordable merchandise that employs a material in an unexpected way. In these pieces, you can hear the designer enthusiastically describing an *aha!* moment or marathon development process. Not every one of these objects is a visual spectacle, but even the more muted accomplishments convey a story about concept or fabrication. The story may even change with the teller.

Furniture and decorative arts that embody this power should be treated with similar thoughtfulness. If there is integrity inherent in an object, then there is integrity in the way those objects are composed.

In my work, the integrity of objects reinforces a restrained approach. Namely, I make sure that every single freestanding element references its architectural context. In a minimalist Colorado house, furniture and textiles echo sparingly used timber, for example. Those in a converted Connecticut barn bear visible construction details, evoking the uses for which the structure was originally intended. Whereas defying architecture involves layering in new information, engaging the setting in a dialogue reinforces the feeling that an occupant has entered a safe, orderly domain.

When two different objects accommodate function and client taste perfectly well, I advocate for the object that harmonizes with the architecture. If all three variables are equal, then narrative power determines the selection. Insisting on these qualities is how, I believe, interior designers elevate their discipline from service to art.

And this may be why I am haunted by that side table. Looking back at the decision, the little accompaniment did have function,

Demure and feminine, the sheer ruffled curtains soften the masculine Dunbar sofa and daybed in this city aerie. A custom-made coffee table relates perfectly to a side table designed by Jacques Adnet.

the client's taste, and architectural harmony to recommend it. But its voice was silent.

To be sure, other professionals may place less priority on factors like the clients personally identifying with an object or its architectural harmony. But just as there is a sea change toward restrained interiors, so integrity's tide will rise. Whatever we call it—from narrative and voice to authenticity, pedigree, or soul—we're hungrier for meaning than ever before. And our hunger is driven by the same impulse that seeks a peaceful domicile. Objects of integrity are deeply conceived, slowly made, and rarely shared. They are antidotes to daily life.

Sophisticated textures abound in this living room. A pair of swivel chairs, originally designed by Ward Bennett, are covered in a slate-gray printed velvet. The sofa was custom designed for the client; a vintage Stilnovo chandelier and a Caste side table complete the space.

Teachers

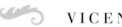

VICENTE WOLF

An ellipsoidal wooden screen in this Westchester County, New York, home separates the kitchen from the living area. Verner Panton's S-shaped chairs surround the dining table.

OPPOSITE: Dramatic club chairs in blue sateen flank an animal-print ottoman in this crisp living room. A Sputnik-style ceiling fixture and three intricately carved candlesticks provide a soft glow after sunset.

Seeing requires much more than just opening our eyes; it requires awareness and the presence to appreciate whatever we are observing. When the light filtering through the leaves of a tree becomes visual poetry, several shades of green come into view, and the shadows the branches project onto the earth have dimension and depth. That is when a simple act of noticing becomes a moment of inspiration—we figuratively breathe in the light, shade, and color of the tree, and in so doing, we acquire an understanding of its essence.

Many of us are oblivious to our surroundings. We spend our days multitasking, or we're so absorbed by a virtual world that we overlook what's directly in front of us. Consciously recognizing how we are affected and influenced by everything we have around us enhances our lives.

It goes without saying that my career is based on being sensitive to aesthetics, but I began noticing my surroundings at an early age. As a result, my life is richer because I relate to objects and environments experientially. My travels constantly educate me, but I'm equally impressed by the mundane and the exotic. It's true that Egyptian columns taught me about scale and proportion, but the pebbles on the beach close to my weekend house perpetually expand my definitions of gray and taupe.

When I'm designing, I often put down my pen, leave the studio, and go for a stroll. At those times, I'm open to anything and everything presenting itself as an idea. It's all fodder for inspiration. The grid of a manhole cover could influence the pattern of a carpet I'm designing for an Upper East Side townhouse; a Balenciaga ball gown in a department-store window might affect how I resolve a color palette in a Paris apartment. A stone carving on the facade of a building might lead me to experiment with a textured wall treatment in a dining room, and reflections of skyscrapers in a puddle on a New York City sidewalk draw me into yet another narrative. All of this inspiration is gleaned in a short walk.

This way of looking at the world isn't exclusive to designers. Any one of us can practice focusing on the amazing everyday details of the world. But first we have to agree to perceive every object that wanders into the peripheral vision as a teacher. In this way, the world becomes our classroom, and its everyday moments our lessons. Everything we see and encounter becomes a valuable learning experience. When we approach the world with a spirit of curiosity and openness, there's no telling where we'll end up.

Taste

DAVID KLEINBERG

To define taste as an aesthetic idea is like trying to describe the color of oxygen. It is ephemeral in every sense, personal in every way, and influenced by the vagaries of society and fashion, yet it is a constant we somehow recognize, like perfect pitch.

How was it that the Greeks were able to create an order of architecture in ancient times that resonates still with modern man? While all has changed around us thanks to industrial revolutions and technology, somehow a perfectly proportioned room is still a pleasing environment, a Doric column an emblem of stature and stability. And surely when Edith Wharton and Ogden Codman wrote *The Decoration of Houses* in 1897, they had very specific rules of what was considered good taste and what was not. How much of their taste would hold true today—is taste all in perspective, street style vs. the royal court, avant garde vs. old guard?

My life's work is based on this challenging-to-define notion of taste, and yet it is clear that even for me, taste is difficult to adequately define or quantify. Taste should not be confused with style. Style is easy to define. It is a clear-eyed view of fashion and economics blended with a casual disregard for convention. Style is mutable; taste endures. Yet with all of these caveats, I inhabit a world of endless options, multiple opinions, and no wrong answers. Or are there?

I have always had confidence in my taste; my aesthetic sense is my bread and butter, and my job is to convince others to join me in that point of view. Good taste is based in suitability and comfort, and I still truly believe these to be the ultimate defining goals.

What allows for the wonderful degree of variation in this interpretation are an individual's interpretation of acceptability and the appropriate. A city dwelling for a young family is highly different from a seaside retreat

A Cubist canvas by Fernand Léger brings gravitas to this New York City library, the walls of which are paneled in ebonized mahogany. A nailhead-trimmed sofa and a pair of leather club chairs are balanced by the set of card-table chairs by André Sornay on the other side of the room.

for a retired couple, a residence for formal life contrasts with one for a freewheeling bohemian existence, and yet each of these many ways of living can exhibit good taste if the same principles of suitability and comfort are applied. It's as simple as that.

While I have never subscribed to a fully eclectic aesthetic, as I find it leads to an unruly visual result, I do believe that if it feels right, it looks right. A discerning eye will lead you to review and edit what you have selected. Like a cook with an innate understanding of spice and flavor, one examines the scene with a view toward proportion, texture, and color in order to create harmony. It's the inner ear that keeps us balanced. Taste works in the same way, creating visual balance and harmony that is simultaneously recognizable and unknowable.

I had the extreme pleasure in my career of working directly with Albert Hadley and Sister Parish, two people of resounding taste who influenced everyone within their reach. Mr. Hadley had the gift of erudition, and with words and sketches he could explain his reasoning to describe what went into the mixture of the tasteful environment. Mrs. Parish was all instinct. She could no more explain why the room was right as to how to build a spaceship, but her instincts were always on target and everyone appreciated the results of her taste. While each of these great decorators had a distinct style, their taste was never in doubt.

We all know the expression "beauty is in the eye of the beholder." But the eye is a muscle, and to that extent it needs to be exercised and constantly worked. Diana Vreeland was right when she insisted the eye must travel, and seeing is surely the path to knowing. So there you have it: at its core, taste is a jumble of influences—including politics, economics, and technology—that are edited by an innate third eye. Trust me, you'll know when you've got it just right.

A hand-painted Gracie wallpaper on a silver ground reflects the ample light in this bedroom on Manhattan's Upper East Side. Chairs by Diego Giacometti and a photograph by Robert Mapplethorpe complete the tableau.

Passion

My first real adventures in interior design began when I was a freshman at the University at Albany, in New York, where I lived off campus with four roommates in an unfairly small house. Obsessed with Jackson Pollock, I hid the dark wood paneling with bluegray paint and followed that with layers of black and white, which I splattered across the walls. Young, inspired, and fearless, I had my first opportunity to run wild.

After I graduated, I read *The Artist's Way* by Julia Cameron, which sets forth a path for the creative person in twelve lessons. For me, it was a revelation. Like many young people, I began working a less-than-exciting job while attempting to figure out who I wanted to be. By week five or six of Cameron's program, I knew where I needed to go. All the untamed impulses I had felt as a student began to coalesce, and I had no choice but to follow my heart—and the advice of Cameron. In the course of just a few short days, I registered for the interior design program at New York City's Fashion Institute of Technology and landed a job with industry leader John Rosselli, diving headfirst into a career of interior design.

In the same way that my quiet impulses guided me through the formative years of my career, I've grown to believe it is essential to learn everything possible about someone before designing their home. Interior design is truly personal, and I take great pride in personalizing the interiors that I develop. Great design is a translation of our deepest desires, untapped energies, and loftiest aspirations, an individualized visual language crafted to resonate with the client in ways even the designer can never fully understand. A home

is not simply a physical space, but an outline that guides, invigorates, and inspires us to live passionate lives every day.

From a practical point of view, I start each of my client relationships by spending time with them in social settings as well as in their homes. I follow that up with a twenty-five-point questionnaire. What did they love about their childhood bedroom? Are they a Mac or a PC? St. Barts or St. Petersburg? Each question is written in the hopes that my team can craft a portrait of the individual so their unassuming answers become uncovered truths, their passions made tangible. The smallest details inform decisions that breathe life into richly nuanced spaces.

It is not enough to sell a style, no matter how exquisitely achieved. One succeeds as a designer through finetuned communications with the client, by translating his or her passions into physical reality—creating rooms that join his or her passions with the instincts of a passionate designer. It is the process of applying one's own zeal for hunting and gathering ideas about design and decoration as guided by the untapped id of the client.

We can change lives without even knowing it by simply following our passions in everything we do. As Cameron changed my life, I hope I might, in the smallest way, change a client's, with a wallcovering that causes a guest to pause in the entryway or a view of Central Park framed with luxe draperies that emphasize the blooms of early spring.

When executed properly, design is about interests and expression; it's innate. You just have to pay attention to what you're passionate about.

This living space on New York's Upper East Side is a nod to the past with a current sensibility. The room is swathed in tones of chocolate brown and cream, and more lively colors are derived from the art and accessories.

Aspiration

Growing up in Oklahoma, I was attracted to visions that I did not understand, and I made it my work to figure it out. From childhood, I was interested in artists and designers: Billy Baldwin, Cecil Beaton, Charles Sévigny in Paris, Francis Bacon, and Cy Twombly. Family friends were using Baldwin as their decorator in Dallas, so I was exposed at an early age. At sixteen or seventeen, I recognized that Charles James's work was genius—a teaching inspiration. A friend of mine worked for the de Menils, so I went to see them and their Philip Johnson house: it was magic and strange, with big Victorian Belter furniture done in eggplant velvet and doors covered in silk velvet. I'd never experienced anything like it; it triggered my imagination. The design was intelligent, sophisticated, and way beyond.

In spite of this, I was always trying to invent my own style. I spent three years in Europe after college. It was a struggle, a creative quest that was painful. I was constantly striving and thinking, How do I make this room unusual and beautiful, something people have never seen before? That process—that leap into the unknown— served me well till my late thirties, when something strange happened: it became easy, like riding a bike.

Now when I embark on a project, I ask the usual questions just to get the clients talking. How do they see themselves in this house, how do they want to live, and how do they want to feel? They all have different answers and different personalities. But in the back of my mind, I always want to give them my idea of what they should live up to and grow into—not what they want today, but what they'll want in five years: their aspiration.

I take tidbits from what they say. For example, "I don't like floral prints, but I can take a vine pattern." I then have to give them something they say they want and at the

same time coax them to a higher level. It's a psychological thing to say, "This vine on this cut linen velvet is so beautiful, it would be wonderful all over the walls!" Persuasion is a slow process, consuming months and months.

I create my interpretation of what I think they want on a board pinned with tear sheets and fabrics. The clients look at it, and sometimes they're apprehensive because it's not what they had in their head. But because I decorate in layers, I don't scare them off by presenting the whole concept in one fell swoop. Instead, gradually, we work with fabrics, colors, and pieces of furniture. In the back of my mind I know what I want to achieve, but it's an incremental education. As Diana Vreeland said, "Don't give the people what they want; give them what they don't know they want yet." When it all comes together, you see stars in their eyes: they understand.

I did a wonderful house in Tulsa, Oklahoma, designed from the ground up for some exceptional clients who collected Abstract Expressionist paintings. They had a ranch house and a lot next door where they wanted to build. Within the house, their huge paintings, by Mark Rothko, Morris Louis, Cy Twombly, and Joan Mitchell, hung floor to ceiling.

The clients' only imperative for the new house was high ceilings to showcase their art. The house I designed was tall beyond their expectations with outrageously high ceilings—twenty-four feet! Yet it was not a big house but a comfortable one. I designed the house for the paintings—itself an exceptional opportunity—then began collecting antique furniture. The style of the house resembles that of Hugh Newell Jacobsen, white-painted brick with huge windows, the walls now overgrown with ivy.

The very first step in furnishing this house was buying a monumental rug that became the

With its hand-painted burlap walls, this bedroom in the Midwest beckons for stylish repose. A 1920s-style French chair and settee and a canopy bed inspired by an antique birdcage take center stage; the fireplace warms the room seasonally.

centerpiece of the living room. A seventeenth-century indigo-and-red Venetian carpet, it is the pivotal complement to the modern art. It's kooky, and it looks like an American rag rug. In the space, it turned out to be a home run.

I want a project to be as great as it can possibly be, and I really work to push the client to attain quality. Things needn't be expensive, but materials must exude honesty. They must be a true representation of what the client wants, whether a simple basket or a gilded bronze statue. Honesty in materials and purity of objects are very important.

Aspiration, when it succeeds, promises the client something beyond good taste. It invests the daily tasks of decoration with meaning, pleasure, and vision, elevating interior decoration to the place of high art it deserves.

The cigar room in this Georgian house in upstate New York features a collection of noble Turkish portraits. The gold tones and ambient light set the mood for intimate after-dinner conversation.

Perspective

BENJAMIN NORIEGA ORTIZ

Creativity depends a lot on the way you look at things and your personal perspective.

How many times have you admired a design solution simply because the solution feels familiar but out of context? Most of Philippe Starck's designs—if you study them closely—come from looking at things in a decidedly different way, like his juicer that stands on its own over the glass. What we consider ingenious design solutions come from people who, in one way or another, opened their eyes to a "fresh" way of looking at things.

In interior design, the happy marriage between architecture and decorating, the way you look at things makes a big difference between a pleasant solution and a transformative one. For example, if you're going to watch TV in the living room and possibly fall asleep, why not put a bed in there? Or if you watch TV in your bedroom with all your children and friends, why not design an eight-foot-wide mattress that can allow everyone to view your programming comfortably? Even more radically, why not make the entire room a bed? If we forget the labels and functions that we apply to rooms (and the furnishings that typically inhabit them), our interiors become more exciting and appropriate. All that's required is a shift in perspective.

In a dining room, the reason that benches instead of just chairs became popular might have been because someone felt that chairs looked too busy, or that guests liked to be seated closer together, or there weren't enough places to seat guests in separate chairs. The fact is that the function of a chair was translated into a singular horizontal surface to accommodate several people at the table. Open a copy of Charlotte and Peter Fiell's *1000 Chairs* and you'll find 1000 perspectives on seating.

Although the kitchen must be the most practical and functional space in a house, calling to mind several restrictions, one can also

Thought of as counterintuitive by some, white is actually one of the best colors for decorating if the materials are chosen carefully. All of the upholstery, including the Mongolian lamb pillows and the leather on the Barcelona daybed, can be spot-cleaned in this Paris pied-à-terre.

An assortment of silhouettes combines in this light-filled living room to form an alternate take on a classic seating arrangement. Voluminous and translucent, the window sheers diffuse what might otherwise be harsh Western light, while the white-painted floors reflect throughout.

look at things differently. If you use the freezer only once while cooking, can't it be in another room? We put something in the oven, and it might stay there for an hour or more, so again, why have it so prominently displayed? It's not as if you're giving a cooking demonstration—or perhaps you are, which would call for yet another shift in perspective, like putting your stove in a center island surrounded by stools. When you look at all the elements that make a kitchen, they can be rearranged in a way that gives us a more interesting, yet still practical, space.

Color is another element that deserves a second look. When designing for kids or pets, I think white upholstery is best. That sounds counterintuitive, but if you think about it, white can be bleached and colors can't; white tells you when it has to be cleaned. Why use fabrics that disguise dirt? We need to see the dirt so we can clean it.

Then let's consider the home office. A friend once told me that wherever he worked in Scandinavia, his big business deals happened in dry saunas, which gave me an idea: Why not design a steam room in his home that

accommodates eight friends with enough room for a sofa covered in a waterproof fabric and well-designed outdoor lounge chairs? A small kitchenette for beverages and maybe a TV could complete the unusual yet perfectly suitable space.

Nowhere is this concept of being creative with perspective more apparent than in hotels, those temporary homes in which we allow ourselves to be different, to think differently, and to experience the extraordinary. Hotelier Ian Schrager calls it "hotel as entertainment," and he couldn't be more right. When we're relaxed, we don't care if the bathtub is at the foot of the bed or if the sink is a seashell sitting on a ledge outside. Away from home, we accept that a room is open to the elements and birds can fly in and out. The reason why we don't allow ourselves this flexibility at home is because we're not looking at things differently, as we do when we're relaxed and on holiday.

So I suggest taking a vacation from mundane reality when designing spaces and remembering self-help guru Wayne Dyer's oft-repeated adage: "When you change the way you look at things, the things you look at change."

STRUCTURE

Symmetry

MARK CUNNINGHAM

One of my favorite books is *Let the Great World Spin*, by Colum McCann. Although it's a work of fiction, the plot was inspired by an actual event: French high-wire artist Philippe Petit's 1974 tightrope walk between New York City's Twin Towers. Each of the story's imperfect characters is searching for balance in life, a kind of personal symmetry. It's a theme that resonates because it's so universal.

Balance is essential in all facets of life, including the spaces in which we live. One of the greatest challenges in interior design is to find the right balance—of light, of depth, of texture, of color. This is typically accomplished with one of three methods: symmetrical balance, asymmetrical balance, and radial symmetry.

Symmetrical balance is a straightforward way to gain visual balance within design. This type of mirrored symmetry can be achieved through the use of different elements, from architecture to furniture, evoking a sense of stability and dignity within a room that could not be achieved otherwise.

Asymmetrical balance requires careful thought and meticulous curation. This approach tends to appear more vibrant, eclectic, and interesting. It can also be more challenging to achieve—a process I find compelling. Creating layers of elements with varying visual weights results in an outcome that harbors balance, depth, and harmony.

Radial symmetry is used to highlight a particular element in a space—a work of art, special antique piece, or profound structural element. The challenge here is to create that symmetry around a single focal point with items radiating inward or outward. The success of such an approach lies in being able to control the direction of one's attention within a space.

All three types of symmetry have a purpose and importance, but I admit to a partiality toward asymmetrical balance.

Growing up in the Southwest, I was surrounded by mountains and mesas, plateaus and plains. Coming to New York City as a young designer was an acute lesson in contrast. The open spaces I'd been accustomed to were now towering canyons of granite and limestone. The emphasis in New York on imposing visual order was unlike anything I'd experienced. It was a change that required adjustment and adaptation, but I appreciated the experience for what it taught me about beauty.

During my tenure at Ralph Lauren, I was further exposed to the importance and excitement of contradiction. The mixture of high and low elements, whether on the runway, in an advertisement, or in a store window, was standard practice. The result was always a unique but accessible authentic sense of style. I was responsible for creating asymmetrical balance within a retail space using layers of strategically placed elements and different sensibilities. Thanks to the brand's ever-evolving collections, different styles had to coexist within the same space in a complementary way and without any competition.

It's my belief that symmetry, in all forms, is as integral to interior design as it is to life. Regardless of the method of symmetry used within a livable space, each element is carefully and intentionally placed. Whether the flow involves large objects to small objects, smooth materials to rough ones, light to dark, or high to low, it is always created with the most favorable result in mind: an appealing and pleasing balance.

Some of what appears to be white is actually pale blue in the master bedroom of this residence on Manhattan's Upper East Side. The symmetry of the spare four-poster bed, upholstered in blue silk, is echoed by the proportions of the cabinetry. The artwork above the headboard is by Milton Avery.

In a duplex apartment in Greenwich Village owned by a chef and writer, the living room is open to the kitchen and features walls and cabinetry clad in stained oak; the dark-colored upholstery mirrors the coffered ceiling above. The three pieces of art hanging behind the sofa are by Ellsworth Kelly.

Floor Plans

ETIENNE COFFINIER *and* ED KU

Nothing comes before the floor plan. It's the absolute truth in our design philosophy, because the floor plan is the guide to how you will live in your space.

We think the best floor plans reflect a true understanding of the who, the where, and the what of the project: Who will be using the space? Where is the space located? What will be in the space?

We begin by asking questions of our clients: Who lives in this space? Do the parents want their kids' rooms near their own? Do the children do their homework in their rooms, or do they need a separate work/play area? Do the parents entertain? If so, formally or informally? Do they enjoy having overnight guests? Do they want an open kitchen or family lounge area, or do they prefer a more traditional kitchen hidden away from guests? How do they relax? Do they read a book in a quiet corner or exercise? The answers to these questions and so many others will help us deliver a plan that meets our clients' needs and even allows them to live in ways that they may not be able to articulate.

While we are better understanding who will be using the space, we also must think about the space itself, the "where." There can be some very obvious differences in developing floor plans if we are working with a one-bedroom apartment or designing a house. But all spaces have their challenges. With small spaces, we have to make every inch count, so we often plan for flexibility of use. With very large spaces, we face a different issue in terms of scale, so we need to make sure the users still feel human inside the space and not overwhelmed. Each space also brings its own physical environment. What is the orientation with regards to light,

to views, and to neighbors? Your floor plan must certainly reflect those attributes.

The last major piece in developing a floor plan is the "what." What are the pieces that will become part of the space and our clients' lives? Be it furniture, floor coverings, lighting fixtures, plumbing, appliances, or cars, we take measurements of everything that will be in the home and then we include the projected measurements of any new pieces. An empty room on a floor plan tells you nothing. But a floor plan with furniture and fixtures allows you to understand the seating arrangements that will encourage conversation; the kitchen that works efficiently and allows for family interaction; the master bathroom that provides privacy and luxury at the same time; and the garage that can accommodate family vehicles.

When we begin a floor plan, we picture ourselves walking through the space as if we were the client. We imagine living how they told us they would like to live with the objects they have or will have. We try to think and articulate their actions: Here you enter your apartment and find your mail in a tray on the console. This is where you can put your dripping umbrella. Here is a bench where you can sit and take your shoes off. Here is the mirror where you can check that your tie is knotted correctly. This process continues throughout the entire home as we try to anticipate the various parts of their lives. Every good floor plan contains life, and you should feel a flow from room to room and from floor to floor.

Without the specificity of the space, the things, and the people, there is no successful floor plan. Architects are taught that form follows function, but a great floor plan magnifies and transforms a simple checklist into a blueprint for how to live.

Mirrored mosaic tiles refract the already abundant light around this living room, which is painted in subtle shades of white. A baby grand piano, near a floor-to-ceiling window, is anchored by a Jay Kelly collage titled *Breathe (Don't Fool Yourself)*.

Portals

RICHARD MISHAAN

Portals free our imaginations to move. They carry us from one place to another, acting as conduits through which a scene can be entered and brought to life. Our vision reaches out and travels ahead of us into the aperture of a window, a corridor, or a mirror.

The first and most significant portal designers must consider is the initial viewpoint through which a person will view the space. This gives us the envisioned whole through which we can better discern and manipulate each individual part. This technique treats portals as a basic principle in the constructive technique of designing rather than a mere ornamental flourish. The eye's tendency is to seek the most aesthetically commanding point, and our responsibility as designers is always to direct the viewer's eye. Portals, then, give us the artistic power to guide and articulate that visual journey.

Architectural space consists, if nothing else, of continuous portals. The construction of interior space depends as much on the transparency of its portal as on the opaqueness of its walls and the closure of its ceiling. When looking into a doorway, window, mirror, or painting or past a proscenium wall, we encounter an opening not only of light and space, but also of imagination. We are looking into another world, a world that stakes a claim on our attention in the same way that we lose ourselves to the drama on a movie screen.

There are, of course, different approaches by which designers can construct and impose the framing effect of a portal. One approach employs formal order and adheres to strict measures that define a more precise end result. Another allows for a serendipitous outcome, generating an impressionistic picture or following a free-form manner of composition. Whatever the style or character of the final product, the viewer, upon peering into it, may forget the frame altogether. And it is that immediate sense of traveling, of forward momentum, that is driven by the portal's structure.

When photographing a landscape or a vista, we position the lens to frame our view and capture that moment, perfectly preserved, from the continuum of time. For designers, however, framing is rarely a matter of static images or frozen perspective. Our medium is dynamic. Changes occur as the viewer travels around the room, so it is only the portal—not the image—that remains unchanged.

My own approach to design is to understand framing the way a director might make sense of setting a scene. I adjust the central theme and then step back, again and again, as if looking at a vignette or a still life. Only in this zoomed-out perspective, as I peer into my imaginary lens, can I create balance and harmony within the scene as a whole. But whereas a painter relies on illusion to create the impression of depth and movement, the lived-in situation of interior design must take into account the evolution of its appearance across time and space, an appearance through which the camera of my eye can move around and explore.

That freedom of imagination is essential to the portal. When creating these vignettes and adding, arranging, and editing elements, I imagine myself to be watching a film rather than staring at a still image. The next time you look through a portal, find the image that was placed there for you by the designer. See how the frame shapes not only your perspective, but also the entire visual field. You will then discover how portals bring together artistic vision and everyday life.

The circa-1840 pews in the entryway of Mishaan's home in Cartagena, Colombia, are from an Episcopal church. Saffron-colored stucco and a contemporary light fixture set a welcoming tone.

The dining table and chairs in this Manhattan apartment, as well as the slipper chairs in the foreground, were found at one of the designer's favorite shops, Homer, in New York City. The windows afford remarkable light for dining, and the gallery wall contains works by Italian photographer Massimo Vitali.

Proportion

Proportion is all about perception. Beauty may be in the eyes of the beholder, but when it comes to interiors, the space between things is just as important as the size of the objects themselves.

When I was training as an architect, a professor once said everything designed should have a minimum of three layers of scale. For reference, imagine an impeccable men's gray flannel striped suit: first you notice the silhouette, then the pattern of the stripes, and finally, as you move closer, the nuances of fabric texture that reveal themselves upon close inspection.

That simple rule stuck with me for a long time, until I began to really investigate proportion in my own designs. I realized that the delineations were not so clear between the layers of actual versus perceived scale.

Let me explain further. I often tell my clients to do the squint test: stand at the edge of a room, knees slightly bent and relaxed with a slight smile, and imagine you are Clint Eastwood in *The Good, the Bad and the Ugly*, surveying your interior with an eye to rearrange. This practice strips the room of color and the relative importance of its objects back to the bare and basic proportions of inspiration and the beautiful furniture within it. With this simple method, one can discern not only the grand but also the subtle measure of a room. You can observe how your eyes lightly dance around the room, the ups and the downs, the shadows and the bright spots, and the thick and thin of things.

Since ancient times, we have created an orthogonal world around us, presumably to command and control nature and to forge a book of proportional rules and our understanding of things. Our actual world is a series of subtle fractals of natural creation that both delight and awe our visual sense. Nothing is perfect, yet everything is. Why is

that? One of the answers might be that in creating our modern visual landscape, not only have we emulated the magic of natural phenomena, but we have also learned its tricks. In striving for that perfect interior, we seek to exert a construct where perhaps there should be none, or at least a relaxed one with a series of visually interlocking queues, nodes, and bursts of wonder.

As we move toward a more unified kind of design that supports eco-conscious decisions, I feel like we move closer to nature in scale and proportion. This is not new; rather it is more scientific. The squint test enables one to find the right balance in design, and so to create something ultimately more human, transitive, and evocative.

The ergonomics and limitations of our body aren't changing anytime soon, but the design to fit them always is. While the "a chair is a chair is a chair" mantra still holds, the proportions of ideal delight have changed over the eons. This is due to cultural adaptations and the advances of material science, but also an inquisitive personal need to explore new forms of design that lend comfort and meaning to our evolving world.

Note that in ancient design, individual furniture pieces held much more meaning; each object was usually created for a simple and unique purpose. In the modern context, furniture plays a more ensemble role, and its individual importance has been relegated to serving the whole. One might call this the socialism of design. Fine proportion and certain meaning have given way to a living utility where each piece of furniture may and must have a dual purpose, must be more durable, shippable, and adaptable to many different design possibilities.

When designing in this amorphous world of proportions, one should always try to have some fun, delight, and marvel.

A grandfather clock and a pair of antique side chairs lend an air of history to this entryway, which features a marvelous fireplace. Globe lanterns, featuring clear and etched glass, and an antique copper ship's weather vane at the top of the staircase complete the tableau.

Perhaps the objects can create the wonder, but their proportions must be at once pleasing and compatible and have a dash of simpatico for their brethren nearby.

As designers, our eyes are always composing, creating perspective, filling in the shadows, and connecting the lines. This may be why a pencil or watercolor room illustration is more tantalizing than any detailed computer rendering. Our minds love the mystery of the negative space, energized by the void, unknown or yet to be revealed. Like a wrapped gift on your birthday, happiness derives more from the mystery than the actuality.

Take these tools, be inspired, and adopt the guise of a Western film hero, dancing through the design of a room with your eyes until all the pieces and their proportions come to rest in perfect harmony.

The proportions of the ceiling beams above the living room in this Water Mill, New York, house set the tone for the rest of the subdued furniture and furnishings. Note the dimensions of the fireplace surround, which stands in perfect balance to the other darker notes in the room.

Silhouette

JAYNE *and* JOAN MICHAELS

A beautiful silhouette is a still-life composition: elegant, refined, mysterious. Subtle details matter: the curve of an arm, the splay of a leg, the imposing mass of a chunky sculpture, the attenuated outline of a delicate sconce. Silhouettes are the ballet of shape, proportion, scale, balance, and texture.

Perhaps the best example of the purity of silhouettes is the work of painter Giorgio Morandi, known for his simple groupings of vases and bottles rendered in neutral tones. However, what Morandi achieved was anything but ordinary. The silhouettes and placement of objects were painstakingly deliberated: subtle colors, pure shapes, objects that overlapped, objects that stood inches apart. He referred to them as "intimate landscapes." The tiny movement of an object could make or break the meaning he was trying to convey.

In the same way, the design of a room should convey meaning. It should be livable, not purely decorated, but it must also possess the drama of silhouettes. Lines and shadows create the dynamic tension, and they should play, not wrestle. Look around a room. Is there harmony? Is there breathing space between the furnishings? Do the pieces work together effortlessly? As in a Morandi painting, the negative space is as important as the volumes.

Rhythm keeps the eye moving: background, foreground, and profile. The clean surface of a coffee table should curl into the gentle curve of a sofa; the sleek face of the fireplace should contain a heavily carved screen or geometric fire tools. A pair of upholstered armchairs should be balanced by a wooden side table or footstool. A smooth white wall should hold a heavily textured painting or large-format photograph.

Light is an important aspect of silhouettes, as the paintings of Johannes Vermeer remind us: the northern cast, the filtered dust, the haunting outlines of everyday objects of Dutch seventeenth-century life. The plain decor, black-and-white floor tiles, heavy draperies, and wooden windowpanes create quiet drama. Vermeer's compositions keep us transfixed, wanting more.

Scale is also critical: the relative heights of seats, backs, coffee tables, and end tables should be balanced and counterbalanced like weights upon a scale. The furniture of architect and industrial designer Franco Albini was provocatively contoured and stripped of all decoration, its scale calibrated and refined. A spiral staircase became an abstract sculpture, a bookcase a floating world.

Proportion is elemental. The stark beauty of the San Jacinto Mountains is a perfect setting for the modern houses, such as Bob Hope's wacky, spaceship-like house designed by John Lautner, that stands proudly against the hilltop, defying explanation and context. Richard Neutra's Kaufmann House floats magically against the desert oasis.

Light, air, scale, and proportion constitute the mathematics that make an object work or not work. The perfect silhouette must appear effortless, even though it is the result of equal parts calculation and inspiration. The designer must be minutely attuned—with the eye of an artist—to the interplay of the outlines and negative space created by the arrangement of furniture and objects in a room. Silhouettes are a visual, often sculptural, language that, like Vermeer's interiors, invest rooms with drama, poetry, and artistic meaning surpassing mere function.

A Ward Bennett sofa, a pair of upholstered chairs by Kerstin Hörlin-Holmquist from the 1950s, side chairs by Tomlinson from the 1960s, and a daybed by Carl Malmsten have streamlined silhouettes that harmonize perfectly in the living room of this Greenwich Village, New York, apartment. The artwork above the sofa is by Timothy Paul Myers.

Scale

JUAN MONTOYA

I remember looking at a photograph of the former president of France, Nicolas Sarkozy, and his wife, Carla Bruni. In all their public appearances, Bruni never wore high heels, only flats, so that she would never look much taller than the President. Scale surrounds us!

Proportion is the relationship of parts to a whole—for example, the legs of a chair to its back. Scale is also the relationship of that chair to the room in which it sits. A designer should not be afraid to plant large pieces of furniture in a small room. Better to have one stunning piece by Jean-Michel Frank or a grand relic of the nineteenth century than myriad small pieces without resonance or importance.

In designing the grand salon of one of the historic Villard Houses for the 2014 Kips Bay Decorator Show House, I chose to let the scale of the room speak to me when choosing furnishings. There needed to be a direct relationship between the scale of the room and the scale of the furnishings—for example, the seventeen-foot serpentine sofa I designed for the center of the room. While it was in production at the workroom it seemed enormous, yet within the architectural envelope of the salon it was perfect. When the implied relationship between space and furnishings is successful, the finished space feels effortless, and everyone entering the space feels at once at ease.

It became an exercise in allowing the existing architecture to dictate the scale of not only the furniture, but the art as well. Learning to embrace scale, and to let it express itself in a room's furnishing, is one of the most important lessons a designer must learn.

When I think of scale in relationship to architecture, Le Corbusier comes instantly to mind. He relates the size of the human body to the scale of a room, and, in turn, to the architecture of a building. The greatest buildings I have visited are always predicated on notions

A seventeen-foot-long, double-sided serpentine sofa is perfectly scaled for an enormous reception room in this mansion on New York's Upper East Side. Equally at home is a twelve-foot-wide stainless steel desk, which was designed and fabricated for the space. The red painting, *Choir*, is by British artist Christopher Le Brun.

of beauty based on proportion and scale. For instance, the library by Erik Gunnar Asplund in Stockholm poses a beautiful relationship between human function and its relation to its environment, with classical orders simplified to reflect modern-day use, such as open shelving to facilitate readers' access to books.

The best rooms I have encountered are those that read simply. This is not to say that they are empty, but that the furniture bears a very exact proportion to the total scale of the space. One element always complements the other; there is a fine balance between them that works like a well-choreographed ballet. A good room or building is like a symphony, with all the parts combining to make a harmonious sound to the ear.

My six-year-old nephew once told me he hated his room. I said, "But it's so beautiful. What wrong with it? The colors are soothing, the carpet is great." Then it struck me. I realized that the room lacked fantasy: there was no place to hide! Everything about the scale was perfect for an adult, but not for a child. When designing, we should always look at who our inhabitant is. A child perceives his or her body in space differently than an adult does; the volumes and scale of my nephew's room needed space for play, for secrets. This simple lesson can be applied to any demographic.

Whether one is decorating a grand country house or a small city apartment, the same principles of scale apply. Create a focal point from the best pieces you can muster; dare to be imposing. Even a small room may take on majesty if one orchestrates, sparingly, significant pieces within it: large in size, superb in style, and high in quality.

A sculpture by Swedish artist Eva Hild rests atop a pedestal in front of an imaginative, undulating plaster wall that houses the fireplace. The wall's "waves" modernize the Roman architectural detailing of the McKim, Mead & White–designed structure.

Communication

 WINDSOR SMITH

A room is only truly beautiful if it draws you in. Some call it "good flow," that ineffable quality that moves you to walk a step farther, to peer around corners and find every sight line. In many ways, creating that kind of allure has always been an act of pure instinct. Nevertheless, there are rules anyone can follow: Don't block sight lines; avoid dead ends; never fight a home's footprint when shaping its pathways; and keep the din of high-traffic rooms away from places of respite.

We have to respect how well traditional layouts honor these rules. They thoughtfully sequence a series of spaces from gracious entries to gathering rooms and back down corridors ending in private rooms. But where are the boundaries of privacy in today's instant-messaging world? Who hasn't answered texts from their bedroom or bathroom? Who hasn't pulled out a phone to look up the name of the movie you can't recall at the dinner table, only to see the e-mail you forgot to answer?

Try as we might, there's just no retrofitting the distractions and diversions of modern life into the orderly equations of yesterday's homes. No matter how seamlessly you sequence space, light, and color, life still interrupts.

Instant messaging, urgent e-mails, video chats, and online streaming mean that the devices designed to bring us together are also pushing us further apart. I realized some time ago that the only way I could make clients with demanding lifestyles truly happy at home is to evolve my work to this shiftier new landscape of starts and stops. The flow I need to focus on building is the everyday flow of conversation. Somehow, I need to find tangible ways to put emotion and connectivity into the DNA of rooms I was previously consumed with making beautiful. I had to draw people deeper than the next room. My job was now to inspire clients to express themselves and communicate in a deeper way within their walls.

Home as a safe haven is not a new concept. But designing homes that can feel like a personal retreat while also functioning as a makeshift office, restaurant, gym, theater, or salon is a new challenge.

We used to think open living plans offered solutions. The kitchen became the great room, where Mom could cook while Dad poured Scotch and the kids watched television or finished homework at the counter. But what we learned was that coexistence doesn't necessarily equal togetherness. It wasn't enough for a room to have multiple functions. Instead, that room needed to stir you, quietly and unobtrusively, to live and breathe in a way beyond mere routine.

To be a good designer today, you must be part shaman, mixing those ingredients that lead clients back to the nuances of human communication. You have to think beyond function and toward ritual. How can a room host game playing, music making, art, sewing, or cooking competitions? How can certain colors, textures, and spatial alignments inspire intimacy and togetherness in a master suite? As daunting as it seems, when you shape someone's home, you provide the architecture for his or her relationships.

I suppose the ultimate goal is a moment of stillness. We have to interrupt the interruptions, rousing families to feel firmly placed in those moments when memories form. In my own family room, that meant moving a Ping-Pong table in front of the mantel. For another family, I pulled the grand piano to the room's center. In most rooms, however, cues to connect are less obvious. That's the mystery of our craft. Mixing airy expanses with dark corners, reassuringly familiar silhouettes with dazzling new forms, or the tactile with the ethereal, design is, at its essence, relationship building. And the rationale for its many juxtapositions remains an instinct for greater, deeper, stronger human communication.

A careful balance between antique and modern furnishings is found in this room, which is anchored by a large table topped with books and a mirrored globe. The corners of the room are places for the occupants to retreat for intimate conversations, and the herringbone parquet floors, which lend purposeful symmetry, were reclaimed from a seventeenth-century château in Lyon, France.

Framing

SALVATORE LAROSA

The inherent duality of a picture frame has always fascinated me. The finite surround places a viewer on the outside looking in. And yet it also invites him to dwell in a mental space that the artist has conceived.

When I was a young designer, every photo shoot with my mentor, Joseph D'Urso, was a master class in the art of framing a view. Photography, as he saw it, should aim beyond merely documenting the appearance of a finished work: "Construct an image to relive the *intentions* that moved you to make it." Joe had me peer through the camera lens and study Polaroid test shots, a must in those pre-digital days, to gauge how even the subtlest rearrangement of objects within a specific field of vision—"An inch more table here . . . less water in that vase"—can reveal powerful relationships within a room.

The eye, I learned, has emotions, but the hand needs a steady frame of reference if it is to communicate intensely personal feelings and elicit a response from others. "Frame of mind," as Joe taught me, can be far more than a figure of speech. This was a lesson that, centuries earlier, an artist like Johannes Vermeer might have conveyed to his pupil through the mirrored microcosm of a camera obscura.

Establishing boundaries to concentrate attention, the essence of any frame, is a fundamental way of ordering experience. Our bodies, the frames we grow into, give us an instinctive sense of physical limits as well as mobility, like Leonardo's Vitruvian Man. Our anatomical optical lens is curiously flexible as we navigate our worlds. Watching a sunset on the beach—or facing the artfully framed allées of an André Le Nôtre landscape—we perceive infinity even though we cannot literally see it.

Depending on our innate sense of scale and the relative stature we wish to project, we gravitate toward the coziness of a low armchair or the grandeur of a high-backed throne. Just as a chair frames the posture and demeanor of a human being at rest, a doorway fixes the afterimage of a figure in motion, momentarily framed within it, providing the foreground to an emotionally charged vista through a room and, sometimes, far beyond it. Inside a large, open volume, the mind's eye extends bedposts or the borders of an area rug to raise conceptual walls, staking out a comfortable room within a room. A pool of lamplight, a flickering fire, the halo of a candle—each defines ephemeral boundaries and moods. The roofline of a courtyard brackets the sky.

Whether sketching the layout for a sofa and coffee table or the elevation of a colonnade, I consciously define a series of frames to direct one's gaze along an eventful pathway. I still prefer the tactile intimacy of drawing by hand on draftsman's tracing paper. The transparent sheets let me shift various elements within a given area until they home in on the "hot spot" I've been seeking. One of my favorite examples centers on a pivotal corner of the refectory in a client's family compound. A chaise I designed exudes repose while gesturing toward a majestic copper beech tree on a hill outside the grid of adjacent windowpanes.

This tableau links every coordinate in a complex intersection of architecture and landscape, rationality and romanticism. A moment of quiet intensity, it also evokes the recumbent nude and pastoral terrain in Giorgione's *Sleeping Venus*.

I have often found inspiration for expanding my architectural perspectives in the narrative works of Proto-Renaissance painters. Age-old story lines—the Annunciation, the Nativity—miraculously spring to life across the multiple framed panels of an altar's predella. Strangely akin to Eadweard Muybridge's

A doorway focuses the solid geometry of an interior view while measuring the path of ephemeral sunlight overhead. The tall, narrow portal tapers to amplify the depth of a wall and the drama of penetrating its mass. When empty, the frame conjures up the sense of an invisible human body passing through.

nineteenth-century motion-study photographs or a contemporary graphic novel, the sequence of static frames only intensifies the dynamic sweep it contains.

The objects I favor for interiors frequently take the shape of diminutive buildings, tabernacles both religious and secular, and constructions that amplify nature and contemplate our place within it. Many pieces are vessels, essentially frames in the round. Regardless of whether they are pitcher, urn, or chalice, whether they are literal or figurative, the frames we employ in our homes hold the substance of this world, as well as our thoughts about what lies beyond.

Rhythmic window frames invite the eye to move within a room as well as outside it. In this Long Island, New York house, composed furnishings against a horizontal grid of panes are like notes on a musical staff. Anthropomorphic chairs extend their arms for a pas de deux.

Definitions

In this regally proportioned paneled dining room, a monochromatic palette of whispery taupe allows the architecture of the room to set a stately mood. A Greek-key pattern is stenciled around the border of the floor to accentuate the neoclassical feeling.

OVERLEAF: Butter yellow is the order of the day in this high-ceilinged salon in a Washington, D.C., home. Hand-painted trelliswork, twined with ivy, serves as the reverse pattern of the upholstered chairs and throw pillows (left). A meditative mood prevails in this library, which features Regency-inspired furniture, including a black lacquer–and-gilt table and white-painted chairs (right).

The professional titles "interior designer" and "interior decorator" are commonly used interchangeably; as a result of this confusing convention, most people find it difficult to distinguish between these two closely allied fields.

Both the interior designer and the interior decorator deal with the aesthetics of interior spaces, and while both the decorator and the designer are motivated by the creation of beauty, it is the scope of work that principally distinguishes them.

Interior designers most often propose and shape spaces, which they also typically decorate. The interior decorator is not the delineator of new architectural plans, but the talented producer of well-schemed and fully furnished rooms. Interior decorators are mainly concerned with surfacing and the selection of the movable objects within an existing architectural context.

The divide between design and decoration has everything to do with the ability to manipulate and architecturally detail interior spaces. Indeed, interior design is a discipline of architecture, although it involves a narrower scope of interest and expertise than the broader field of architecture. The interior designer commonly focuses on the planning and detailing of the interior, having the skill to both conceptualize space and prepare the architectural drawings required for general or specialty contractors to build out or renovate the space. In creating design documents and specifications, the interior designer is often providing the same services and drawings an architect would, as well as those a decorator would supply.

A decorator, on the other hand, should have a high level of expertise relating to furniture (both selection and arrangement), surfacing, floor coverings, window treatments, and the selection and placement of all movable decorations. The decorator can, of course, change surfaces and trims as part of an overall decorative scheme, but typically he or she does not prepare the documentation to the same degree as an interior designer.

A further distinction between interior design and interior decoration is regulatory. In many places, the practice of interior design requires a license, while the practice of decoration does not. The "product" of the designer, creating the interior architecture of a dwelling or commercial building, often touches on safety issues, and as such, it is regulated by local codes and standard building practices. Designing can require building permits and may be subject to inspection by the relevant municipal agencies. Decoration typically does not require permitting, nor inspections.

The *Encyclopedia Britannica* gives a great definition of interior design, pointedly differentiating it from decoration: "One of the key considerations in any design must be the question of whether a design 'works' or functions for its purpose. If a theater has poor sight lines, poor acoustics, and insufficient means of entry and egress, it obviously does not work for its purpose, no matter how beautifully it is decorated."

Edith Wharton's classic book *The Decoration of Houses* was first published in 1897, and it ushered in the century that gave rise to the specialized fields of both interior decoration and interior design. Before Wharton's book, decoration had traditionally been handled by painters and upholsterers, but the rising affluence of Americans opened the door to a quickly growing specialty field, interior decoration. The decorator was a purveyor of taste

and style. Interior design gained a foothold in the mid-twentieth century in response to the proliferation of multistory office and apartment buildings and the rise in importance of the American kitchen and bathroom. Interior design is now so specialized that the work of commercial interior designers is quite different in its focus from that of residential design.

Interior design engages planning, aesthetics, and decoration, and it is at the beginning of the twenty-first century no longer limited to the wealthiest, but considered important to most.

Juxtaposition

MATTHEW WHITE *and* FRANK WEBB

*"Creativity is that marvelous capacity
to grasp mutually distinct realities and
draw a spark from their juxtaposition."*

—MAX ERNST

Juxtaposition is a wonderful, tongue-twirling term frequently heard in interior design, and understandably so. Apart from the fact that it possesses an erudite ring, its successful deployment is every designer's goal and what elevates your average well-designed room into something that surpasses all expectations.

At thirteen letters, *juxtaposition* is a long word for a very basic concept: putting things next to each other for the sake of comparison or contrast. Although it sounds more like science than art, both are equally at play. When you think about it, the designer is a bit like Dr. Frankenstein, trying to create life from inanimate objects. Our science is the knowledge of historical styles, available materials, and fine craftsmanship, not to mention the continual experimentation inherent in the design process. While this science lays an important foundation, it takes the lightning bolts of a designer's artistic vision to bring our creatures to life. Fortunately, ours tend to be much more attractive than Dr. F's, and they rarely kill anyone.

And on the subject of lightning, electricity is exactly what successful juxtapositions produce. Whether furnishings are complementary or contrasting, their pairing generates a palpable current that evokes a desired feeling or ambience. In the same vein, rooms are called lifeless when poor juxtaposition either fails to generate a pulse or electrocutes with overenthusiasm.

The late Albert Hadley was a master at juxtaposition because his interiors were said to produce a wonderful frisson—a brief shiver of excitement—for all who experienced them. It was energy at its finest.

Igniting that spark also involves a certain degree of risk; informed chances inject a degree of freshness, and ideally a whiff of welcome imperfection. Even the most tailored interior benefits from the errant extravagance, and the most sumptuously decadent from a touch of austere rigor. For us, we find our risk taking typically involves the introduction of a bit of humor or wit, and it's fascinating where it can lead. If you respect the medium but never take yourself too seriously, you'll give yourself the freedom to create risky pairings that can truly break new ground and surprise you in delightful ways.

Through juxtaposition one can create harmony or tension, and even harmony through tension. A fairly common example of the latter is when antiques are blended dynamically with contemporary art and design, but the mix requires a deft hand. While anyone can study period interiors and attempt a historically accurate room, the outcome can be less than inspiring. What takes things to another level is the artful juxtaposition of period pieces with those from completely different places and times. Similarities in line, form, material, or color can induce harmony, whereas variances in the same can inject exciting tension. Like an accomplished director, a great designer knows how to cast, block, and balance his talent so that the ensemble delivers a scintillating, ovation-worthy performance.

At the very heart of juxtaposition is the nature of give and take. Each design element contributes something to the mix,

The original mantel in this apartment in a prestigious Stanford White–designed building was retained to bridge the old and the new, a classic juxtaposition. Two Lucien Rollin chairs sit across from a custom sofa based on a Jean-Michel Frank design. The contemporary chandelier was produced by Venetian glass artist Massimo Micheluzzi.

with an eye toward the whole being greater than the sum of its individual parts. Operating as a design partnership, we live and breathe this aspect of juxtaposition on a daily basis. Two people, two perspectives, and two egos converge at the design table, and most days, no one gets hurt. While some might figure a classicist (White) and a modernist (Webb) to be forever at odds, nothing could be further from the truth. We each have our preferences, but we see the value in our differences and often marvel at our similarities. Most importantly, like any partnership, we recognize that something in the other person makes us even better. In the end, isn't that what successful juxtaposition is all about?

Intimacy

BOBBY McALPINE

Bringing intimacy into the design of a house is something I do on a regular basis because, frankly, most people forget to ask for it. Often when I meet with clients, they speak about rooms intended for the gathering of friends and family. Very few talk to me about the solitary spaces where they will be alone or with just one other person.

It's easy to forget about the places which you will ultimately love the most—the kangaroo pockets where, closely held, you're invited to drop pretensions and explore the truth of yourself. In this posture of vulnerability, you become connected to all those characters inside and outside of you who deserve a voice; you unlock and free them. This same entreaty is issued to all who enter, calling them to wade in and wander out and dance. When the heart expands, it's easier to recognize the same cues in others. Typically, the ego builds the house, but the heart is the one most desperate to be housed.

Intimacy begins in the lap of parents where we once sat, held close but also emboldened to venture out, knowing that we were backed by love. In architecture, this experience is found within alcoves, bays, a fireside inglenook, and the spaces beneath low mezzanines or beams—all sheltered spots existing adjacent to loftier ones. Without thinking about it, we are drawn to them. In the language of cathedrals, we are more likely to allow ourselves to be vulnerable in chapels and side aisles; a timid person who might evaporate standing alone in the middle of the nave thrives along its shadowy edges. We experience this constantly and unconsciously in restaurant booths, which are far more intimate than tables in the middle of the room. When we sit buried in a banquette, we dissolve in safety and the conversation changes.

A vaulted loggia with limestone columns leads to the antique front door of a Nashville house. An arched niche is sculpted into the rubble-stone walls, offering a chance to pause and view the pool and lush garden.

OVERLEAF: The seating area of a Nashville master bedroom is nestled beside windows at one end, and the bed sits atop a dais of antique wood. This simple gesture and a change in floor material separates the two zones. The room is furnished with antique artifacts, modern lighting, and a chaise fabricated from a pair of antique lounge chairs.

In the house, this attraction to being held is witnessed strongly by canopied beds and draped bedchambers that invite you to turn inward and rest securely like an animal in its den. Compression of space creates a sense of comfort and containment.

Subtle messages of texture, tone, and light and the reflective qualities of surfaces are just as expressive. Texture can be an emotional friend. Compared to harder surfaces that reflect light, drapery and soft woods have the capacity to drink you in and receive you. Their capacity to absorb sound quiets you.

The level and quality of light also has a strong effect on what happens inside a space. Old glass turns light molten and liquid, encouraging contemplation. The graphic shadows cast by Venetian blinds and shutters create a film noir atmosphere in which confidences can be given and received. Light imitating candlelight or originating from a low source—firelight, lamps, sconces, or lowered chandeliers—reduces scale and corrects chilly volumes. It warms and enriches texture, color, and focus, creating a sensation of containment that shifts and hones the conversation. Introduced into a larger, more expansive space, these aforementioned elements create islands of intimacy.

Bringing the center of gravity down to the lower third of the room with wainscoting, banquettes, and even wing-back chairs intensifies this sensation of containment. In a very large, gregarious room where everything floats and there are no walls to lean against, your primary relationship is with the floor. It becomes your nearest companion, and the rug is a raft to which we cling.

In any room where our most intimate possessions are arrayed, others are called to show and tell. There is an invitation in the submissive gesture of tenderly exposing those bits and pieces that house our stories. In the safety of such places, our emotional walls begin to dissolve. That is the irony of creating containment: When the walls come up around us, our internal walls slip away. The architecture takes over the job of the psyche, becoming our armor and expanding the territory of the heart in a subtle but important way.

Planes

DANIEL SACHS *and* KEVIN LINDORES

Planes—walls, floors, and ceilings—are the building blocks of architecture; they connect us as human beings to the most basic shelter or dwelling. Walls contain and protect us, and they direct us where to go and what to do. The roof is protection from the outdoors and suggests civilization, a sanctuary from the elements that is an enclosed world in itself.

Modernists tend to use planes to create a path rather than a place, dissolving walls. The modernism of Le Corbusier, Mies van der Rohe, and Frank Lloyd Wright was intended to make the wall go away—in the case of Wright, it obviated the division of indoors and landscape. When the barriers that compose traditional containment are dissolved, how do you create a sense of place? The difference between traditional and modern is not so clear-cut, but one might say that in the modernist interior, containment is signaled more by doors and windows than by planes.

In our work for clients, we try, first of all, to create a sense of place. Most good interior spaces do that by calibrating the relationship of where a wall is to the wall, ceiling, and floor next to it. The twenty-first-century designer has a range of choices, from the seventeenth-century language of rooms, hallways, and enfilades to that of early modernism, with its paths and transparencies.

In an 1850s New York City townhouse, we adopted a modernist approach, dematerializing the walls by painting their elaborate baseboards and crown moldings in a single light color. The texture of architectural detail remained, but the walls became a suitably blank background for the clients' important collection of modern furniture and art.

When you build from scratch, you can dictate how a space feels with the architecture. But when you're working with an existing space, you have to use illusionistic devices such as wallpaper and color. In another New York interior, we had to contend with an entry that was dimly lit and narrow, and which we could only slightly open. We decided to keep it dark, so that the space onto which the entry opened appeared much lighter. We sheathed the ceiling in a rich, gilded wallpaper which made the entry seem less bounded and hung artwork—images are an important means of expanding tight walls. Planes become agents of space not only in their relationships but in their surfaces.

When one designs and builds a house from the ground up, the relationship of planes and the sculpture of volumes is more freely addressed by one's own aesthetic, but it is also of course shaped by the clients' needs. An interesting case in point is a studio we built for a New York artist moving his family to rural Connecticut. The artist asked us to take the actual proportions of his New York studio—an old gymnasium in a nineteenth-century building where he has worked contentedly for thirty years—and re-create them on his new property.

On the new site, these dimensions are part of a one-story house built from scratch, no longer enmeshed within a city block. But instead of nineteenth-century masonry, we used prefabricated construction materials and techniques to erect the building on the forest floor. It is simply built and beautifully designed, but what is most important about the new house are the memories and emotions the client feels about the dimensions—the planes—that comprised his former studio.

The origin and purpose of planes is to create a sense of place that expresses dwelling and protection. The task of the designer, whether working with an existing space or creating a new building, is to fulfill that purpose and do something more—to evoke a sense of human aspiration, whether grand or intimate, temple or cottage.

A custom-made white oak–and–steel table rests beneath a Noguchi ceiling lamp in this Manhattan loft owned by photographers Inez van Lamsweerde and Vinoodh Matadin. The couple's art collection includes works by Andy Warhol and Louise Bourgeois.

Destinations

ALAN TANKSLEY

"All journeys have secret destinations
of which the traveler is unaware."

—MARTIN BUBER

The way I see it, the role of an interior designer is not only to create order out of chaos, but to make a special effort to provide subtle, sometimes secret, destinations along the way as well.

I believe the first consideration with any project should be to establish the hierarchy of spaces, which is generally based on the function each space serves; this runs the gamut from the initial approach and entry through the shared communal spaces to the most intimate and private realms beyond. Of course, this can be accomplished in a relentlessly clinical manner—think of Louis Sullivan's oft-repeated edict "Form follows function."

Alternately, if one chooses, there are opportunities to create interesting, useful diversions or delightful distractions along the way without compromising efficiency and functionality. For instance, when creating a place to pause along a passageway by recessing a console table loaded with curious, eye-pleasing objects into an alcove and useful items, you add immeasurably to the experience of trudging from point A to point B with little or no added expense.

To further illustrate the subtle importance of this perspective, consider experiences we've all had when arriving at and moving through a house or apartment we've never been to. The most successful experiences are those that begin by being intuitively guided from the street, sidewalk, or parking lot to a welcoming front entry, ideally through a garden, forecourt, or intimate public lobby. Along the way, one may have encountered a place to pause, and though we seldom

The monolithic fireplace, open to both the living room and the dining room, forms a strong visual centerpiece unifying the public spaces of this residence in Vail, Colorado. The appeal of a comfortable gathering around an open fire invites both family members and guests to pause and relax.

In the vestibule of a master bedroom suite in this Vail, Colorado, house, a chaise longue is a perfect spot to curl up on a blustery afternoon.

OPPOSITE: This Snowmass, Colorado, house was purposefully designed with an unconventional flow, which provides a sense of anticipation and discovery when traveling between its rooms. The outdoor seating area here has unparalleled views up the adjacent mountain.

do so, the very idea of it is intriguing and thought-provoking. Moments such as these might evoke memories of peace, tranquility, or security—not a bad thing for an otherwise eventless transitional space. When we perceive that an otherwise unremarkable approach has been transformed through skilled planning into an exceptional experience, we feel that something special lies in store, something akin to an adventure. If all goes well, the same effort undertaken to provide a nuanced and welcoming sense of arrival will be revealed throughout the rest of the home.

Recently, I was given the opportunity to work on a house in Jackson Hole, Wyoming. It turned out to be culminating in the delivery of one of the most unique

and dynamic residences I've done to date. The house had a spectacular setting and a challenging but attainable roster of needs and desires to be accommodated. Having previously built or renovated several residences, the clients were engaged and decisive throughout our collaboration. Most importantly, they were experienced in the design process, therefore they understood and appreciated the complexities involved in designing and building a handcrafted house and complementary property.

Chief among our conversations throughout the experience was the importance of creating destinations, both obvious and subtle, that over time would reveal themselves to those who passed through their home. Places created for the purpose of gathering communally are balanced by intimate spaces tucked away for smaller gatherings. Movement through the house is marked by a progression of corridors, vestibules, and level changes that quietly delineate the public and private areas. Access to the exterior is effortless, with organic pathways to the terraces, gardens, and stunning views beyond.

In addition to the brick-and-mortar examples given, there are many less tangible destinations one can strive to create when designing a house or room, or even a tabletop vignette. Some are born out of practicality, such as the need for at least one sturdy armchair in a sitting room for those seeking a secure destination to relax in. Another is considering the importance of appropriate lighting in all cases, whether it be for reading, working on a computer, or general ambience. Although most people don't consciously recognize it, when presented with well-considered options, they are destined to position themselves where it best suits their needs at that moment.

Finally, as legendary *Vogue* editor and style icon Diana Vreeland famously said, "The eye has to travel." This endures as timeless and prescient advice to be heeded by all who strive to create environments that impress us with their thoughtfulness, that have subtle and detailed considerations for function, or that are unexpected visual destinations, created simply to delight one's eye.

Geometry

ERIC COHLER

Although numbers have always been challenging for me, I love geometry.

As a child I built cities out of wooden blocks and Legos that included spheres, circles, squares, cones, rectangles, and triangulated forms. Later, my parents gave me an Etch A Sketch; I was fascinated by what I could create using simple lines. Once I discovered that I could transfer forms to paper just as easily, I never looked back, utilizing a ruler, a compass, and an antique drafting set that I was given as a teenager. This was the beginning of my obsession with lines; those doodles eventually became floor plans and facades, leading me to follow a career in design. To this day, I can recall almost every space that I've been in throughout my life and re-create the plan with ease.

For simplicity's sake, an informed examination of geometry starts with the Egyptians around 2,500 BC and the Great Pyramid of Giza—a perfect example of the golden ratio, a number intrinsic to the understanding of proportion within geometry. Without correct proportion and balance an interior oftens falls flat as a cohesive dynamic is missing. Personally, I can't create "magic" without these keystones.

Two thousand years later, Euclid, known as the father of geometry, proved that a line has zero width, is purely one-dimensional, and is the shortest distance between two points. Fast-forward a few centuries to the Roman architect Vitruvius and his ten-book treatise *De Architectura* on planning, design, and construction methods. The work was incredibly modern for its time and, in fact, was the first to include descriptions of measuring devices, whose later incarnations remain in use today. In my interiors I use measurement daily. For example, the distance from sofa to cocktail table must be carefully measured to ensure that any drinks are within reach.

Finally, Venetian architect Andrea Palladio was considered one of the most influential individuals in Western architecture. His treatise, *The Four Books of Architecture (I Quattro Libri dell'Architettura)*, is based in part on the solid foundation laid down by Vitruvius. Palladio also mastered the perfect cube, a form of Platonic virtue. Due to the rapid adoption of styles and the strength of empire building through the early twentieth century, Palladian windows, arches, and details can be seen from the Veneto to St. Petersburg, Sydney, Mumbai, and Harare.

Wondering what all of this has to do with interior design? Everything. None of the world's greatest builders, architects, or designers—spread across thousands of years—could have created structures without geometry. Without basic geometry, the tension between solids and voids would fall flat, and there would be no floor plans, elevations, or structural detail of any kind.

In my practice, I rely on geometric forms to balance and cancel one another out in interesting and different ways. I ascribe this to pure tensile strength. Without a certain amount of stability, things fall apart literally and figuratively. Geometric relationships are integral to the life of a designer in creating plans and elevations and hanging art. Not only are a tape measure, level, hammer, and hooks essential, a strong sense of how the works will relate to one another and as a balanced whole is also necessary.

Geometry comes into play in arranging furniture and accessories, as without proper spatial skills, all is lost. And considering the adjacencies of forms requires geometry: how close a table should be to a chair, and at what height. In addition, geometric relationships become evident when planning lighting—in the way light illuminates or casts shadows over a space—and in specifying fabrics, stone, tile, and other materials.

A bold assemblage of artwork is hung salon-style from airline-grade steel wire in a room with few walls. Geometric patterns are found throughout, such as on the checked cut-velvet club chairs and the bolster on the purple settee. A turquoise gourd Christopher Spitzmiller lamp, a Revlon-red lacquered coffee table, and a carpet with coral formations add whimsy and charm.

Geometry explains and enhances the three-dimensional nature of our world. Without it, the world would be a pretty flat place. Geometry directs us toward the beauty of shapes and forms, paving the way not only for the "cities" created by a small child, but also the sophisticated interiors marked by a sense of sculpture that the designer well versed in geometry can create.

This towering, templelike bathroom, with its banded tile and round shower area, is a study of perfect proportions. The windows high up in the rotunda bathe the space in abundant natural light. The entire tableau is softened by a linen shower curtain with a mouse-gray band that repeats the stripe of the tiles.

STYLE

Style

SUZANNE KASLER

For me, it's all about style. Style is fascinating. I know it when I see it, but it's hard to describe. That's because it can take so many forms and cross all the boundaries between art, architecture, fashion, and design. And it's not any one look or a particular thing: style is more than trends. It's about attitude, and anyone can develop it.

Look around. We do this naturally when we travel. Paris is the epicenter of style for me, a place where I can walk into the ribbon store and come out with a whole new palette. Even a stack of luggage on the sidewalk outside Goyard is a work of art. We are primed to soak up the sights in a foreign country, but the trick is to keep your eyes open.

At home in my bedroom—my favorite place to work—the sunlight streams in and warms up the creamy white walls and the pale blue silk curtains, which are the same lovely shade of blue-gray as the vintage Georges Braque poster I found in a bin at the Avignon flea market and hung above my bed. On Sunday afternoons, I surround myself with magazines on fashion and current events as well as interior design. I tear out pages, and you might be surprised at the things that catch my eye. It's not the dress on the model in *Vogue* but the beautiful hardware on the French doors in the background. That's the detail I want to remember. I always ask my clients to bring in pictures. It's a huge part of determining what they like and developing a design style that will suit them.

Style is very personal. Out of all the unique people, places, and things you come across, you want to pick out the ones that are right for you. We do this all the time, whether we're buying a dress or decorating a house. When you find your style and embrace it in your work and in your life, you feel more comfortable because it will be authentic to you. Style is about expressing yourself.

As Coco Chanel once said, "Fashion fades, but style endures." When it comes to my own wardrobe, I feel more comfortable in classic pieces. But I add an accessory—a colorful purse or a whimsical piece of jewelry—to make it feel fresh and updated. I like mixing the traditional and the modern.

I do the same thing in houses. I have clients who come to me because they want to give a traditional house a younger look. Sometimes I'll do it through editing, paring down possessions to the strongest pieces. Or I might change the palette, strategically adding shots of clear, bright colors. I may use turquoise or pink or lavender paint in a dining room or a powder room, so you see it when you pass by. Then the living room will be in shades of champagne, with perhaps a few turquoise pillows, so it still feels colorful but is actually restful to the eye. You can use several different colors in one house if they all have the same value. But you don't want to overdo color—you don't want to overdo anything—because then it won't feel quite so special. Design is a balancing act.

I'm balancing fabrics, too. In the same room, I might use sisal and linen and silk. Composing a room is similar to the process you go through when you're putting a stylish outfit together. You might mix something dressy with something casual—for example, a silk shirt with your favorite pair of jeans. It's a nonchalant look that creates a sense of stylish, casual elegance—the perfect balance of high and low.

One thing I love in working with clients is being able to help them define their own style and then translate it into a three-dimensional space. When a home reflects your personality, you're more comfortable there. When you choose things that have meaning for you, in how you dress and what you bring into your rooms, you feel confident

A luxuriously deep armless sofa, two Lucite tables, and a pair of Fortuny throw pillows create a welcoming spot to relax in this Atlanta living room. Sixteen Kris Ruhs prints, hung with the frames touching, appear to be one significant piece of art. A Turkish Oushak rug anchors the space.

and happier with life. People sense that, and it also makes them feel more comfortable with you. Having identified your own style, you come across as completely yourself.

To find one's own look, in design and in fashion, is what makes life special. Being authentic to yourself is what defines timeless style.

Reflective lacquered walls, which create drama and intrigue, invite conversation in this expansive dining room; lacquering the trim and baseboards finishes the architectural envelope. A Louis XV limestone chimneypiece, and an ink drawing by Franz Kline complete the room.

Vintage Modern

THOMAS O'BRIEN

I am often asked what, exactly, is the meaning of vintage, particularly vintage modern? Is it a relative era from which things date, or is it more a subjective statement of style? Is it an ambience versus a provenance?

In design, there are typical distinctions between what is antique, what is vintage, what is modern, and even what is contemporary. In defining terms, it's common practice to say that an antique is an object or form that is at least one hundred years old. So by that measure, vintage things are of the past, but not as old as antiques. Yet I think of vintage more in terms of this idea: as a synonym for classic, a lasting contribution of a past time that we want to bring into the present. Vintage means adding the value of history to what we collect and live with, so that the world isn't untethered from who and what has come before. It's part of the perfect ecology of design, recycling the old to make it the new. In some ways, it's the cinema of a particular past that we're drawn to, when life seemed more wholesome or glamorous—or both.

On the other side of the timeline, the notion of modern is equally complex: it can be what is happening now—the contemporary— or it can refer to a movement and a style beginning in the late nineteenth century, a period that is itself more than a century old these days. But it's never antique. It's the opposite of traditional.

Modern is really by its nature a mind-set; what fascinates me in design and history is that every age thinks it is modern in its own time. Something ancient or something Georgian can look and feel modern through the generations because it has the virtuous form and innovation in the way it works or the material from which it's made. But at its root, modern is simply what creative people were inventing by sifting through and essentially loving older ideas, mixing them differently, adding new technologies and improving on them, and always designing the leading edge.

A vintage modern piece features ideas that become layers in the DNA of a design that materializes at a later date. It's how something of the 1920s can have echoes of eighteenth-century France, which borrows from Greek or Egyptian antiquity. It's how intriguing it is to play with that heredity in the choice of a material, the colors and the proportions of a room or a piece of furniture, when designing for the time of now. It's how the same forms get reinvented over and over, because they work the best.

I'm interested in the ways that history adds this depth and grounding to newer things. It's the collective memory that makes even the most chic interiors feel familiar and accessible; it's literally the reason we are all, instinctively, born collectors. This is a contin-uum that I try to bring to what I design: adding the vintage—as a lineage and a classicism— to new things being made today. And this is the bridge I cross with each of my clients. Everyone needs his or her own particular connection between past and present.

A perfect example of incorporating vintage modern is the interior architecture for a Manhattan penthouse I designed using an edited palette of just five basic materials in different combinations in each room. The varnished linen, shagreen tile, nickel, plaster, and walnut each come from the tradition of French and Italian luxe modernism of the 1920s. In this residence, the goal was to use the simplicity and warmth of these special finishes to let the modernism of the space become sensual, vintage, and very European in a way, rather than austere.

Many vintage lofts have surviving classical architectural detailing that can feel surprisingly romantic and ornate. For one project, the object was to build that history into a new

A spare fireplace surround, one of several in the apartment, signals a casual and welcoming place for entertaining in the living room of the Central Park West pied-à-terre of fashion icon Giorgio Armani. Parchment-colored linen on the walls, leather seating with patina, and rich, dark woods extend the invitation to relax.

raw, duplex loft, with all the formality of a traditional 1820s townhouse. A long, serene entry hall was constructed with intricately paneled doors and fine millwork, while a minimal staircase brings the space into the present. A few carefully selected nineteenth-century antiques add a spare balance, so that the old is seen in a new light, yet the new is still about something old.

The magic of design is the chance to create something that will be its own vintage in the future. That's the difference between reproduction and the imagining of history.

In the entryway to this elegantly modern Soho loft, a refined staircase is paired with a beautifully carved Swedish settee upholstered in sage-colored silk velvet with tiger-print silk velvet pillows. In its detailing, scale, and form, this space has the European sensibility the clients had requested.

Modernity

 ALAN WANZENBERG

The shelves and mantel in this Upper West Side, New York, apartment were designed and built to mirror a George Washington Maher fireplace surround that was donated to the Art Institute of Chicago. Red tiles lend an air of modernity; the volcanic glazed vessels on the mantel are by Marcello Fantoni, and the sculpture on the coffee table is by Klaus Ihlenfeld.

Modernity is more than an attitude. It is a look at the world that incorporates all its myriad elements into life in a way that is essential, giving pleasure and meaning. Modernity demands an edit of all that's available, paring the choices down to what's necessary. It's not about novelty or trend. It can be about what's contemporary, but that is not its preoccupation; it is about determining how, and with what, we live. It is the here and now. To possess modernity, one must live in the present.

I plan for the future and reflect on the past—as we all do. But I don't let those activities overwhelm my living in the moment. Some planning for the future is necessary, but, as experience has shown, much of it is a waste of time. Life is volatile. Knowing this, I believe you should strive to live each day with an outlook that embraces whatever is going to come your way. Developing confidence and strength in your abilities and coping skills is the best way to manage this.

Modernity and its manifestations in the physical world—what is considered "modern"—can be easily misunderstood. Modernity is not about minimalism or everything being white and reductive. When this happens—and the pendulum often swings in that direction—modernity falls into a style or, worse, a cult. It then has the potential to become tyrannical and intolerant, unaware of all the potent and fascinating forces in design that brought the modern world, as we think of it, into being. True modernity in design can reference the past and allude to the future, but it always exhibits a confidence and resolution that is completely understood in the here and now.

Throughout my career, I have been fascinated by the way people live, by their homes and the objects they surround themselves with, reflecting all the variety of experiences we have in our private worlds. Engaging in the creation of those worlds has been my lifelong passion. Thinking about how families naturally interact on a daily basis, I attempt to understand the familiar and the foreign, the private and the public. My concerns are with how people want to live, what they want to surround themselves with, and with that sweet spot that integrates function and aesthetic pleasure in a subtle manner to reinvigorate and renew. This is the essence of modernity.

Planning, often overlooked in much of contemporary design, is one of the basic tenets of modernity. How an architect or designer lays out a home and how it ultimately gets built has a discreet but significant impact on the way people occupy it. The iconic "glass box" house, now ubiquitous throughout the world, is in most situations unlivable. There is a balance in design that measures what's open against what's closed, with the purpose of creating something harmonious to the life intended. Modernity is incompatible with the poor planning that causes conflict; it's important to create layouts and details that avoid the issues that are detrimental to any sense of a modern way of living.

A successful designer works to create details and elements that will give a sense of confidence in history, in a way that is modern and contemporary but not reductive. He or she designs so the result has been distilled into its essence. There are numerous examples of seemingly disparate elements that resolve into a sophisticated and modern whole, not unlike the best of modern life. This is modernity.

Tradition

ALEXA HAMPTON

As a lifelong student of design, I love its traditions. I love the established canon, from the styles of ancient Greece, right up through the modern tradition. Whether I am admiring an Adam room's fan motifs or the pared down, deconstructed shapes of a building by Frank Lloyd Wright, our traditions are like our parents. We take from them, we discard some of their teachings, or we can plain rebel against them. However, everything we do in design, as in everything else, speaks to our relationship to the traditions that have come before us and what we have learned from them. As a second generation designer, the metaphor for me is even deeper, and often literal.

Tradition in design can mean a lot of things, both visible and invisible. In the most obvious sense, tradition in interior design is an anchor. It doesn't drag a room down, or tether it, I hope; but rather, tradition can connect and locate a space in a context. It can save an interior from arbitrariness and help to create an experience that feels authentic and personal to its owner.

Often, tradition presents itself overtly in architecture, which powerfully assists in the design of the interior. When I am working in a Georgian house, I use that fact as my springboard to envision rooms that would make sense in such a setting and then adapt those ideas for our modern era. In New York apartments, floating above gridded streets, with little to no relationship to their exterior, tradition is frequently imported to create meaning and impose order where there is none. It is a place to start; an answer to the endless options available. In some locales, tradition emerges as color palettes: the reds that pigment temples in Asia echo the color of indigenous trees' leaves, pastels that soften the glare of relentless sunshine appear over and over again in the Caribbean, and the cooler tones that speak to visions of water

and the reflections of northern light are in evidence in the blues and periwinkles of Scandinavia. Conversely, in a Venetian palazzo, or a Parisian apartment building, the very surfeit of visible tradition in the embracing architecture has given birth to its opposite in the interior furnishings: the sleek silhouettes of the International Style. In effect, there is no Barcelona Chair if there is no Gaudi.

In design, traditional elements are loaded with the meanings they have accumulated over time. The iconography that accompanies neoclassicism, for example, has always spoken to power and those who would seize it. Greek, Roman, Napoleonic, Federal, Fascist: their not coincidentally shared imagery is meant to convey strength and mastery. The dynastic decor of the caesars, the sinister visual domination of a mammoth monolith in the era of Mussolini, the suggestion of solidity and security in the decorations of a Federal Bank in the American Midwest—traditional cues can function as tropes that help invest a space with a thought, a sensibility, or a hope, their meaning immediately identifiable to a passing glance.

The robust shapes of Chippendale and Regency furniture have always connoted masculinity to me, as has the unrelenting simplicity of most things Biedermeier. Likewise, the whimsical curves of Louis XV pieces, or Victorian furniture, just to name two, telegraph femininity. Little transmissions of meaning abound in traditional furnishings far beyond the spoken purpose of any given item. These silent messages are as much a part of the designer's toolbox as any can of paint or swatch of fabric. They are our essential means of communication. A rococo chair placed, just so, in a room is a fast way to establish a sense of grandeur and decadence in a space, simultaneously functioning in a sculptural role, all while executing a primary and practical function: offering a place on which to sit.

A bust of Brutus, purchased from a dealer in London, holds court on a William Kent table that belonged to Mark Hampton, the designer's father. The scrolled carvings of the table are echoed in the photograph of a window in the Castello di Sammezzano taken by Massimo Listri.

American design has always appealed to me especially, American that I am. It easily demonstrates its democratic openness to picking and choosing from among the many traditions available in the pursuit of a style, whether genetically connected to our past or not. Its very eclecticism illustrates our melting pot identity, just like everything else in America does, from our religions to our cuisines. I don't think it marks us as ahistorical barbarians. Instead, I like thinking of our approach as affirming us as perpetual pioneers and mix masters, with our unfettered connection to architecture and interior design and how we choose to articulate ourselves through those disciplines. Sometimes American design succeeds, and sometimes it fails; but it is moving, morphing, developing. The best traditional design today has a light touch. Slavish devotion to period decor seems to be of interest only in museum installations. For me, the use of traditional elements helps me to better describe who my client is, what his or her interests are, and how he or she would like to live. While I have probably used the recently coined phrase "traditional with a twist," American traditional design has always been twisty and creative.

Dynamic and ever changing, the employment of traditional design should never be mistaken for stodginess. It is pregnant with meaning, and that is its value. It is a way to get where you want, but never the destination.

Symmetry and order prevail in this New York City living room. The bookcases flanking the mantel hold a surprise: the left one is actually a hidden door that leads to the dining room. The painting of Palazzo Corsini above the mantel is by Marc Dalessio; the pair of rare bergères are covered in sailcloth to provide a playful juxtaposition.

135

Glamour

KELLY WEARSTLER

Glamour is an emotional business. Glamour is personal. Glamour itself is not the property of a certain style or bygone era; rather, it is defined by the *feelings* it evokes.

My philosophy and aesthetic are deeply entrenched in trusting my instincts and embracing anomalies. If there is one thing I have never lost in my career, it is my insatiable thirst for newness; my disposition as an artist is one of perpetual romance with the new. Travel, history, my sons' artwork: the world is constantly bubbling with fresh and exciting inspirations to revamp my tastes. When I was just starting out, I insisted upon acquiring a wide breadth of skills. I installed my own hardwood floors by hand in my first apartment. I feel deeply that it is imperative for any artist to, above all, stay curious. The hunger to explore is everything. Glamour, to me, is also about learning.

In defining glamour in design, there are the old tropes and fallbacks: chandeliers, sweeping staircases, a virtuoso use of color, floor-to-ceiling anything. And I can never stress enough the importance of lighting. Lighting is *essential* to glamour. The right glow can make a closet glamorous.

Glamour within a home calls for thoughtful attention to detail, the simple act of curating a vanity or well-appointed kitchen. Mystery plays a prominent part as well; there must be something left unsaid, a demureness that leaves the ineffable in its wake.

I always say Mother Nature is the best designer. Her austere beauty is full of enchantment. Nature reminds us that glamour can be quiet and unaffected. The perfect location effortlessly encapsulates its own raw magnetism. There is no substitute and no trump for a fantastic view. I might choose marble patterns that echo the movement of foliage outside a window or implement quiet tonal blondes to highlight the blues

Gold-leafed wood paneling, inset with antique mirrors and trimmed with antique brass, lines the walls of the wife's dressing room in a Bel Air, California, house. A pleated-leather sofa and lacquered-frame club chair underscore updated Hollywood Regency style.

OVERLEAF: In the entryway of a house on Mercer Island in Washington State, three different marbles intertwine to create a graphically dynamic floor. The walls are sheathed in onyx-black paint, while the striped ceiling completes the glamorous space. The ceiling fixture is vintage.

and grays of an ocean waiting outdoors. The environment informs the dialogue.

The quiet drama of nature is a marvel to me—for example, a marble quarry in Italy with its symmetry and raw organization or the streamlined sense of economy inherent in a shell. Such things accentuate the point: that which is iconic is often simple. The magic happens in transcending the everyday, from mundane to emblematic, something graceful and efficient, but with much to say. In a day and age where casualness is the norm and comfort reigns, it begs the question: Is real glamour a thing of the past? How does one elevate the everyday to art?

Cleverness and fortitude are my favorite tools as a curator. I am a firm believer that anything in a home may be beautiful without losing its functionality. Every room deserves to be a work of art. And it's paramount to remember that great style flourishes at any price point. What is glamorous to me is the history behind a thing, the story in its bones. It is why flea markets remain my favorite source to this day. Give me a chair that has some soul, because if interior design is storytelling, I believe in choosing pieces with a voice.

In the modern world, glamour might sometimes be dismissed as frivolous or condemned as artificial, as an illusion. Admittedly, it is a form of escapism, a meditation on fantasy. Yet our ideals as a society can be powerful and uplifting. The notion of a glamorous life embodies the promise of our best selves. It stokes our imaginations, validates our ambition, and baits our desires. Glamour is confidence in transcendence; it is a place full of wonder and excitement, where mediocrity and boredom live in exile. The deepest definition of glamour is that which makes us feel as though our ideals might one day become our reality.

Talking about glamour feels as elusive and vague as talking about love. It is something set apart, glinting in appeal. Individualistic. Unexpected. Supernatural. My favorite spaces are those that evoke strong feelings. If your home tells a story, why not tell a magical one? Glamour reminds us that there is enchantment in the everyday. It celebrates something larger than a thing itself, acknowledging an ideal and holding it as attainable, albeit elusive. Its magic lies in its ability to blend ambition with hope.

Simplicity

JESSE CARRIER *and* MARA MILLER

Simplicity is a state of mind, not just a visual style. In essence, it is ease—a life concept that translates into decorating. How do people live effortlessly? How do we, as designers, fulfill that? Since everyone understands simplicity in his or her own way, how individual clients define it is the designer's job to discover. Simplicity is not necessarily about living with less, living without clutter, or just plain living without. Simplicity is the editing, the logic and focus a designer uses to decide what to include and what to remove or omit.

There is some deep part of human nature driven to amass possessions to make a home feel cozy and finished. Yet with too much of too many good things, environments become oppressive, regardless of how beautiful each individual object may be. A space that is overly dense and weighted with—fill in the blank: furniture, objects, color, pattern—tends to be physically and visually uncomfortable both because it is confining and because it lacks the necessary moments of visual relief that the eye requires in order to appreciate what it sees. The condition of too much or too many always leads to the loss—or at least the blurring—of composition, which is that artful arrangement of forms that a designer uses to direct the eye and create energy and movement. As a result, even the most lush and detailed spaces come to feel stagnant over time.

The urge to simplify, to pare away, may be less an aesthetic choice than an emotional and physical one. A pared-down interior not only looks right, it feels right. Step by step, piece by piece, a designer assesses, adds, and subtracts, always considering how the combination of components works together from different vantage points. Finding the right balance is one of design's great challenges, in part because it varies from person to person and project to project, but especially because so many possessions come laden with

meaning and memories. The editing process usually happens organically and in layers. As pieces are removed, relocated, or clustered, the tangible result both looks and feels better; this improvement converts clients, sometimes quickly, sometimes gradually, sometimes item by item. The resulting simplicity may be hard-won, but it complements the variety and makes it sing.

Every style lives on a spectrum of simple, decorated, and more decorated versions. The monolithic, architected, perfectly refined space is clearly an icon of simplicity. In minimalist spaces, precision and exactitude are necessary because every tone and every texture matters. The more exclusive or refined something becomes, the harder it is to achieve that kind of ease. When a design is so selective, so edited, refined, and stripped of detail, the eye will focus on what remains and be less forgiving.

Country or rustic interiors represent the other end of the style spectrum and another very specific type of simplicity, one that stems from the naive and utilitarian. These interiors can also be extremely refined and very sophisticated; when they are, the effect is often due to spare layouts and even sparer decor. This way of simplicity feels genuine, charming, and easy because it embraces the beauty of life's imperfections. The furnishings do not try to be anything other than what they are; they are perfect in themselves, in their own way. What is simple to see—and feel—is the authenticity and inherent beauty of furnishings and objects created entirely for function and utility. Their surfaces are likely to be raw or unpolished, and they very often tell the stories of their use and the hands of their maker.

For some people, the concept of simplicity has everything to do with the use of the space. Everything in the space must function exactly as needed: surfaces are wipe-able; upholstery, spill-proof; and the carpet matches the dog

The dining room in this Caribbean colonial–style home on the west coast of Florida is simply furnished with a plaster-dipped Flemish-style chandelier, which looks fresh paired with the antique French dining table. The vintage chairs offer a sharp contrast in the otherwise pale scheme, and the Frank Stella lithograph imbues the room with tropical colors in the most sophisticated way.

hair. For other people, simplicity is having a fully staffed home that runs like a machine. It's about a lifestyle that preserves a certain scale, graciousness, and formality. For still others, simplicity is luxury—perfect details, perfectly refined—rooms where everything is important and just so. And for some, simplicity means not having to think about design at all.

Creating true simplicity is a very complex process, one that requires an enormous degree of conscientiousness and refinement, which should not be confused with discipline. While the intent of discipline may be simplicity, discipline takes energy and the will to maintain it. And that is the real test: life may not be perfect, but simplicity in design makes it possible to live beautifully, effortlessly, and with ease.

In this New York apartment, on the Upper West Side, a traditional English Bridgewater sofa, upholstered in linen, provides both comfort and tradition. A custom linen-wrapped Parsons coffee table is a clean-lined foil to the seating, and a Stephen Antonson bust, featured on a tall pedestal, is formal and elegant yet playful upon closer inspection.

Exuberance

ANTHONY BARATTA

Great decorating is powerful. Interiors, from the subtle to the demonstrative, have the ability to change the way we think and the way we feel. And while I appreciate a quiet, understated room, I am happiest in a clever, uninhibited room that is filled with color and pattern. A room that is, in a word, exuberant.

I am often asked what makes an exuberant interior. One need only look at an Odalisque painting by Henri Matisse to answer this question. The master's bombastic use of color and pattern, his looseness of line combined with the sensual and the exotic create in a painting what the mere mortal decorator can only hope to bring to the decor of a room. Matisse takes risks in what he paints and how he paints it. The tension between the elements of risk and familiarity makes his paintings come alive. Risk taking is also a key component in the formula of an exuberant interior.

Architecture is always the starting point when designing a space; it generally reveals how best to furnish. While it is true that designing a room is easier with good architecture, one must always remember that good decorating has the power both to hide the flaws and celebrate the strengths of the architectural background. The most high-spirited rooms result from a well-mannered and imaginative union between architect and designer. My favorite example of this marriage is the Paris apartment that Le Corbusier designed for Carlos de Beistegui in the 1930s. The clean, simple modernism of the great architect combined with the over-the-top baroque furnishings of the patron was simply smashing and would influence such designers as Dorothy Draper and everyone who worked in the Hollywood Regency style.

Color is, of course, the easiest way to make a bold statement. There are no bad colors, but it is a lot easier to create an exuberant interior with red than it is with

An irregularly shaped canvas by American minimalist painter Frank Stella takes pride of place in this exuberant living room. The vivid geometric rug and throw pillows are balanced by the clean lines of a pair of midcentury armchairs and the custom ottomans.

OVERLEAF: Perky orange furnishings populate this generously proportioned family room, which is grounded by alternating squares of bright colors and muted neutrals in the custom rug. To the left of the asymmetrical fireplace is a painting by Enoc Perez, while a black chalkboard painting by Joseph Beuys hangs above a sectional sofa on the right.

beige. Nancy Lancaster's butter yellow room at Colefax and Fowler, David Hicks's drawing room using ten shades of red, Billy Baldwin's sublime blue room at the Villa Fiorentina, and Mark Hampton's chocolate brown room in a Kips Bay showhouse will always be a huge influence, because although each room is unique, they all share a clarity and sense of purpose expressed through a strong color statement. Love of strong color is a personality trait, and like an MGM musical, I choose to decorate in Technicolor. There are no rules when using color to foster exuberance, but I like using a classic combination like blue and white as a jumping-off point and then adding in the spice—such as orange.

Comfort is an equally essential element for exuberance. Furniture should not only feel delightful, but also be arranged in a way that makes for easy conversation or reading a book or gazing at the view. There is nothing quite like being enveloped in beautiful fabrics and carpets and, yes, I still love drapery.

I am as obsessed with pattern as I am with color and comfort. Perhaps the trickiest part of decorating is the layering of pattern, and yet to me it is the most interesting and most fulfilling part of my work. Plaids, florals, stripes, geometrics, and everything in between are fair game. Pattern comes from all elements in a room, from the flooring planks and windowpanes to the books on the shelves, and this should never be overlooked.

Lastly, scale is a key component. For a big, bold look, you have to use large-scale furniture. The great California decorator Michael Taylor knew that magically, big furniture makes any room look bigger. His work truly exemplified what a bold, exuberant room is all about. Pushing the boundaries of proportion has always excited me, because it impacts all the other elements of a design.

In the final analysis, all great rooms tell a story, and the exuberant room's narrative speaks of the comfort, color, and style of a life well lived.

Family

The dining room in an apartment for a young family with four girls is heavily used; it hosts everything from formal gatherings to birthday parties. The pendant light is by Lobmeyr, and the table, custom designed for the room, is made of Macassar ebony. The striped painting is by Callum Innes; the red canvases in the background are by Kate Shepherd.

Our homes are laboratories of creative expression and social engineering, and for families, a home is not only a manifestation of personal tastes and interests, but also the means by which values—through design—are communicated from one generation to the next.

A large part of my practice is designing for families. I come to each project with a developed set of principles for what makes an attractive, comfortable home. The interiors I design are modern and whimsical, yet timeless and fad-averse. Like families themselves, designs should have longevity. I believe homes must have a strong sense of order and place with careful attention paid to scale, balance, and proportion. Objects must have room to breathe. Homes should incorporate elements of the past that add balance and deepen the present. Color should be used to enrich, unify, and warm the space.

With a style all its own, every family reflects its members' genders, ages, personalities, habits, interests, quirks, obsessions, and beliefs. When you think about the design of your home, it is important to consider how your family lives and what rules you follow. Do you take your shoes off when you enter the home? Is food allowed outside the kitchen? Does your cat have claws? Does the dog shed? Are any rooms off-limits to the children? What activities do you all enjoy doing together? How do you like to entertain? The answers will guide your design choices, so the home reflects who you are and how you can function best.

One of the most common complaints I hear from clients is that they have rooms in their homes that never get used, or which they do not feel comfortable in. In an era where many parents want to be involved in every aspect of their children's lives, each room needs to be a dynamic part of the family. As we all know, the kitchen is once again a central space whose purpose has expanded far beyond cooking and eating. Gone for many are stand-alone dining rooms, replaced by open floor plans combining work, play, lounging, and entertaining.

Just as homes can be laid out to maximize social interaction, an individual room can be designed to positively reinforce parent-child bonds. The placement and relationship of each piece of furniture to another affects how human connections are made. For instance, adding an L-shaped sectional to a family room with an ottoman in front invites everyone to gather to play games, do homework, and converse. Having an inviting, comfortable, well-lit place to read to a child fosters intimacy. Including trundle beds in children's rooms makes it easy to have sleepovers, promoting socialization.

Contrary to what one might think, elegance and practicality are not irreconcilable for families. Throughout a home, materials can be aesthetically pleasing as well as durable. In my own apartment, I designed a Roman-style mosaic floor for the foyer. The polished surface reflects the light and adds a sophisticated glimmer to the entrance, but nothing could be more resilient to withstand scooters, bicycles, and muddy boots, nor so easy to clean. A regal but rugged Anglo-Raj wooden bench is the perfect place for putting on shoes and piling knapsacks, footballs, and catchers' mitts. Chic can serve everyone quite well!

When you live in a place like New York City where space is in short supply, storage, lots of it, is essential so that everything (clothing, books, toys) has a place. Custom cabinetry helps; integrating beds, desks, play areas, and storage means that order can easily be restored at the end of the day. Living in an uncluttered, well-designed

home with carefully chosen art encourages children to appreciate beauty and nurtures their imagination.

As a parent of older teens, I have learned so much from my own children about what good design means for family living. First and foremost, design needs to appeal to all ages. Kids like to have fun, and therefore home design can, and should, reflect this. Children have inspired me to be playful with color and shapes, not just in their bedrooms but throughout a home, without sacrificing refinement and style. Design for families need not be dumbed down.

Like families themselves, designs evolve over time. Design should always be looking ahead and anticipating a family's changing needs. But regardless of age, children, through their daily immersion in a well-thought-out house, gain an appreciation of good design and learn what it means to incorporate beauty into their lives. A home is a place to share, create, and nourish the best in each of us as individuals and as a family. Design is one of the finest means to accomplish this.

A colorful photograph by Olivo Barbieri hangs above a Jens Risom sofa in the center of this modern family lounge. The pair of bronze-and-glass coffee tables afford space for everything from coloring books to best sellers, and the ombré curtains are made from alpaca.

Nuance

SUZANNE RHEINSTEIN

When I first began buying my own design magazines, rather than reading from my mother's neat stacks of *Flair*, *House & Garden*, and *Vogue*, the style of the time was a swirling sea of bright color with startling combinations. I jumped right in. I painted the living room of my first apartment chrome yellow, the kitchen Tiffany blue with orangey-red stained chairs, and the bathroom shiny chocolate brown with tortoiseshell bamboo shades. The mix of unexpected and luscious color combinations is still quite popular today, and it can work wonders to create an arresting impression of liveliness.

But among the many ways of approaching the decoration of rooms, there is one that I have come to favor. It is about creating an atmosphere where the individual parts make up a harmonious whole and an aura of calm, with subtle color shifts, interesting juxtapositions, and the smallest of details that can make a huge difference to the feel of a room. It is one that favors nuance over a wow factor.

I came to fully appreciate nuanced interiors when my design clients, who live jam-packed lives, began to express the desire that their homes serve as retreats from their overcommitted, overstimulating worlds. The use of understated colors, fabrics, lighting, furnishings, and accessories all combine to create a soothing and sophisticated environment.

Assuming the architecture has been attended to and the preliminary floor plans made, choosing the furniture must be done carefully. When considering pieces old and new, pay attention to finish and textures. The antique chairs I buy often have beautiful old and rubbed (not chipped!) paint with the wood showing through or faded gilt or mellow fruitwood frames, which look very attractive in the same room, with none of

them standing out more than another. The tables may be small shapes from Asia, with forty applied coats of lacquer creating the characteristic soft undulations in the surface. Or it can be a bespoke modern table with a smooth lacquer finish and simple bronze legs. I sometimes order extremely plain tables or desks with very finely woven raffia or glazed linen applied for texture.

In this kind of decorating, the details of the upholstery must be subtle, too. They matter, but they shouldn't necessarily stand out. Fabrics can be contrasting in their finish, such as roughly woven matte raw silk, fine cottons and Belgian linens mixed with waxed leather or kid leather, and short-piled silk velvet, but tonal in their color. The occasional print can be a Fortuny cotton or a hand-blocked linen used on the wrong side, its colors bleeding through to look like a dreamy watercolor. Choosing a workroom that is excellent with tailored dressmaker details is essential. And other details, like micro welts or flat ones or the braid to use at the bottom of a skirt, should be well thought out.

Straw matting is very good to ground all these elements. It comes in every natural color, from the palest cream to grays and medium browns. Using beautiful old rugs that are faded with age, either on top of the matting or by themselves, is another way to bring a subtle pattern into the room.

Thinking of the whole room—ceiling, floor, walls, and trim—as a unified background works especially well with contemporary architecture. Painting everything one color with different sheens—for example, dead-flat walls and eggshell for the wooden trim— looks intentional and can have the feeling of being in a cloud. If well done, it creates a perfect space in which to arrange the furniture.

Art can be older or more contemporary, but the rooms are not about the art. The art

The Baguès sconces from Rheinstein's husband's childhood home in New York are affixed to walls covered in squares of painted Chinese paper. A Dutch kettle stand sits in front of the Swedish Gustavian settee upholstered in an embossed silk; artist Bob Christian painted the floor in a design from a Venetian church.

is part of the whole that creates a great space for living life. There might be recessed lighting built in, but there should also be lamps to create soft pools of light. Lamps made from old Chinese jars with a pearlescent surface or carved urns are very beautiful. These look good with simple shades made from silk or linen in soft colors. Mixing these with minimalist contemporary bronze or patinated-brass standing lamps is an interesting juxtaposition.

Other objects used in these rooms can also contribute to the nuanced atmosphere. Mirrors with very old, "dead" plates, all gray and tarnished silver with barely a reflection, are something I admire, along with the soft shine of antique Sheffield silver and the way it quietly gleams with the copper bleeding through. And silver lustre pottery—developed in the late eighteenth century and known as poor man's silver—that has turned black at the edges has great beauty.

The longer you are in nuanced rooms, the more you realize the details that make up a harmonious whole and create an aura of calm. Nothing should stand out, but it should all be beautiful and part of the atmosphere.

The sepia mural enveloping this room was also painted by Bob Christian, and the chairs and wooden chimera on the Louis XVI marble mantel are eighteenth-century. The painted, gilded, stained, and waxed wood surfaces and various fabric textures bring a subtle interest to the space; the ceiling was lacquered off-white to reflect light.

Welcoming Spaces

TIMOTHY CORRIGAN

We have all walked into one of those spaces that subtly whispers, "Look, but don't touch!" This is either because the rooms are so fancy that you can tell they weren't intended for the likes of you, or because they are so serenely clean, stark, and curated, they quietly communicate that you and your things are not needed here.

As a designer, I have always felt that no matter how beautiful a room is, if it does not welcome you, it is not a well-designed room.

The secret to all good interior design is in that subtle but elusive sense that the space is welcoming; indeed, it must beckon you in to become *a part* of the room.

When people spend any amount of time in a space that I have designed, they inevitably come away saying, "That is one of the most inviting and comfortable places I have ever been." Yet, oddly enough, when people look at photos of those exact same rooms, the feeling of relaxed welcome is not the first thing that comes to mind. I have always believed that the rooms that I create actually need people in them to make them feel complete and finished.

So what are those seemingly intangible things that communicate a sense of welcome, those items that are not immediately evident when you first enter a room?

First, you have to be sensitive to the psychology of the room. Color plays a huge role in the emotions that are evoked in the space: use color to maximize intended emotions for the area. The furniture plan and flow are also important; not enough furniture—or too much—can kill a room's mood. Getting the proportions of the furnishings right is also essential. For example, low furniture in a room with tall ceilings can make its occupants feel diminished and unimportant.

Next, pay attention to comfort. We've all seen beautifully designed chairs that feel like torture devices when one sits down.

When it comes to seating, ergonomics and comfort should come first. Getting scale right is also important; you don't want the chair to be under- or overscaled. If you want statement pieces in a room, choose something other than seating.

Then, consider practicality. Who wants to worry about the inevitable spilled glass of red wine or water ring on the antique side table? One of the most important aspects of a welcoming space is that it has been designed to really work for the way that you live. Today, with so many terrific options in terms of high-performance fabrics, you don't have to squirm at the smallest accident. Using marine varnish on even the finest of antiques takes the worry out of every glass or coffee cup that gets set down on a table.

Lighting is also critical to a welcoming space. Nothing looks less inviting than a room filled with overhead lighting that deadens a space and makes it feel flat. Lighting, even in daytime, can be used to accent an area or object to make it feel special. Lamps placed around a room provide pools of light that help define areas, and just like moths to the flame, we all seem to gather toward the warm glow that only a lamp—even the newly improved, color-corrected LED bulbs—can give. Make sure that you have overall lighting for mood as well as specific task lighting for places where you read or work.

Finally, consider the power of personality. The most welcoming spaces are those that are interesting but not overpowering. This is achieved through layering of objects into the space: art, books, items collected from travels around the world or just your neighborhood. Don't be afraid to mix the finest of objects with the most common, such as an old wood carving with some shiny, new piece of engineered metal. Sprinkle a space with visual treats that surprise and

A seemingly paradoxical mix of formal architecture and casual decoration are found in this grand salon in France: deep down-filled seating, upholstered in an outdoor fabric; an antique Tabriz carpet; and objets d'art from many periods. The result is a room that feels relaxed and welcoming.

provoke curiosity. And don't stop with just the visual senses: music and scent play a key role in making a space feel special, alive, and welcoming.

Anyone can have a beautiful space, but the most successful rooms are the ones that welcome, nurture, and allow everyone who comes into that space to truly become his or her best self.

In a guest bedroom of the same house, pieces of cognac-colored furniture stand as the complement to a palette of blues inflected with gray. The purpose of such a room is to make guests feel that they are in a special place, and it is accomplished here with luxurious Fortuny curtains, a Portuguese rug, and an eighteenth-century Swedish chandelier.

Luxury

TOM SCHEERER

Luxury has always been synonymous with interior design. In fact, the quest for it is an utterly unavoidable aspect of our work. Clients seek out designers because they want something superior to what's normally available, and that specialness is generally thought to reside in rare or expensive furnishings and finishes.

But societal aspirations toward ever-increasing extravagance have accelerated. Our heritage of puritanical restraint in all matters of consumption—a heritage that has led to some beautiful design solutions—has been overwhelmed. Advertising and the media promote luxury so relentlessly that most Americans who hire a designer crave it, and they all seem to desire the same things: silks, velvets, fashionable art, marble-clad bathrooms, and $10,000 kitchen ranges—not to mention architecture done on a grand scale with a stupendous amount of square footage.

But luxurious interiors can be conceived without using any of these elements. In fact, it would be a good exercise to design a sensuous, indulgent house without them, and here's why: if you avoid all the clichés bobbing around in the cultural soup, you'll be forced to come up with your own definition of luxury. And if you can redefine luxury in your own terms, you will have clarified the essence of your personal style.

Luxury properly starts with a fantasy. My own notion is clearly fixed in my mind; it doesn't waver. It starts with a house high on a bluff in a car-free village looking westward over the sea. There are white walls, a stone terrace shaded by vines, and fruit trees. There's a kitchen with a hearth for cooking over wood. In the bedroom, I sleep facing windows open to the salt air.

Now, truth be told, none of my clients would want a house that stark or primitive.

But it helps to know my fantasy, because it informs all of the more finished or elaborate design solutions that I come up with for other people. I push from the direction of less shine, less opulent pretense, and more appreciation for the inherent sculptural silhouettes of tables, chairs, and sofas.

I let clients know that while they should have the marble bathroom or the fancy refrigerator if they want it, they should also know that these trappings are just the tip of the iceberg when it comes to living well. The marble is not nearly as important as having a window. The kitchen appliance doesn't matter as much as the food that comes out of it, or the way the food is served. A lot of what I give to my clients is my experience and my take on what might be luxurious and what might be a bill of goods.

In my own career, I've steered clear of most of the clichés. The occasional velvet sofa aside, I'm not sure I've bought a yard of silk in thirty years of decorating. I start with the premise that true luxury resides in the siting or orientation of a house, the flow of its rooms, and the arrangement of furniture within them.

The materials are the final layer. Good-quality materials will always be attractive, but there are different ways of thinking about quality that lead to vastly different kinds of rooms. If you consider fabrics, for example, there's a sensuality inherent in rough ones as well as in smooth ones. Mohair and linen are as luxurious as silk and satin if you appreciate their characters. For me, luxury often has to do with the hand of the maker. A hand-blocked cotton or hand-looped alpaca blanket has an aura of luxuriousness that a textile produced on a mechanized loom will never have.

Are there inexpensive luxuries? That depends on your thinking. The word *luxury* suggests that you're going a little further for

A vast living room in this Jupiter Island, Florida, residence has the luxury of multiple seating areas, including this corner banquette tucked in between the entry and a set of windows. The combination of French furnishings and exotic elements makes it the perfect room for conversation and entertaining.

it. You're stretching. But it can be something as simple as a free-range egg instead of the supermarket variety.

One thing is certain: luxury will look different in the future. The world's population is exploding, and natural resources are shrinking. Consequently, younger designers are making a style out of austerity. They're embracing modernism, which has a cleaner aesthetic, and they're using vintage furnishings, a form of recycling. This is all positive. But even in this context, there will always be small luxuries. Cashmere, leather, animal skin, precious stones, and gold leaf may be the expected ways to communicate luxury quickly and in no uncertain terms, but I believe it's a designer's task to ignore these kinds of easy answers and come up with a new definition of what it means to live well, both for themselves and for their clients.

The corner room of this apartment in Brooklyn Heights is a classic red library, often seen as a cliché. However, it's made fresh here by an overglaze of semi-transparent brown. A linen-velvet sofa, which has been reincarnated several times, mixes beautifully with a pair of midcentury tub chairs covered in a coarse sky-blue linen.

Trends

Au courant. Outré. The latest thing.

The notion of being stylish and on trend is certainly appealing—particularly when applied to fashion. Who would choose to appear unfashionable? But what relationship should being in vogue have to interior design and architecture?

Does an interior designer need to subscribe to current trends in order to appear modern? Or when the work represents something of permanence—interior architecture, for example—is timeless design more important than the next new thing?

I've built my career based on what I consider to be the essential elements of timeless design. My approach to living, decorating, and architecture embraces a philosophy that reveres understated decor. I regard myself as an anti-trendsetter; I seek to create environments that can't instantly be identified with a particular year, let alone a single look.

The great designer Billy Baldwin once said, "Nothing is in good taste unless it suits the way you live. What's practical is beautiful, and suitability always overrules fashion."

So how do we, as designers, remain relevant in a world where styles and tastes change with alarming frequency? How can we continue to respect the past while incorporating a degree of modernity into our work?

If you study the history of design, it's impossible to judge much of the work of our decorating ancestors without wincing. It's a challenge to imagine a time when American Colonial was considered the height of good design. (A vintage spinning wheel as a decorative element, anyone?) And I'd love to know who was responsible for convincing the masses that a sofa with rolled arms measuring sixteen inches in diameter was a good look—if you doubt that such was the case, pick up any issue of *Architectural Digest* circa 1988. In fact, rifle through back issues of all the decorating magazines from the 1940s through the turn of the century, and you'll find truly cringeworthy examples of designers desperately seeking to be of the moment.

Yet for every distressingly cheesy and dated spread, you're certain to find an interior that seems reassuringly lovely and appropriate—and somehow still fresh in spite of a detail or two that might give away its true age. The overwhelming majority of these timeless interiors contain classic elements: iconic Chinese tables, a Japanese screen, a French fauteuil or English antique chest, a period mantel, and, often, modern artwork.

We can't help but be influenced by current fads, whether it be a mad passion for orange or a resurrected yet somehow less severe iteration of the overscaled 1960s drum shade.

It's only through the study of history, art, and the decorative arts that we can develop an understanding of how and why certain trends emerge and which ones will last. Interior design is a relatively new discipline, but there are numerous precedents that inform what constitutes timeless yet distinctive design. Some of the great practitioners—Frances Elkins, Jean-Michel Frank, Elsie de Wolfe, Albert Hadley, and the aforementioned Baldwin—had a real understanding of classic forms and periods, but each was able to reinvent those components and establish a style uniquely his or her own. When you peruse the books celebrating these major talents, what distinguishes their interiors is a modernity that doesn't seem to correspond to a specific time. They freely incorporated elements that reflected the era in which they worked while still managing to instill a timeless sensibility to the houses they decorated.

Ultimately, determining what might be considered timeless is a subjective exercise. What I view as chic and stylish might be deemed dull by someone else. I don't feel

The entry hall of this house in Los Angeles features a marble floor designed by Stuart that welcomes guests in high style. The artwork hanging in the stairway is *Landscape No. 556*, 1998, by John Virtue; an Italian walnut stool and a seventeenth-century commode complete the setting.

we all need to adhere to the same dictates of design, but I often reflect on how certain decisions I make might be evaluated in the future. A wall can be repainted and a sofa recovered, but some of the actions we take as designers are likely to survive us well into the future. Will that mosaic tile we're selecting be considered passé next year? Does the cabinetry pinpoint what will one day be seen as a regrettable moment in design? The consequences of our efforts and choices are significant and long-lasting—or at least I think they should be.

In a house originally designed and built by the legendary Hollywood set designer Cedric Gibbons for his wife, actress Dolores del Rio, this second-floor salon is more than forty feet long and has commanding views of the Pacific Ocean and the Santa Monica Canyon. The space is warmed by rich colors and soft textures like velvet and mohair.

Comfort

BUNNY WILLIAMS

Many years ago, when I was beginning my design career, I had the most extraordinary experience that really framed my philosophy about comfort in design. On a trip to London, Mrs. Parish, whom I worked for at the time, arranged for me to have tea with Nancy Lancaster in her flat above the design firm of Colefax and Fowler, of which she was a partner.

I was shown upstairs to wait, almost breathless with excitement, in Nancy Lancaster's famous yellow drawing room. What struck me first was what a comfortable room it was. Deep English sofas were slipcovered in linen, and one could tell that they were well used. Then I began to take in every detail. The amazing yellow-lacquered walls, the huge paintings of Elizabethan queens, the crystal chandelier, and the William Kent furniture were all of amazing quality yet only added to the room's inviting feel. It was a room that made you just want to curl up on the sofa by the fireplace and have a nice visit, which is exactly what we did when Nancy Lancaster arrived.

This room made me think back to my childhood in Virginia. Each Sunday, our extended family would gather for lunch at our favorite Aunt Bertha's. Twenty or more cousins of all ages would sit in her large living room filled with overstuffed furniture slipcovered in red-and-white toile and miscellaneous chairs pulled into three or four seating groups. There was an amply stocked bar in an antique corner cabinet. We loved this room that was welcoming to all. Though it did not have the elegant yellow silk curtains or high quality of furnishings of Nancy Lancaster's drawing room, Aunt Bertha's living room was still one of amazing comfort.

The comfort in a room comes from thinking about the occupants in the planning stage. Where will they sit to talk to one another? The seating group should be intimate and the sofas and chairs not too big or too

Down-filled upholstered pieces, covered in a mélange of vintage and antique textiles, are the linchpins of comfort in this library, where French doors open onto a verdant garden. The soft light of numerous lamps illuminates a room filled with mementos that tell the story of the owner's travels.

OVERLEAF: A bevy of throw pillows on a generously proportioned sofa beckon guests to converse. A suzani draped over the sofa and carved chairs of different styles and periods augment the sense of informality so necessary to comfort.

small—just right, as Goldilocks said. There should be small tables for drinks and soft lighting at eye level. A welcoming table or cabinet with a cocktail tray lets guests feel at home and enables them to help themselves. Even in rooms that have a more modern, minimalist sensibility, it's the thoughtful details that indicate the room has been planned for people, not for a photo shoot.

Rooms need to be functional as well as beautiful. Thinking first how the room will be used is essential to creating a comfortable space. Is one's lifestyle formal or informal? Is there an art collection? Young children or grandchildren? Pets? All should be considered. Then the personality of the room can begin with the selection of colors, fabrics, furniture, and art. What is always important to remember is that rooms are for *living*, not just for show.

Furniture groups need to be created to allow people to talk to one another. They cannot be too far apart. They should be made up of sofas and chairs of various sizes. There should always be proper light for reading. There should be a place to put a laptop, play a game of cards, or do a jigsaw puzzle. Once the furniture plan is set, a scented candle wafting through the room, a cashmere throw over the back of a club chair, soft throw pillows on sofas and large chairs, and interesting books and magazines piled on a table or a bench in front of the fireplace bring an added layer of warmth.

Everyone who decides to become an interior designer does so for his or her own reasons: it can be about the passion for space, or it can be about a house for great collections of furniture or art. For me, my first thoughts are about the people I imagine living in the rooms I create. I learned at an early age that a house is for enjoying life and sharing with others. I want to think of different age groups gathered around with lots of chatter and laughter filling the room.

A well-thought-out room will be inviting for a single person, a small family gathering, or a large party, and it will be a room you will never want to leave.

Humor

HARRY HEISSMANN

Have you ever wondered what appeals to you about an interior that you've seen in a magazine or in person? What is your eye drawn to as it travels through the room? What makes it personal and memorable? For me, it's often humor.

Some rooms have the best layouts and furniture plans and are professionally layered and accessorized, yet they still feel incomplete. They need wit to go from house to home. Design and style doyenne Iris Apfel perhaps said it best: "One major fault in American interior design is the lack of humor. There should be humor with everything, because if you don't have it, you might as well be dead."

Looking at an interior by Tony Duquette, one finds not only comfortable furniture and carefully arranged objects, but also special touches not necessarily obvious to the average eye: his humorous use of hubcaps and egg cartons come to mind. Duquette recycled long before people started talking about it, and while the egg cartons morphed into a ceiling treatment by being finished with shimmery gold paint, they remained an inexpensive and witty material only recognizable upon close inspection. However, one should be cautious: this hidden humor must be executed judiciously; what is humorous in the hands of a master like Duquette might fall flat elsewhere.

So how do you infuse an interior with humor? How can you make it more amusing, personal, and interesting?

A good way to start is to be curious and inquisitive in daily life—you will see that humor abounds. For a designer, the practice of keen observation is de rigueur: search out amusing, provocative objects to place strategically in an interior to animate a room.

You can find humor in the pieces of Claude and François-Xavier Lalanne, where a sculpted animal opens to reveal a desk,

In this apartment high above the streets of Manhattan, a whimsical garden snail—designed by Tony Duquette and realized in resin—inhabits a living room landscape. The symbiotic mushroom, one of a pair, was purchased on Dixie Highway in Palm Beach, Florida.

bathtub, or stove, or in the murals by Ludwig Bemelmans at the Carlyle Hotel in New York.

Humor can be hidden or subtle, obvious or in your face, but as with everything in interior design, it is about the combination with other pieces, the dialogue, the juxtaposition. Sister Parish famously placed an antique carousel animal in a showhouse room—an instant sculpture—something to make guests smile upon entering. Meanwhile, in the celebrated living room of Elsa Peretti's residence in Porto Ercole, Italy, a fireplace shaped like Neptune's mouth was designed by Renzo Mongiardino.

Humor happens in more subtle ways, too. It can be the multicolored shoestrings master Albert Hadley used as the trim on a friend's period French chair, an amusing and unexpected application, or the carvings of ballet slippers *en pointe* on the legs of an antique chair French doyenne Madeleine Castaing had in her house in Lèves.

When Hadley visited the apartment I had just finished for myself in 2003, he sat down, looked around, and then lit a cigarette. He remarked that the apartment should be called the House of Friends. When I inquired what he meant by that, he said: "Well, look around kiddo—everything you own has a personality or eyes!" To me, his comment meant I had succeeded.

Albert Hadley understood so well what all interior designers should learn: that a room is not only an arena of smart planning decisions and a rigorous aesthetic, but also a place for pleasure, for the enjoyment of life's lighter moments in the company of both friends and objects. The latter, if they possess wit and express spirit, can immeasurably enliven our human coteries and conversations. Decoration is not a matter of life and death, but a matter of life. Humor is the salt in the soup.

Inspired by a sixteenth-century Italian fireplace, the custom mantel injects a bit of wit into a Manhattan loft apartment. The lettuce-leaf chairs—spotted in the window of a Manhattan boutique—enhance the room's playful sensibility.

Reinvention

MILES REDD

Picasso reportedly said, "Good artists borrow; great artists steal," and to that point, I have always looked to my peers, past and present, for inspiration. But I have found that even if you boldly copy something deliberately, as I did when I borrowed Albert Hadley's design for Brooke Astor's red lacquer–and-brass library, it rarely turns out the same. In fact, it is always slightly different, for such is the nature of hands and materials: lightning never strikes in the same place twice. Even when a room draws inspiration, however literal, from an existing space, it will always have its own personality, either that of the creator or, hopefully, the inhabitant. Like *les jeune filles* wearing a party dress, the effect is not quite the same when worn by a grown woman. Rooms take on the personality of the person who is living in them, so I say copy away.

I have never been one of those decorators who designs everything. I believe in the great collective unconscious and building on ideas that have been around for thousands of years. Maybe those Romans did invent something, but one is hard-pressed to find something that has not been done before; and although I do attempt to interject new ideas, my rooms have always been an amalgam of many different influences and references. For example, I have a pair of upholstered zebra doors in my living room, and I have often said that they might be the only original idea I have ever had; and yet, one must give a nod to the El Morocco nightclub, Elsie de Wolfe, and Ralph Lauren, for they all used zebra in cunning ways before I was even born.

I try to look to the past and reinvent it for the future. Time and ideas push us forward, but there is always a reference in the past that, as a designer, I can point to for influence. One of my absolute favorite things to do in decorating is to find something good but slightly overlooked and make it great. I found a fabulous David Adler bathroom that was all mirror panels from a

A painting by Agustin Hurtado hangs above the seating area of this vibrant living room in Houston. The walls are covered in satin, while the striking yellow curtains, red-striped upholstery, and black-lacquered doors call to mind Dorothy Draper, who influences Redd's work.

fantastic house in Chicago and installed it in my apartment in New York. In the process, the floor was simplified to a Directoire pattern of a large silver X and slabs of inky Belgium black marble; a 1950s Venetian mirror was layered on top of the vanity area; and an immense bust of Zeus was placed in a corner to add wit and curiosity. The essential room is the same, but because I am now living there, it is simultaneously a new creature.

Take a piece of good brown furniture, something that maybe belonged to your grandmother or great-grandmother, something that might not be to your taste but that you cannot give away. Revitalize the old, dull finish: ebonize it, tortoiseshell it, change it! Take an old Bombay chest and lacquer it

pale blue, then silver-plate all the hardware. Something that seemed dowdy is now fresh and up-to-date, yet it has all of the beautiful craftsmanship of generations past.

Creativity is a marvelous thing for the human spirit, and it is certainly one of the things that gets me up in the morning. The process of reinventing an idea or object is, in many ways, the essence of my personal creativity; it allows me to create rooms that don't feel like showrooms stamped out of an assembly line. Look at my work and allow these musings on decoration and reinvention to percolate; perhaps you will find an idea that you can reinvent by pushing it a wee bit further.

I encourage you to do so, because imitation is the highest form of flattery.

With its teal taffeta curtains and walls sheathed in a stately scenic paper by de Gournay, this dining room sets the stage for lively conversation. Blue-and-white Chinese porcelain lends an air of cross-cultural influence.

OPPOSITE: Several reinventions are in evidence in this high-style space: a plain table has been given a dose of verve with a faux-tortoise finish, and robin's egg–blue curtains have a ruffle reminiscent of fashion designer Oscar de la Renta's dresses.

Sex

MARTYN LAWRENCE BULLARD

I'm often thought of as a creator of sexy atmospheres in my interiors. Perhaps that's because I believe a successful room is *only* successful if someone actually calls it sexy, or, better still, feels sexy in it. Now obviously what's considered sexy differs from person to person. It's all a matter of taste.

But can good taste induce such emotions? Can it, in fact, put you in an amorous mood? I can't say I've found any scientific proof, yet I can honestly attest to the power of a beautifully decorated space: a Paloma Picasso lipstick-red living room with enticing, deep velvet-covered sofas; a bedroom in a Venetian palazzo accessorized by a copper bathtub floating romantically in a corner; a fireplace crackling magnificently in a darkened library stuffed with well-worn leather-bound books. All of these are decorative tricks and luxurious decorating recipes that elevate the sex appeal of a space.

Naturally sexy rooms are those layered with textiles and textures, a heavy use of color in graduated hues, purposeful overscaling of soft furnishings, abundant down-filled throw pillows, and cozy cashmere blankets. And let's face it: if all else fails, there's always the dimmer switch, that miraculous little invention that will change the mood of a room, spice up the ambience, and create instant "decorative sex appeal"—even if the rest of the furnishings are lacking that certain je ne sais quoi!

I have, however, had requests to make certain spaces especially sexy, like a bathroom shower cubicle wrapped in golden mesh that was placed in direct view of a master bed. The mesh was woven so tightly, it allows one to see the outline of a naked body when the candlelit chandelier above lusters its glow.

Whether or not a client may actually verbalize it, the wish for a room to be sexy is always the underlying current, the unspoken key, and the ingredient that spurs the

Fantasy was the directive—an Indian fantasy, to be exact. In the master bedroom of Cher's Malibu, California, home, a nineteenth-century ivory-painted tablet depicting an Indian deity was the inspiration for the room's decor, which features a palette of textured creams, tea-stain browns, ivory, chocolate, ebony, gold, and bronze.

OVERLEAF: A generously scaled copper bathtub by Waterworks anchors this Balinese-inspired bathroom in Malibu, California. Teak columns support an intricately carved cornice of eighteenth-century Rajasthan design that extends the ethnic reference. Colonial lanterns provide seductive light, while a tropical garden softens the architecture.

envy of friends and family. Whether a room has neoclassical proportions, a traditional structure, midcentury madness, or sleek, modern lines, the sexiness factor is key to its successful execution.

You might ask the question, How does one create a sexy interior without making it sleazy or tacky?

In fashion, the line between chic and distasteful, provocative or provoking, is often very narrow. The same is true for interiors. As I've said, I never actually start out thinking that an interior must be sexy; I believe the vibe must be organic, like the blossoming of a relationship with a person you are attracted to. Never force anything is the number-one rule. Let the nuances of the room guide you.

Find the color you respond to, that makes you feel good and look good. I've found that if a client likes to wear blue, then they will love a blue room, because it's a room they will feel the most attractive and confident in. If you've got green eyes and you're sitting in your green-lacquered living room, you know your eyes are reflecting the color that's around you, flashing seductively like emeralds in the window of Harry Winston! This is immediately your very own room, a stage where you are the star and the world is yours to seduce and be seduced in. This is a successfully sexy interior. No real tricks, just good decorating and an understanding of color and when and how to use it. Whether you have a country cottage dressed in simple cottons; a high-rise penthouse with tailored leather-clad walls and sleek furnishings; or a beach house casually dressed in loose linens and wicker, it's all about understanding who you are.

Once you can interpret your decorative dreams, the rest comes naturally. Each layer will amp up the vibe. But remember the words of fashion's greatest heroine, Coco Chanel: "Always take one thing off before leaving the house." The same is true of the home. Interiors are always chicer and sexier when you don't over-gild the lily.

Scandinavia

RHONDA ELEISH *and* EDIE VAN BREEMS

The luminous simplicity we associate with Scandinavian design is a virtue born of necessity due to the harsh and unpredictable northern environment that dictates a careful balance of the elements of nature. Over the centuries, Scandinavians have learned to embrace their own geographically unique light, woods, water, metal, and earth. They craft these elements, using forward-looking aesthetics and technology, into houses of enduring elegance. The Scandinavian quest for balance and peace with nature is rich in lessons for designers from all countries.

Today, we are familiar with the great Scandinavian pantheon of midcentury furniture and textile design: Finn Juhl, Hans Wegner, Alvar Aalto, Poul Henningsen, Kaare Klint, Josef Frank, Bruno Mathsson, Märta Måås-Fjetterström, and Armi Ratia. These masters hail from a heritage of functional design that has its primitive beginnings on the isolated farmsteads of the countryside. The farmer's survival depended on the durability of his longboat, hunting knife, oxen yoke, and even the hand-hewn wooden bowl his family ate from. Life in such homes was often in close quarters, hence the ingenious furniture hybrids that did double-duty: beds with built-in clocks and cupboards, or chairs that unfolded into tables.

Respect for materials, the love of native woods, metal, linens, pottery, and wool runs deep in Nordic countries, manifested today in design schools, guilds, and agencies, and in regional and international design competitions that foster innovation while honoring the past. The Scandinavian emphasis on durable and ecologically sound materials has led, in recent years, to advances such as roping made from recycled wires and bicycle tires or nano-engineered cellulose fabrics.

Through the centuries, the design of the Nordic home has balanced the often dark, cold climate that surrounds it with applied and decorative techniques, still used today, that foster light and warmth. Scandinavia is dotted with brightly painted buildings, from city dwellings to rustic summer cabins. Painting also had a practical purpose: seventeenth-century interior and exterior paint was developed as a fungicide, insecticide, and wood preservative, with deep, saturated exterior colors derived from local mining by-products—copper, cadmium, iron, and chrome oxide—which, when mixed with lime, produced rich hues of marigold and reddish coral.

In the interior, mellower versions of the exterior paints were used in the eighteenth and nineteenth centuries. Today, casein and egg tempera are enjoying a revival, for they offer an appealing environmental alternative to harsher chemical paints. The richness of mineral pigments is valued for light-reflecting qualities. The white palette widely associated with Scandinavian design, a counterbalance to the long winters, derives from the Swedish Gustavian classical influence. It is a sophisticated layering of many whites, grays, and mellowed wood surfaces, including floors: bright and reflective, yet not cold, accented with the bold Scandinavian primaries that create an enlivening tension, an equilibrium.

The Scandinavian love of light as balance to dark winter days is manifested also in the use of glass and glazing. Glass is revered as an art form that punctuates interiors with its beauty and reflective qualities. King Gustav III's 1787 Pavilion at Haga possesses one of the first modern glass walls, conducting the outdoors in. This architectural strategy continues, whether it be in the massive mirrored glass siding on a museum, reflecting Norway's coastal landscape; in a simple family *lusthus* (garden gazebo) on the edge of a Swedish lake; or in the sculptural glass domes for viewing the Northern Lights on a floating hotel off the Arctic. Window treatments in Scandinavian interiors are minimal, and

In Scandinavia, pale hues are chosen for their ability to reflect the light, which is in short supply. This charming living room follows suit, with walls and furniture painted in delicate shades of gray, green, and white. The natural waxed oak floors anchor the room, much like the pine needles in a Nordic forest.

reflective glass, crystal, brass, and iron light fixtures provide poetic electric light. At night, torches, lanterns, and votives burn romantically in doorways, windows, and the streets alongside conventional lighting, imparting an extra sense of warmth.

The Scandinavian countries do not shrink from life's fragility. Like Odin hanging himself on the universal tree of life, balancing upside down in order to gain the wisdom to save it, Scandinavian design is a search for a dynamic balance between the self and the environment. Its lessons—use of local, ecologically sound materials, rich color derived from indigenous sources, light-giving techniques, and the exaltation of art forms such as glass that have arisen in response to a dark climate—may be translated into other environments, even ones radically different from that of Scandinavia. Where light and heat are abundant, the balance celebrated by the north might dictate an opposite aesthetic: an architecture of cooling filters, loggias, screens, and shadows, with interiors in which, for example, window treatments figure prominently rather than minimally. The essence of Scandinavian design is not the ubiquity of a particular color scheme, style, or material, but the sensitive maximization of resources that are scarce through the environmentally intelligent use of ones that are plentiful. Scandinavian design provides an enduring touchstone and philosophy, no longer confined by geographic boundaries, that designers everywhere may look to for inspiration.

Plaster walls, unadorned and weathered, meet hand-hewn beams on the ceiling of this sitting room. The carved nineteenth-century Swedish furniture is upholstered in several different stripes, which echo the linear pattern of the broad-planked wooden floors.

Fantasy

RAJI RADHAKRISHNAN

Making the impossible possible is what great interior design is about. The beginnings of a project are precious: moments when I give in to lofty dreams and the most cherished desires. I don't let anyone inhibit my first thoughts which, like sweet early morning dreams, are rife with possibilities. Even later in a project, when reality has set in, I find there are always several tangible takeaways from my earliest thoughts. So at this early stage, the premise I work from is one of no boundaries, no budgets, and no restrictions.

Flights of fantasy must start somewhere: a trip to a favorite museum, a couple of days spent foraging neck-deep in art books, or hours staring at a work in the Metropolitan Museum of Art at the risk of looking quite silly to passersby. Getting lost in these forays results in the creation of something rich and new.

I honestly believe that when conceiving design concepts, you have to run your course—go deep, get lost, confused, and exhausted, and finally abandon everything you've learned, because true learning comes when you *unlearn* everything you think you know. Let go, so that what comes after is not only your most original idea, but also one which is inherently adaptable to your now well-informed reality.

A favorite artist's work is never forgotten, not if you've studied it deeply enough. Trust that it will rise at the opportune moment, summoning a far-out idea that translates beautifully to reality.

The murals you see in my work are a perfect example; each represents a figment of imagination or memory. A sliver of Versailles, a breathtaking view of the King's Chapel, a memory of a crazy trip to London that involved hopping from one tube to another, refusing cabbies and double-deckers, an unforgettable view of the Acropolis from a hotel window.

Works on paper by Matisse, Yves Klein, and Don Kunkel are grouped and hung together over a sofa by Ettore Sottsass. The dining table, an early-twentieth-century barley-twist style, is paired with 1940s French chairs under a Gaetano Sciolari chandelier.

An Al Held serigraph is hung above a custom console made from an eighteenth-century French balcony. The artwork is flanked by a pair of Jean Perzel sconces; a Marc Newson Felt chair and Willy Rizzo cocktail table complete the tableau.

Fantasy can be found in other places as well. Fantasy can make even an average-sized room with little architectural interest unique: for example, grooved plaster walls coupled with five-inch-thick dentil moldings, plus more intricate layers added above to the ceiling and below at the wall, create an illusion of detailed richness that doesn't feel new but as if it was always there. Look down and trade that tired old eight-inch parquet

floor for hand-hewn four-foot Versailles parquet—now you have a shell with its chin up and square to you. Fill that room to your heart's content, and you'll see how much of your fantasy has become a reality.

Fantasy or reality, the point is that we should never shy away from grand dreams and possibilities. Open yourself up to the best of your imagination every single time, even if it is pure fantasy.

PROCESS

Trust

MEREDITH HARRINGTON

All good relationships are built on trust.

The practice of interior design involves a network of relationships: designer and client, designer and architect, vendor, tradesman, and dealer. In residential design, creating a home for a client necessitates a personal relationship between client and designer. We come to know how a person, a couple, or a family likes to spend their time and what makes them happy. Clients share private information about family relationships, habits, tensions, anxieties, and hopes. Discretion and empathy are invaluable here. Respect for the eccentricities of our clients and guardianship of their privacy is key.

Caring for a client's money is another equally important level of trust that must be gained by the designer and carefully guarded. Clear business terms, transparency in the practice of markups and discounts, and creation of good budgets and billing practices are essential to winning client trust and building lasting relationships. I have one client for whom I have worked on eight projects over a period of seventeen years. Although project budgets are produced and agreed to, and detailed and voluminous monthly billing is still prepared, this client now requests that he receive only one e-mail from my office each month indicating the amounts that should be transferred to bank accounts. Trust indeed.

Our clients also need to develop faith and trust in our vision and our ability to deliver lasting and beautiful designs. Working diligently to communicate design concepts and making sure consultations occur throughout the design and build of the project helps clients understand our process. I worked on a three-phase beach-house renovation over several winters. In the last phase, I strongly urged the client to change the orientation of a back stair to the kitchen, but it meant eliminating a cloakroom under the stair. She was adamant

about keeping the cloakroom for her children, and at one point, she actually told me not to bring it up again. Undeterred, I persuaded her to incorporate a cloakroom into a small foyer off the kitchen. She has thanked me ever since for insisting on this room-altering change. Good design solutions, persuasion, and open communication lead clients to trust in their designer's ability.

Learning to listen to and correctly interpret client wishes while helping them achieve these visions in a coherent design are essential. But so are being honest about the limitations of a design due to physical or budgetary constraints and managing client expectations with regard to the reality of project timing and completion. I once advised new clients to sell their small mews house and look for something that would let them fulfill their vision for a more spacious lifestyle. They had been working with an architect for some time and at considerable expense, trying to make the very small house into something it couldn't be. Instead, they found a stunning property that we have since worked on together twice.

Designers are nowhere without lasting and trusting relationships with architects, employees, consultants, vendors, artisans, dealers, and contractors. Knowing one can rely on—and be relied upon by—our colleagues is absolutely critical to the success of any project. Cultivating these relationships is an ongoing part of a good design practice.

Finally, we as designers need to trust ourselves—our education, our inspiration, our energy, our training—as well as our instincts, as they are often the source of very good decisions. The *Oxford English Dictionary* states that the origin of the word *trust* means "strong" in Old Norse. Strong ties don't break, and neither does trust if it is believed in and cultivated.

This gallery is a transition space from an enormous great room into a cozy family room. The light sculpture is by Lonneke Gordijn and Ralph Nauta of Studio Drift in Amsterdam and is made of copper, real dandelions, and LEDs; it sits above a sideboard by Philip and Kelvin Laverne. The bespoke games table is from Soane.

Problem Solving

CELESTE COOPER

Designers are problem solvers. We operate at the nexus of strength, function, and beauty described by the ancient Roman architect Vitruvius. But at that crossroads lies a maze of problems—whether of vision or execution—that we must solve.

The first step is to create a vision for an interior and vividly transmit it to the client. The designer must, with unassailable logic, solve aesthetic problems to create what John Saladino called "a walk-in still life." We deal with composition, shapes in space, figure and ground, volume, rhythm, symmetry, proportion, juxtaposition of objects, color, and vistas. I often say a floor plan should look like an abstract painting. This is the initial vision we present to the client.

Yet unlike art for art's sake, the interior designer's exquisite tableau must be more than a satisfying vision; it must be practical, outfitted like a ship, for whomever we are serving. We must contend with the minimalists for whom no amount of hidden storage is enough, who insist that the smallest space must function as a library, office, media room that seats sixteen, *and* guest room. We must create kitchens for those who have perfected takeout as an art form, provide a television in every room for avid viewers, and outfit a telecommunications-and-security system that could be on the *Enterprise*. We must write specifications for every surface and draw every detail.

Once we have forged a plan detailing function, we must execute our vision with things, purchasing what will satisfy both form and function. The items are the medium for the message. These items must be carefully thought out, wisely chosen, and sensitively realized. Editing for message is key, as eclecticism can be a license for chaos.

We must know what's out there, a breadth of knowledge that necessitates endless study, research, making judgments, avoiding clichés, and exploring alternatives, all the while knowing, of course, that the client wants it all to "go together" and to arrive quickly.

Translating to the client our selection of things is the next step in the problem-solving process. Design finds its unique language in the drawing. Most clients can't read architectural plans, much less working drawings. The designer must translate this knowledge, making it clear that everything is there for a reason. Good design is not just a function of likes and dislikes. The designer must conjure a yet-to-be-built environment with pictures and words. We must convey not only how it will look, but also how it will feel and why.

Now that the client has absorbed the lessons of vision, function, and things—the latter in the most detailed possible sense—problem solving shifts gears to behind the scenes. There are purchase orders to generate, oversee, and expedite. There are also never-ending site-supervision problems full of unforeseen complications. The designer must have a high level of organization and a mind for minutiae to orchestrate a labor-intensive pas de deux. The length of this phase can rival the gestation period of an elephant.

The installation constitutes the long-awaited moment when our vision for the client becomes reality: the contractor is done, the purchases arrive, the furniture is arranged, the accessories are in place, and the art is hung. The space becomes that abstract painting first foreseen in the plan. When the scale is right, when there is harmony and balance and rhythm, interior design evokes the frisson of meaningful art. It can also evoke a strong emotional response from the client: "I never imagined it would look like this."

For the designer, it is the realization of that walk-in still life, the culmination of all problems solved.

An enormous picture window facing Central Park in this Manhattan aerie floods the space with Western light. The challenge was to extend the light throughout the apartment, and this was accomplished by using a neutral taupe palette and carefully chosen reflective surfaces, including the ceiling and floor.

Texture

TIMOTHY BROWN

According to dictionary.com, the actual definitions of texture range from the obvious—'the visual and especially tactile quality of a surface, as in rough texture'—to the technical: 'the characteristic structure of the interwoven or intertwined threads or strands that make up a textile fabric.' A third definition is more subtle: 'the characteristic visual and tactile quality of the surface of a work of art resulting from the way materials are used.'

Texture is not just about the tactile feel of an object—the chunky rug, the rustic weave of a Belgian linen, or a slab of subtly honed marble. Texture in a room is also created by the interactions of pieces, like a high-pile rug on a satin-finish hardwood floor or a rough-hewn glazed vase on a polished marble table. Shape and size can also be tactile; together, they create a landscape in a room that can be seen and felt.

Anyone who has ever seen a Gerhard Richter painting up close understands how implied texture creates dimension; it is the same when designing a space. What you can feel and touch become equally important: the silky, rough, nubby, or furry bits are what make the scale of a room usable and pleasing.

These are several ways the use of texture can enhance an environment. Texture leads to visual interest. For example, the secret to producing an all-white room successfully is the appealing interplay of textural elements. Soft paired with coarse, matte paired with shiny, and heavy combined with light—these amalgams keep a neutral room from becoming boring. A rough texture in a room generally lends it coziness. Silk shag rugs, velvets with a thick, plush pile, and slubby woven cashmere throws don't reflect light in the way smoother surfaces can, but they envelop a room in a feeling of

warmth. More polished surfaces—sleek chrome or a supple full-grain leather, for example—can create a cooling airiness that feels modern. The exact same sofa upholstered in a light silk will become a completely different piece when covered in a thick tweed.

Balancing reflective surfaces with matte ones adds depth. A decorative plaster finish will interact with light to create shadows and movement all on its own, but marrying it with the absence of movement, such as a flat painted surface, will create another level of visual texture altogether. Color, too, plays a role in visual texture: melding two or three shades of the same color in a space creates tonal interest as opposed to using one single color alone. If the shades are varied with a glaze for a subtle glow next to a flat finish, you have both light and color working in your favor to create a greater scope of interest.

In the same way that rugged, craggy mountains show more texture than a gently sloping hillside, the scale and height of all the pieces in your space contribute to create an overall sense of form and, in turn, texture. A tall table lamp flanked by picture frames, several sculptural vases in varying heights and widths, or a vignette of picture frames play with proportion and create their own scheme of visual texture. The simplest combinations, such as a low ottoman paired with a high-backed sofa, can be what is used to create interest without being obvious.

Texture is never just one design element. It is the combination of elements—the softness of the silk, the irregularities in the surface of a stone wall, the different sizes of throw pillows—that work together to make texture the most important ingredient of every room.

Texture becomes, in a word, everything.

White paneled walls and a white tongue-and-groove ceiling unify a relaxed, airy foyer in a Wainscott, New York, beach house. The stripped antique pine floor, Noguchi hanging paper lantern, French woven-rope high-backed chair, and green-and-white ceramic lamp all add to the modern textural tableau.

Materials

 TERRY HUNZIKER

I often think of rooms as landscapes with horizon lines, shifts in elevation, the play of natural light, and, perhaps most important, varying qualities and textures of materials. There is great variety in nature; in the forest, one can find every conceivable material and texture, from the cold, smooth surface of a river rock to the rough, mossy bark of an ancient tree. In the same way, every well-designed room should feature a multitude of elements that combine to make one harmonious whole. What we ultimately see and feel tells a story.

The materials we select for our interior furnishings play a major role in how we perceive and inhabit a space. Of the five senses we use to relate to all things in the world, sight and touch predominate in our relationship to materials. We see and touch them every day. It's an intimate experience.

A very distinct example of the importance of materials comes from a concept I had twenty years ago when I bought two apartments in a converted historic brick hotel, circa 1898, merging them into a 4,000-square-foot raw space that I wanted to keep fairly open, without too many walls or doors to pass through. The space was to be very much about materials; it was to celebrate the beauty of common and not-so-common materials and to use them in unconventional ways, creating a friendly visual tension.

The materials I worked with were characterized by contrast: raw hot-rolled steel, hand-troweled Venetian plaster, cerused-oak panels, cast concrete, translucent glass panels, limestone, and automotive lacquer. Most importantly, the walls, ceilings, and floor planes were all separated by a ⅜-inch gap so that no two planes would ever meet. The gap emphasized the different materials while also easing the transitions in a clean and obvious way. These essential breathing spaces between contrasting materials suggested hallways which no longer had walls to contain them. You see this in abandoned buildings: floor surfaces that change abruptly because the walls once separating them are gone.

Taking the concept a bit further, I thought, How would it feel if, in total darkness, you could make your way through these spaces by the feel of the materials underfoot? Transitions would need to be subtle, yet obvious.

For an entry, I complemented the smooth polished-concrete pavers with a hot-rolled-steel entry wall and door. Fifteen feet in, a shallow step up onto an embedded steel "runner"—surprisingly velvety in feel—approximated a phantom hallway leading into the living space, where a Venetian-plaster floating wall is smooth and glossy to the touch. Oak plank floors overlaid with warm, soft wool area rugs demarcate the living room and library, whereas sisal, somewhat rough but with good traction, covers the stair treads and risers.

Building materials are the defining elements of living space. They announce, with each step, exactly where you are. There are few rules regarding material or finish selection, but the interior designer should keep in mind that opposites very often attract: light materials with dark accents; smooth with rough, glossy with matte, warm with cool, refined with industrial.

A great amount of thought to materials must go into every project; it is crucial in creating an environment the client will want to live in for years to come. The intelligent, authentic, and creative use of materials, in all their wonderful variety, is the basis of an interior that speaks to us daily and will ultimately endure.

A mélange of materials, including a custom leather-wrapped door with bronze hardware, a leather headboard, a campaign folding screen by Richard Wrightman with custom boar-skin panels, and a wood-framed nightstand, create a restful environment in this New Zealand bedroom.

Limestone floors, a metal coffee
table, a leather-and-cerused
oak daybed, a wool area rug, and
beautiful neutral textiles are the
finishes that coalesce to create
this rich, subdued living room.
The tray in the foreground and the
frames in the bookcase contain
Maori artifacts.

201

Light

VICTORIA HAGAN

Even as a child, I was fascinated by light. My first childhood bedroom was yellow with a large window. I remember on sunny days, I loved how the light streaming through the panes would create a vivid, graphic sea of rectangles against my yellow carpeting. And on nights when there was a moon, the soft, muted light would cast a silvery glow on the large, twisted maple tree outside my window, transforming it into an exotic, modern sculpture. It was magical to me. What I don't think I understood back then was that what delighted me most was not the light alone, but the *interplay* of the light with other objects. Light could transform the shape, color, and mood of everything around me. It is this transformative power of light that is a dominant force in my design work today. Light is my muse—in my life and in my work.

As a designer, one can glean inspiration from all areas of life. I once came across this quote from the late, brilliant Swedish cinematographer Sven Nykvist and was compelled by it: "Light can be gentle, dangerous, dreamlike, bare, living, dead, misty, clear, hot, dark, violet, springlike, falling, straight, sensual, limited, poisonous, calm, and soft." I couldn't agree more. And it can be countless other things. That's the amazing and miraculous thing about light.

It is an interior designer's job to advance light's power into a client's home. Everyone has had the experience of living in a space that they either loved . . . or did not. And my hunch is that if you loved it, it almost always had something to do with the light. Conversely, if you didn't love it, it probably also had something to do with the light. And very often, for most people, it's on a subconscious level. As a designer, light is something that's at the very top of my consciousness. It's the first thing I notice when I walk into a space. I don't just see light, I *feel* light.

I've always loved doing puzzles with my sons—spreading all the pieces out on the table, starting with the four corners and the outside frame and working inward. It's a process. Interior design is much like a complicated but fun puzzle of moving pieces—color, texture, scale, juxtaposition of materials—and then light comes into the picture of that puzzle and changes it. Again, it's a process. Something that light definitely affects is color, as color and light go hand in hand. I'm often amazed that my reputation as a designer is one who works with light colors and muted tones, when in fact I can honestly say I have only done one purely white room early in my career.

While my work does include subtlety and nuance, I aim for my projects to have exuberant, varying color palettes customized for each client. I think what people actually perceive in photographs of my work is the light, and that is deliberate. Light is a known variable that changes throughout the day, and with it, the saturation of color changes, too. A deep burgundy can become a Revlon red, a lobster red, or an undersea coral, all depending on the light. Light is constantly changing—minute to minute, hour to hour, throughout the day, throughout the year—just like life, and you must take its power into consideration when making your design choices.

I remember my mother taking me to museums in New York City as a child; I was particularly awed by Vermeer. Of course, Vermeer's paintings are famous for his depiction of light. But for me, what I intuited was that he was depicting a time of day—that *life* was happening within the frame. There was an experience going on, and one could not help but feel a part of the scene. As an interior designer, creating a pretty picture is not what motivates me; I want to create an experience for my clients. Whether it's a rustic hideaway in the mountains or a

Exceptional natural light from French doors and a skylight floods this townhouse living room in New York City. The black-and-cream color scheme is complemented by a pair of Lucite Karl Springer chairs and a strappy vintage chair found at an antiques dealer in the neighborhood. The artwork above the sofa is by Joseph Kosuth.

Someone who does not

breezy beach house or a sleek Manhattan penthouse, light always inspires my choices. I love that the color and the quality of the light on Long Island, New York, is distinct from the color and quality of the light on Nantucket, which is distinct from the light in Los Angeles, which is distinct from the light in Paris—and on and on.

I have been quite lucky in my career to work with extraordinarily talented architects, and I'm sure they would all attest, much as I do, that light is neither traditional nor modern. It defies design categorization, yet it is transformative to every interior moment and transcends time and space. I see light as the only truly timeless element of design.

Relationships

BARRY DIXON

The American system of government, the Holy Trinity, an equilateral triangle: when successful, these all share a special balance of three. The ideal home is no different. When it works, it is a perfect balance of person, place, and structure.

Interior designers of the highest order possess a knack for such balance, a capacity that allows them to intuit the complexity of the intangible, the mood of the invisible, and marry that with the obvious surface of things. We all do it differently, as our designing minds are the product of our individual histories. The aesthetic truths we learn are shaped and tempered by intrinsic preferences and acquired tastes, by indelible associations and peculiar perspectives. These are then all melded into the collective unconscious of our decorating cerebellum to emerge as our personal style. Clients hire us for our style, our one-of-a-kind filter. All the decisions that must be made in designing the clients' homes pass through this filter to be transmuted to the definitive end that will be *their* home—and no one else's.

To achieve this, we must effect a designer's system of checks and balances that is best achieved via a triumvirate of important relationships vital to decorating success.

First, there is the relationship between home and place.

The home may be a house, an apartment, a mansion, a cottage, a room, or a maze of rooms. The place may be in the city, on a farm, up in the air or down on the ground, hot or cold, arid or tropical, in the woods, by the sea, or far up on the side of a mountain with an endless view. One of the designer's principal roles is to marry home to place. What a home sees through its "window eyes" needs to be considered and brought into the interior, abstractly or otherwise, for the realm to take root and belong. A home must know and honor its place on earth.

Second, the designer must consider the relationship between home and inhabitant.

The spirit of the home, now at one with place, must mesh with the spirit of the homeowner. The designer must cultivate an intimate understanding of the house itself: old or new, large or small, oversize or under-scaled, light-filled or dark, ornate or austere. Is it true to its original aesthetic or layered with eras of bad decisions? Is it an architectural gem or an enigma? These are but the threshold issues the designer must evaluate. There is a deeper, more hidden layer of understanding that the best designers master in service to their clients. What is the essence of this house, its character or soul?

This phase is where the designer's mettle is tested and proven. A knowledge of the history of ornament and architecture, of stalwart truths of scale and proportion, is what allows an interior designer to speak the language of a home. Different homes have different souls. Old houses whisper to us, telling us what they'll be comfortable with in the way of invention. Sometimes they plead for release from tortured renovations, beg for a return to former glory coupled with a boost to modern relevance. Older and wiser, they've lived other lives and know who they were, are, and can be. New homes, by contrast, are new souls, brave and energetic, puppies in need of training and direction. They have no history, no romantic whisper, but they have no battle scars either; they are still pure and closer to the architect's original intent. They have the promise of youth, vigorous and strong.

What constitutes the client's soul? Understanding the psyche of the human being who will inhabit this house, who will breathe life into this realm to make it a home, is paramount. The designer has to marry one to the other in a blessed union that will only succeed when he understands both.

The third relationship at play in the designer's work is the most important of all. that between designer and client. The

An acid-green Murano glass chandelier was a custom commission executed by Barovier&Toso. The whimsical mantel is eighteenth-century Italian, found through Ed Hardy in San Francisco. The seating arrangement, covered in various ice-blue patterned fabrics, invites both casual and intimate conversation.

responsibility for success is ours. Designers design every day. But for the client, seeking guidance, interior design is a rare endeavor he or she may or may not enjoy. The ball is in a designer's court to find out exactly whom we're working with in order to create a bespoke realm for living. To get this right, we must listen carefully to our clients to discern their hopes and desires, especially those less obvious. We chart the basics—family, existing furnishings, budget, formality—to calculate their particular hierarchy of needs. What are they like and what do they like?

Listen, watch, notice, and remember. A basic tenet of haute couture is that a lady must wear the dress, and the dress must not be wearing the lady. And so the rule of "home couture" is that the client should wear the home; the home should suit him or her as perfectly as it does its place in the world. The bespoke success of this endeavor is, in the end, what we're hired to ensure: to avoid general showhouse notions of a perfect cookie-cutter home, the off-the-rack, one-size-fits-all ideals of an interior. The tailored process of creating a one-of-a-kind transcendent realm timelessly melds past and present, person and personality, with the heart and soul of home and homeowner.

A stylized array of Mediterranean influences populates this sitting room and includes Moroccan, Venetian, Turkish, Spanish, and Greco-Roman, all of which are united in a color palette of yellows. The Greek-key pattern articulated in nail heads around the pouf is an inspired decorative touch.

The Reveal

ANTHONY COCHRAN

I love making my clients cry. Thankfully, they have always been happy tears, as I prefer to reserve drama for interiors, not professional relationships. In the business of interior design, there is no greater satisfaction than the climactic moment when a designer welcomes clients back into their newly decorated home and watches them fall utterly in love with it.

I say "fall in love" because just being happy with it is the baseline of satisfaction. The real goal is for clients to find their redesigned space not only exactly what they wanted, but also far beyond what they ever could have imagined. And there's a secret to this perfect, crystalline moment: a project that is really and truly complete. The expected checklist is finished, but just as important, a whole slew of little details that a client would never dream of have been deftly taken care of as well. These details are the icing on the cake, and who wants to eat a cake without icing?

Transforming a house is never just about sofas, chairs, tables, mirrors, and window treatments. They're important, of course, but the real differentiator is how these pieces are brought together in scale and sensibility with accessories, artwork, and the incidentals of daily life—even seemingly unremarkable things like a tissue box cover. For example, will the house be scented? How will books be arranged on shelves? Will there be flowers? What's in the refrigerator when the client first opens it? (Answer: a bottle of champagne. After all, there's a new life to celebrate within these walls.)

Many clients never get to this moment. "You handle the furniture and rugs, and we'll do the rest," they tell their designer. "I already have accessories," they say. "I'll figure it out." They never have the excitement of the reveal, of reentering their space in its new conception. And they also never fully understand why they're vaguely pleased with the results but not nearly as thrilled as they had hoped. What they're missing is the transforming magic that occurs when a home is completely pulled together by one overseeing eye.

Presenting a project in toto did not originate with me; I learned it from two masters. Early in my career, I was fortunate enough to work for John Saladino and, later, Victoria Hagan. About a week before one of their projects was complete, the client would be asked to leave the unfinished construction site, essentially banished for the duration. They returned to a dream realized. And in the days that followed, they would call again and again, excited to report yet another little detail they had just noticed. "How do you do it?" they'd ask. My mentors knew the answer, intangible but very, very real: every aspect of the design had been thought through.

Clients choose their interior designers for a variety of reasons—reputation, referral, similar taste, aspirational taste—the alchemy is always different. But no one chooses someone they don't trust, and that professional esteem is something no designer takes lightly. Interior designers offer not just professional training and years of experience, but also a new set of eyes constantly seeking ways to air out, integrate, freshen and improve the visual and daily lives of their clients. Merging styles and tastes, eras and motifs, and furniture with personal objects is all in a day's work, so letting an interior designer execute from beginning to "curtain up" is worth the trust and extra effort. Because as any great designer can tell you, there's nothing like tears of joy.

A sophisticated color palette of dusty shades, articulated in velvet, satin, cashmere, and linen, draws inspiration from the colors of nature at dusk. The carefully chosen accessories speak to the bachelor who calls this space home.

Pattern

MARKHAM ROBERTS

Pattern to me is interest. It's depth and dimension; it's stimulation.

Pattern is everywhere and seen in everything, from fabric and furniture and artwork to the placement of trees in a landscape or the movement of grass in a field.

Whether I am working on a garden or composing fabrics, I enjoy playing with different types of patterns. This can be done by putting together vivid prints of different scales and colors or by more subtly combining textures in monochromatic tones—or any combination in between. You just have to recognize what works for you.

Pattern can elicit emotional responses, and even if subconscious, these are powerful. Stripes, for example, provide rhythm and calm. Think of the orderly, almost military appeal of the tented room of the Charlottenhof Palace at Potsdam, or how satisfying and handsome the repetition of stripes can be when covering walls or furniture.

Alternatively, floral patterns remind us of the world around us and reflect or interpret the natural beauty we as humans find so appealing. They can be bright, happy, and exuberant or more reserved and somber. Other patterns—toiles, ikats, suzanis, and Chinese scenic papers—can take us to far-off places.

Patterns can even be transformative. For example, the use of an African tribal print on a period Georgian armchair brings new life to a familiar old style and lightens what could be a heavy traditional feel. When used in an unexpected way, pattern can make an old piece of furniture a little cooler or less rigid.

I am very often asked how I mix patterns together, and I never have a good answer. I think of mixing patterns as more of an art than a recipe. There are no guidelines or steadfast rules—aside from not putting hideous things together. Seriously,

it's all relative and particular to each situation, so I tell people to look at things and see what appeals to them aesthetically.

I've done rooms with a very bold and obvious use of patterns in the mix. I love the challenge of a giant room with all sorts of things going on, from the walls and the carpet to the layers of fabrics in the upholstery and curtains. Add in artwork and accessories, and you have a complex system of patterns working together to make a room beautiful.

Alternatively, when working on rooms where the scheme is meant to be completely calming, the use of subtle pattern, quietly detailed, lends visual interest and lessens the risk of monotony. Even where I intend a room to gently coax one to sleep, it doesn't mean the eyes have to be bored by a lack of pattern. I will use textures as pattern and rely more on other things in the room to achieve this interplay my eye seems to crave; the different shapes of furniture, for example, can be as stimulating as the more obvious use of patterned fabrics.

Whatever the case, a room needs this visual interest, whether it's obvious or subtle, to make an overall pleasing result. One room illustrates particularly well how I view pattern holistically. For the forty-second Kips Bay Show House, I chose a small French-paneled room on the top floor of the classically proportioned Villard Houses by Stanford White.

I went for a monochromatic scheme of teal and highlighted the effect of the handsome paneling by upholstering the inset panels in textured wool. This set off the mottled teal glaze on the surrounding woodwork beautifully and made an excellent backdrop for all of the art I hung on the walls. The play of the different shapes and types of frames in addition to the varied artwork within the configuration of the paneling itself

In a landmark Rosario Candela building on Manhattan's Upper East Side, this staircase has a custom banister and stenciled grass cloth (hand-embellished by a decorative painter) on its circular walls. The carpeting on the stairs is also a custom design.

made an interesting arrangement for overall contemplation as well as closer scrutiny.

With the walls essentially covered in varied pattern, I needed to balance the floor and ceiling with more of an overall pattern as a relief for the eye. The tiger rug and cork ceiling balanced each other and complemented the strong teal in the rest of the room. The furniture and accessories provided the final layering of pattern thanks to their mixture of styles, placement, and relationship to everything else in the room.

Whether creating a complexly schemed room with wildly varied prints and shapes or working on a small, serene space, pattern is key, and experimenting with it makes everything come alive.

The walls of the family room in this house in Nashville are upholstered in a cashmere tweed. The brown-and-cream color scheme is underscored by the pattern of a Quadrille fabric on the two club chairs, and the antique Georgian armchair is covered in a fabric by fellow interior designer Suzanne Rheinstein.

Expectations

PAUL SISKIN

There are so many factors that go into the creative process of interior design. The clients' wishes, budget, usage, environment, and spatial boundaries are high among the considerations. Good design must embrace all factors in the equation and incorporate them into a solution that meets not only the client's basic needs, but also his or her expectations, which may contain larger desires for beauty, social aspirations, and wishes for a transformed lifestyle.

Having said that, a designer must evaluate how realistic clients' expectations are.

Case in point: I once interviewed a potential client regarding a new apartment she had bought in Manhattan. The two-bedroom space was located in a Midtown postwar white brick building. I had asked her to bring me pictures of spaces or items she loved, things she would like to have incorporated in the design of her new home. The first image was the grand room from the popular television series *Downton Abbey*. I tried to explain that we were dealing with apples and oranges: very little, short of wizardry, could transform her eight-foot-two-inch-tall rooms into the receiving hall at Downton Abbey, with its lofty ceilings. In the end, the client decided not to work with me, which may have worked out for the best, as I believe a good designer understands the limits of both space and their abilities.

Clients may also have unrealistic expectations for how great an impact a new home can have on their lifestyle.

Another case in point: a young couple had purchased a Beaux Arts townhouse. When

the lady of the house walked me through the architect's plans, she narrated the new lifestyle that would attend this new address. She described how future dinner parties would unfold: cocktails in the living room, dinner in the dining room, then coffee and after-dinner drinks in the library. Of course, their good friends would remain on for the screening of movies in the media room. At this point, her husband stepped in to point out that they didn't really like to entertain.

Part of the designer's responsibility is to make sure the client understands the limits of his or her new space. For example, I can build storage into an apartment, but it is still the client who must organize his or her belongings on a daily basis.

A change in one's finances and environment can contribute to a new lifestyle, of course, but it will always be the people themselves who drive the change, not the other way around. It's an important factor in designing for someone, but a sensitive subject and difficult to convey. As my relationship with a client grows more relaxed with time, it becomes easier to communicate; however, this concept is one I try to explain as early as possible.

My work takes much of its direction from each individual client. I take pride in the fact that my work is unidentifiable: it does not immediately reveal my hand. I help create the canvas that the client completes. It is his or her participation in the process—the clear, ongoing communication of expectations— that will make the home his or her home and not a showcase for my firm.

The comfortable seating area of this Hudson Valley, New York, house, with its floor-to-ceiling windows, literally brings the verdant outdoors in. A subtle taupe color palette furthers the idea by referencing the stone terrace outside.

Commissions

AMY LAU

These days, I can look at a magazine photo of a room and know exactly where most of the elements were purchased. So much of what gets used to furnish houses comes out of manufacturers' catalogs or straight off the Internet. If, however, you have the means and desire for an exceptional home that pushes past the ordinary, artists and artisans will help you create exceptional interiors.

Artist collaborators bring unparalleled craftsmanship and creativity to a room's design. Instead of fabric bought off the bolt for a sofa, why not ask a weaver to craft a unique bouclé in lush cotton blended with silk? And there's no reason that the throw pillows shouldn't be beautiful enough to frame. You can use vintage textiles for pillows, of course, but why not call in an artist? The California-based textile designer Lauren Saunders produces artisanal throw pillows with knitted wool or felt appliqués on embroidered velvet. For the ballroom in a Chicago apartment, she sewed on her own celestial starburst pattern to echo sculptural midcentury art on the wall above.

Though they may seem intimidating, you will find that people like Lauren Saunders are open to custom commissions and find collaboration invigorating. In fact, many small-scale manufacturers relish the chance for creativity. You just have to pick up the phone. The modernist metalworker Silas Seandel might agree to sculpt the bronze frame for a spectacular coffee table topped with a gargantuan slab of agate from Uruguay. Or if you are lucky enough to have a double-height living room, a celebrated painter and sculptor like Malcolm Hill can build a three-dimensional bas-relief for a long swath of wall above eye level.

Sometimes you will want an element unavailable in the marketplace, and an artisan solution can address that need. Perhaps my favorite commission was one of my first, a contemporary mantelpiece for a New York client interested in Eastern philosophy. Echoing nature, its asymmetrical design embraced the rough edge of a solid wood slab that swelled and flowed organically where it once met the tree bark. Tyler Hays, the brilliant founder of the artisanal New York furniture showroom BDDW, used that kind of live edge for the mantelshelf of his claro walnut mantelpiece, giving it a Zen quality that perfectly complements the Asian-inspired loft in New York where I installed it.

When working collaboratively, advance planning pays off. You can sketch a custom carpet idea full-size on butcher paper or stick blue painter's tape to the floor of a room to understand the scale and proportion. Measured drawings can help, but there is nothing better than climbing a ladder in a space to build a chandelier with an artisan. If hands-on design is not possible, supply detailed instructions and photo inspirations to back them up. As you go along, archive sketches from meetings and also note key conversations. Finally, be sure to snap plenty of documentary pictures throughout the process for later reference by all involved.

History supplies evidence of the rewards when furniture is commissioned, especially for great rooms in important houses. You can modernize the idea by working with a furniture designer on a unique suite of pieces for an entire room. It's a real pleasure to have a front-row seat to this level of creativity, and it lends a deeper appreciation for the bespoke elements that result. Beyond any creative rewards, custom commissions can be worthy investments with intrinsic value that will only grow. Some pieces may eventually go into the museums, auction houses, and fine-furniture galleries of the future. Certainly one thing is clear: as they age, these will become the heirlooms of tomorrow.

Lau commissioned the asymmetrical sofa from famed furniture designer Vladimir Kagan. It sits under a spectacularly scaled chandelier, custom made for the space by lighting designer Lindsey Adelman.

Quality

THAD HAYES

The one issue that is rarely discussed in our profession is the mass disposability in our culture, the result of poor-quality items that typically don't last or wear well and end up discarded. We as modern consumers have an unfortunate tendency to jettison and start anew. What happens when sofa fabric becomes soiled after a few years of use? Do we discard the sofa or get a new fabric and have the sofa reupholstered? Of course we don't abandon it: a sofa of good quality should last thirty years; therefore, a new fabric is appropriate. I was happy, for example, to receive two 1950s club chairs from my mother that needed only minor refurbishing and re-covering. The idea of "waste not want not" was common during the Great Depression and weighed on the American consciousness through the 1960s. During this period, furniture was restored, reconditioned, or reupholstered.

Seeking out well-made things that last need not be an extravagance. Rather, it has to do with purchasing quality instead of quantity and properly maintaining what you have. I've seen this attitude practiced countless times with friends and relatives who came from modest means but had the good sense to purchase well-made items, be they a chair or a dress shirt

The highly talented craftspeople who make our upholstered sofas and the shades for our lamps, who lacquer our tables and cast our bronze hardware, are dwindling in number, their work replaced by mass-produced goods of inferior quality.

We recently sat down in my office for our bimonthly meeting. The first order of business was discussing potential new lampshade makers. These are the kind of artisans who are disappearing—they collaborate with us in selecting dozens of silks, linens, and papers of varying colors and textures to cover a wire frame, all of it custom made for a particular lamp shape and style, with tapes, strings, ropes,

A painting by artist Odd Nerdrum is reflected in the mirror in the entryway of this apartment at the Pierre Hotel in New York City. The ceiling fixture, the sconce, the floating shelf, and the bench were all custom designed for the space.

OVERLEAF: The overall neutral palette of this austere Fifth Avenue penthouse sets the stage for a collection of contemporary art, including paintings by Ross Bleckner and Harland Miller. The coffee table accessories are from Royal Copenhagen.

and bric-a-brac, or left plain and simple. The process of designing a lampshade closely resembles the work of a fantastic milliner you would have encountered at Bergdorf Goodman in a bygone era. Yet a large percentage of the specialty lampshade vendors we began using in the mid-1980s, when I founded my business, are no longer around. This is due partly to the lack of technical and artistic training that supports our profession, but it could also be that people are settling for less expensive mass-produced shades of inferior quality that have very little to do with the lamp or its context.

With online product information as our guide and the Internet as our source, we are beginning to dissociate ourselves from the actual things we are looking at and require for our projects, whether these are sink fittings, tile and stone, or antiques. Images of items on a computer screen do not suggest tactile qualities, weight, scale, integrity, and craftsmanship. The more we reference products and goods online, the more disconnected we become from the essence of the actual thing.

Interior designers must be mindful of how things are put together and how they function. We not only make beautiful, interesting, and intriguing spaces and objects, we also need to ensure that the construction techniques are solid and lasting. Our drawings must convey details that inform contractors of the method and means of construction. The shop drawings must show the exact way things are assembled and installed. Increasingly, wood veneers and shortcuts are employed, only to fail or look ragged and worn once the pieces are handled. We must know where solid woods are needed and when a veneer is appropriate without compromising the integrity and longevity of the piece. Ideally, these things we design and create should develop a beautiful patina that makes the piece more tactile and luxurious with age.

In a culture of mass consumption and mass disposability, having something that is substantial, well made, and lasting lends meaning and weight to our existence, solidifying a positive view of ourselves in a volatile world. We need to return to some of the traditional ways of doing things in order to preserve the integrity of our profession and ensure that quality, above all, is maintained and cherished.

Editing

JANE SCHWAB *and* CINDY SMITH

The living room of this Charlotte, North Carolina, house is perfect for small groups or large gatherings. The vast limestone fireplace and plaster walls harmonize with the antique Oushak rug, which provided the basis for the color palette.

OPPOSITE: Palladian windows look out into a garden in this Florida home. A creamy white coats the walls, while the window and door surrounds are natural limestone.

As a nation, we have perfected multitasking and accelerated our lives to a dizzying pace. Our time is at a premium; thus, the occasions on which we are able to share our homes with those we value are truly special. Now, more than ever, it is necessary for our homes not only to enhance our daily lives but also to provide a refuge—a place where we can recharge from the frenetic world or gather together.

We feel rooms should be refined to reflect their owners' personalities, providing a sense of calm and comfort. Interiors should facilitate rather than overpower conversations. The famed designer Sibyl Colefax once wrote, "Everything in a house should be so simply and yet so ingeniously contrived that life flows through it easily," and we quite agree. An interior's ease can only be achieved through careful editing.

Elegant serenity, the product of judicious editing, is a concept deeply rooted in historic design principles. Thomas Jefferson was so enamored of the dignified simplicity and heritage of Greco-Roman architecture that he encouraged its use as the basis for our country's first public buildings. The Greeks imposed mathematical relationships to create a system of proportion that stimulates our inherent sense of beauty and harmony in a space. They also utilized restraint and temperance in their designs. We look to the time-tested Greek principles of clarity, simplicity, and balance when editing today's home. William Morris, founder of the Arts and Crafts movement in Victorian England, stated, "Have nothing in your house that you do not know to be useful or believe to be beautiful."

Editing for simplicity does not result in plainness. Objects may be exquisite and ornamented without being fussy. Whether refined or rustic, they can be a beautiful addition of scale or shape to the composition of a room. When we edit, we ask ourselves if the object is congruent with our vision for the room.

Editing for balance is a spatial consideration. We strive to achieve a balance reminiscent of classical proportions of beauty. We ask ourselves, Does the eye have space to pause? Every item should not compete for attention; a room's composition should allow the eye to rest. When the eye is able to rest, the uniqueness of the items in it is accentuated.

Editing for beauty is a critical component of the process. It takes time and practice to learn how to walk into a crowded market and select the extraordinary rather than the ordinary.

We are awed by objects that convey creation by a true artist, expressing his vision through the turn of a leg, superior carving, or exquisite hardware while exercising just the right amount of restraint. Patina, the finish of an item added by time, makes us wonder about

the lives that have been touched by the piece. We look for pronounced textures that will add dimension or promote movement. We are repeatedly drawn to unusual pieces made of authentic materials—bone, wood, stone, silver, porcelain—that have real decorative value.

The careful selection of innately beautiful objects, when coupled with the removal of extraneous objects, allows a room to breathe and the occupants to enjoy the composition. Editing is not only about what is beautiful but also about the feeling it evokes from its occupants.

Layering

ALEX PAPACHRISTIDIS

Creating layered interiors is second nature to me, but it requires discipline and imagination; whether I am decorating a prewar Manhattan apartment or a contemporary country house, the layered mix of antiques, modern art, and custom furnishings gives a home depth of character.

But a layered approach is not the same as eclecticism; it's more nuanced and considered.

In a successfully layered room everything goes together, but nothing should be overmatched or obvious. The goal is harmony and balance, which demands a combination of textures, a careful mix of matte and shiny, patterned fabrics and solids. A variety of surfaces—whether ceramic, marble, or bronze, crystal or lacquer, steel or parchment—play off and enrich one another. Rooms should have a collected feel, so avoid matched sets. If the dining room table is dark wood, surround it with painted or upholstered chairs. A room should never look like it has too many pairs. However, I do make an exception for sconces and bedside lamps.

My passion for elegance makes me a very traditional decorator in many respects. I am drawn to the eighteenth century, when some of the most beautiful furniture ever designed was made, such as the bold sophistication of a William Kent console and the clean elegance of an eighteenth-century gilt bronzed Gueridon table. To my mind, even the best modern furniture references eighteenth-century shapes and silhouettes, which have a classic, enduring quality. Louis XVI chairs are a surprisingly nice complement to furniture designed two hundred years later by Jean-Michel Frank and Diego Giacometti. I find it is natural to mix classical furniture from different time periods and countries— whether French, Russian, or Swedish—and they can be combined in endless combinations without looking dated or predictable.

English, French, and Portuguese antiques are extremely compatible; they mix beautifully together. They reflect the trade routes of long ago, evoking historical tastes when those who ruled the world would collect the best of the best from every nation. Good taste, after all, has no boundaries.

The play of patterns and textures is integral to a layered approach. Pillows should always have different fabrics on their fronts and backs—so, too, should bergères and upholstered dining chairs. My sofas often have five or six different fabrics: I cut out a motif I like from one piece of fabric and have it appliquéd onto another. Lampshades should be silk or cotton, ideally custom made, and trimmed with gimp or fringe.

You may not immediately notice these embellishments, but they are essential in creating a unique, layered environment.

Rooms should be designed with personality. Draw on furniture and objets d'art that are conversation pieces, and antiques because the provenance of every piece tells a story: they evoke the romance of another time. Furthermore, antiques are "green." They already exist in the world, and clients appreciate that they are "recycling" in the most sophisticated manner.

Even if you are starting from scratch when decorating, your rooms will never look done or brand-new if they are layered correctly. The goal is always to create spaces that can evolve; if you develop a passion for, say, seventeenth-century Chinese porcelain or contemporary art, the new pieces can be added seamlessly.

I believe in contrast, if not contradiction, as a constant in a well-layered design, such as putting a sumptuous embroidered sofa or gilt furniture on a heavy, woven sisal carpet. I love a room with upholstered fabric walls and bare wood floors stenciled with a graphic pattern.

A striking red-and-gray chevron-patterned carpet, warp-dyed silk on sofa cushions, and bright yellow ceramic foo dogs on brackets become all the more vibrant against dark walls in this layered Manhattan library.

OVERLEAF: A Julian Schnabel painting brings a charge of modernity into an otherwise old-world room in this Manhattan townhouse. A blue-gray linen-velvet sofa is accessorized with throw pillows made from silvery satin pieced together in geometric patterns. The claw foot armchair and ottoman assert tradition.

I frequently put simple matchstick bamboo blinds on windows framed by elaborate silk curtains trimmed with passementerie. By placing an inlaid eighteenth-century Dutch table next to a twentieth-century Japanese sculpture on a hand-dyed Indian rug, everything becomes more interesting.

Decorating is an art, not a science. The rules are meant to be broken. The goal is to create a home that reflects your sensibilities. Open your mind to all the possibilities and layer in fabrics, furniture, and art that have been carefully chosen to create a home that is personal, collected, luxurious, and timeless.

ELEMENTS

Collecting

NANCY BRAITHWAITE

Curiosity is one of the wonders of human nature. It is energetic and feeds intelligence; it fuels interest. It is essential to creativity, originality, and uniqueness. Most certainly, it is a precursor for the collector's necessary education, for it is through curiosity that one develops an informed and trained eye that leads to a collection's success.

In order to build a noteworthy collection, collectors must have the knowledge to compare and rate the objects in question. Museums are wonderful repositories of the greatest collections, the best-of-the-best objects that teach us so much about the fruits of human endeavor. Historic houses—grand and humble alike—are equally revealing.

Collecting is passion, pursuit, coming in for the kill, plus the anticipation of acquisitions to come. A collector is always on the hunt. Every serious collector sits and waits for that one great piece—the next.

The range of collectibles is as infinite as human creativity. One can collect for purely decorative purposes, or with a far greater degree of seriousness. All periods of history provide objects that may form a collection's seed or through-line. When one collects antiques, one is acquiring, absorbing, and living with history. One is also caring for objects that have had life before, and will have life after they leave our hands. Collecting contemporary objects can be just as exciting for those interested in the artistic merit of more recent eras and creative culture as it takes shape and shifts into a future mode.

Every serious collector follows three rules: collect what you love, collect at a level you can afford, and, have an expert by your side to prevent costly mistakes.

Collections evolve. As experience, knowledge, and opportunity lead to the acquisition of exemplary objects, the collector may cull earlier pieces as the collection develops its depth of character. This ongoing refinement is continual.

Part of the thrill of collecting is recognizing the value of an item before the rest of the market does. Sometimes the intuitive eye just knows. The response is immediate, and it captures the senses. Many designers are born with what people call "a good eye." This is a gift, and gratefully accepted. Those with a "good eye" naturally seem to "see" and understand form, proportion, and scale. They have a feel for the relationships that make up a pleasing arrangement.

The good eye, however, must be educated, principled, and disciplined. Albert Hadley famously said: "Seeing is a very difficult thing to do. Most people 'look' at a lot

In Braithwaite's home, an important collection of American antiques is an object lesson in material culture and history. The hand-painted walls allude to early American decorative tradition; the daybed is a rare piece from the early eighteenth century.

of things but never 'see' anything. Looking is emotional. Seeing is an intellectual process." It is the method that humans use to evaluate when "this" belongs and "that" does not. Without a trained eye, seeing this way—critically—is virtually impossible. Achieving such discernment is hard work, a lifetime's study and practice. Without it, significant collections—those that lead us into the future by teaching us about the past—would not exist. Many serious collectors assemble their troves with an eye to preserving cultural heritage, and plan for the day when they can bequeath them to the public trust as an addition to humankind's ongoing legacy.

Collecting need not be elevated, however, to infuse everyday existence with pleasures, some expected, others surprising. Amassing a treasury of buttons can encompass the same excitement, enthusiasm, and entertainment as acquiring an archive of Shaker children's chairs. What generates the thrill is the marvel that is the intellect, and the quest to know who, what, where, when, why, and how. If one is not captivated by the evidence of what makes us human—what we have made, are making, and will make—one cannot know oneself, or others, at all. Curiosity is where that quest starts. Without it, there would be no collections—or life—at all.

A pair of late-eighteenth-century fan-back Windsor chairs and a pair of antique wrought iron–and–wood chandeliers give this Atlanta living room a stellar pedigree.

Patina

KATHRYN SCOTT

The true potential of beauty lies not in prestigious products purchased from expensive stores, but in the simple everyday surfaces that speak of life itself.

I think of it as the beauty behind patina. The idea is not my invention, nor am I the only one who prefers imperfect over perfect; the concept is represented by the Japanese philosophy of *wabi-sabi*, which honors the visible wear expressing the lifetime of each object around us. To think of everything having a lifetime worth noting is an interesting idea, and it somehow disallows the human temptation to behave as if everything else is subordinate to ourselves. Suddenly, we are face-to-face with the realization that we are merely a part of our surroundings and participating in an interdependent universe. Every element plays an integral part; the whole makes up a profound beauty found all around us.

The role of a designer is to improve our quality of life by rearranging the environment we live in. What sets one designer apart from another is his or her personal vision. Inspired by wabi-sabi, I search to express the beauty of life through purposeful curation. It requires careful balancing, as being surrounded by too many broken-down things can appear like degeneration and chaos. Selectively using objects or materials with patina, whether antique furnishings or worn architectural surfaces, makes them feel more precious since their condition remains as a cherished memory, a history we wish to remember.

There are times I find myself struggling to re-adjust a client's hesitation when this is a new philosophy to him or her. The expectation that indestructible materials are better, and therefore practical, has caused some to surround themselves with lifeless materials. This is a typical fear that seems quite ingrained in our society, one that has caused many to hesitate to use marble for a kitchen counter to avoid stains and scratches. I respond that only when the counter becomes worn and scratched will it truly be beautiful, as that home will then reflect that it is well loved and well lived in. The desire to keep everything perfect—as if it has never been used—is quite unappealing and makes everything feel dead. Nothing in nature is perfect. The desire to keep everything new reminds me of mass production and synthetic materials, whereas I find more beauty in the handmade and materials found in nature.

I first became enamored with patina in my travels through Europe, when I noticed the way an old stone floor surface wore unevenly. Different colored marbles, inlaid side by side, dip lower at the softer stones and the most traveled pathways. The undulating surface is rich and sensuous; it is something that cannot be re-created without the hand of an artisan. Even a faithful reproduction of a beautifully worn surface cannot be made as rich as the authentic one formed by time because it does not reflect the history of a place.

The visible pathways of old floors, walls, and architectural details are proof of the centuries of people who passed through that exact spot. The worn surface has become an anthropological documentation of the place. If you pause for a moment to imagine the people whose passage left its mark, the place itself feels different; the irregularities remain as a memorial to our ancestors, and imagining them carrying on with their daily activities in the same place we carry on with our own is a profoundly beautiful thought.

The walls of this Brooklyn dining room are finished in earthy stucco, a surface that ages to take on a life of its own. The top of the dining table is raw cypress without a protective sealant, which allows it to acquire an authentic patina through everyday use, and the walnut cabinets in the background are oiled to accentuate the grain.

Antiques

TIMOTHY WHEALON

Antiques may be commonly defined as something old and possibly valuable, but this description does not take into consideration all the emotional elements and connotations that make antiques interesting: beauty, craftsmanship, patina, form, as well as connection to our cultural history and humanity. Antiques make an "imprint" on our lives in diverse ways—as the result of a purely visual experience, a memory associated with the object, or the literal and poetic imprint of the human hand over time. Antiques evoke a feeling or mood; we respond to them on an emotional level.

I was drawn to antiques at a very young age, accompanying my mother to estate sales and auctions in the Midwest where I grew up. My first purchase was a mahogany George I armchair with a needlepoint seat I bought when I was only twelve years old. Later, my love of antiques would lead me to Sotheby's in London and New York. There, I learned to evaluate and catalog antiques, noting quality, rarity, condition, and provenance. These valuable lessons educated my youthful eye.

The intrinsic beauty, the "soul" of an object captivates me. A rich past life is revealed through antiques, but historical context is secondary to their essential visual power. I use antiques in my interiors to elicit emotions from the individuals who inhabit the space.

In *The House in Good Taste*, Elsie de Wolfe wrote, "What charm is to a person, the vague thing called quality is to an object of art. We feel it, though we may not be able to explain it . . . . The age of a piece of furniture is of great value to a museum, but for domestic purposes, use and beauty will do." I believe the quality that de Wolfe speaks of is manifested in antiques through form, proportion, craftsmanship, and patina.

Whether flamboyantly rococo or restrained neoclassical, form and proportion are crucial, as is the craftsmanship that goes into an inlaid parquetry top or a perfectly executed parchment commode with gilt-metal sabots, hand-wrought escutcheons, or perfectly dovetailed drawers.

Over the years, I have watched great craftsmen and restorers building and taking apart objects for restoration; this has taught me more about antiques than anything else. To me, craftsmanship is the key ingredient in all antiques. I always favor careful, sensitive restoration of an antique. What is more beautiful than the layers of paint on a Swedish antique slowly chipped away over time, or the sun-faded top of a well-worn Irish mahogany table?

While knowledge and expertise are important, nothing compares to the feeling one has when presented with something unique or extraordinary in an antique, whether at the Brimfield Antique Show in Massachusetts or one of the small antiques shops on the Left Bank of Paris. I always tell my clients to buy an antique or object because it speaks to them and because they love it and want to live with it.

I was taught that an antique is something one hundred years or older, yet this definition no longer makes sense. Whether it be a Pierre Jeanneret teak-and-caned chair made for Chandigarh in India in the 1950s or a John Vardy gilt-wood mirror made for Hackwood House in the countryside of England in the 1760s, antiques are objects that are dusted with the patina of time and imprinted with the hands that made them, even if they were crafted only fifty years ago. A mixture of carefully edited antiques enriches our lives and the homes we live in with their collective beauty and soul. As John Keats wrote, "A thing of beauty is a joy for ever!"

The dining room of this townhouse on Manhattan's Upper East Side is steeped in historical references. An Italian chandelier from the early nineteenth century and a pair of gilt sconces from the 1940s illuminate the festivities at the Louis XVI dining table. The Swedish-inspired reproduction chairs were custom made for the room.

Early-eighteenth-century English ormolu walnut stools encircle a Regency oak library table in this New York townhouse. A pair of parcel-gilt armchairs from the Palazzo Corsini in Florence are joined by a colossal marble portrait of the emperor Trajan. The painting above the mantel is by eighteenth-century artist Giovanni Paolo Panini.

Curation

I started at the École des Beaux-Arts in Paris shortly after the Sorbonne riots, and I have vivid memories of my French professors and fellow students looking down on American fashion, American culture, and definitely American art. In fact, American art never even came up during our art history course. We were taught that the only way to understand fine art was by studying the classics and embracing a traditional approach. We drew from plaster casts, dissected cadavers, and used the primary colors as a base in every single painting with glazes stroked carefully over grisaille. This rigorous approach prepared me to be an artist, but the unbending perspective also left me skeptical that an appreciation of art needed to be so restricted.

As an artist by training, I have always approached interior design as an extension of the art world. I am fortunate in that many of my clients have fabulous art collections and allow me to design a room with the art as the inspiration. Terrific art can do as much as architecture to make a space; similarly, bad art in an otherwise beautiful space can cause it all to come horribly crashing down. Truth be told, I would rather my clients have amazing art with simple furniture than the other way around.

In my role as a professional interior designer, I am often asked to buy art. I am more than happy to oblige, but I implore my clients to participate in the endeavor. Every collector has to start somewhere. I urge clients to see, think, and ask lots of questions. One should visit art museums, talk to gallerists, read voraciously, and then tuck all the information away in a quiet crevice of the brain. In the end, what matters most is to buy what you love,

as the best collectors have a genuine passion for each and every piece they purchase.

Most people I know who make that first art purchase begin a lifelong love affair; art has the effect of turning people into collectors. Perhaps it's because art collecting presents a rare opportunity to show another side of your personality. Don't let that conservative exterior fool you; some of my most traditional clients are enthusiastic buyers of Marilyn Minter.

Price tags do not define the value of a piece. I have many prints and drawings by up-and-coming artists that stand their ground against far more famous pieces. One word to the wise: avoid fads. Fads typically aren't born of passion, but rather of a herd mentality. Let your heart guide your selection.

Art and interior design should always be in conversation; like any couple, each needs space and air to relate well to the other. They can't be in competition, nor should there be a hierarchy in the relationship. The art will often take the role of provocateur, as it never fails to elicit emotion. Art is not wallpaper that someone might walk by and ignore, although I might argue that some wallpaper is amazingly close to art. Fine art will transport you to another place, and you will know that it's fine because you will find yourself quite happy to be taken there.

Alain de Botton calls art "useful, relevant and above all therapeutic." He argues certain great works offer clues on managing the tensions and confusions of everyday life. I agree. Art provides very real clues that give a period in history—including our own—its richness and texture. Art is a statement about the world in which we live, as is the space in which we eat, sleep, play, and exist.

A soaring gabled ceiling and a white color scheme create a serene, monastic atmosphere in this Marin County home just outside of San Francisco. Two breathtaking works of art, an Yves Klein table and a canvas by Callum Innes, create the alchemy.

Lighting

 JAN SHOWERS

Have you ever noticed how lovely everyone looks in the glow of candlelight? That's because any light that illuminates only the front of the face–including the rising sun in the morning and the setting sun in the late afternoon–is magical. This type of lighting avoids creating the harsh shadows that overhead lighting can bring.

There are certainly instances when overhead lighting is useful, but in general, ambient light is flattering light. A silk or linen lampshade allows light to diffuse through the shade, providing a gentle glow, while a thick paper or metal shade gives light that is dramatic but harsher.

Many years ago, Shirley MacLaine won the Oscar for her stunning performance in *Terms of Endearment*. That same year, she came to Dallas to receive an award from the USA Film Festival. I was on the board of the festival at that time and had the opportunity to sit with her and chat. She simply looked stunning! So I asked her how they aged her for the movie because she looked at least fifteen years older in the film. Her answer came immediately: "Lighting, my dear–overhead lighting is how we age actors in Hollywood." MacLaine went on to say that if we could all walk around with lighting that lit our faces, we would look at least ten years younger.

Have you ever noticed how actors' or actresses' eyes seem to sparkle in films? That's because they know where their key light is and that if they are standing or sitting on their marks, the key light will do its magic.

What is a key light? The key light is the first and most important light that a photographer, cinematographer, lighting cameraman, or scene composer will use in a lighting setup. The purpose of the key light is to highlight the form and dimensions of the subject.

One thing I always tell my clients is that they should look fabulous in their rooms, otherwise why bother going to all of the trouble and expense? Complementary colors for clients and great eye-level lighting are my two favorite ways to make them look great and feel confident in the rooms we design and create.

I find that clients are often surprised when I suggest that we use lamps on a dining credenza or buffet. Dining rooms are notorious for typically having only a chandelier, which often creates a harsh light, unless it has shades made of either fabric or glass. That is why most people use candlelight for dining. Lamps add much more softness to these rooms and another wonderful decorative element.

Dressing tables and vanities in bathrooms are another place where eye-level lighting is essential. In these rooms, one really needs both recessed ceiling lights above and lamps or sconces to light the face.

Recessed or overhead lighting is necessary, of course, to highlight art and objects and to fill dark areas where there is no opportunity for lamps or sconces. There is an art as well as a science to lighting artwork and objects, so I believe that hiring a qualified and talented lighting designer is a necessity when building or remodeling a house.

Always have a lamp by each chair in a room; this may mean a lamp in between two chairs. (There should also be a table by a chair to set a drink or cup on–there's nothing worse than having a lonely chair with no light and no table.)

Mirrors are a brilliant way to bring eye-level lighting to any room, as they create a window on any wall on which they are placed. The use of glass also creates a glow in any room that nothing else can reproduce. Groups of interesting glass objects that are well lit by

This dining room is lit by eye-level lighting from the lamps on the credenza as well as by the French chandelier over the table. There is also recessed lighting focused on the fine Murano glass vessels that are the centerpiece of the table.

directed recessed lighting are another way to bring pleasing light to faces.

The power of inspired lighting, so often underestimated, is the secret ingredient that enhances our painstaking creation of rooms that suit our clients' individuality as well as their needs. It is the design element that softens and beautifies, casting client and interior designer alike in the most positive light possible.

One of the seating groups in the main living area of this home has the advantage of natural light provided by the window behind the settee and the glow from Murano glass floor lamps. The antique mirror and mirrored commode reflect light into darker parts of the room.

Textiles

KATHRYN M. IRELAND

It's a mistake to underestimate the role that textiles have played in domestic decor through the ages, not to mention in everything else, from warfare to religious sacraments to political celebrations.

Textiles are ubiquitous for a reason: they pack a punch, concealing imperfections or highlighting a sublime form. Even Michelangelo, renowned across centuries as a cranky curmudgeon, revered textiles—see his extraordinary sinuous marble drapery on the *Pietà*. One might say fabrics are ephemeral, while the bones of everything else endure. But that only tells part of the story.

It's actually thought that woven cloth predates Jesus by more than 5,000 years. Originally, woven fibers were used for simple clothing as well as storing food and portable provisions. But it didn't take long before textiles were being adapted for other uses. From the immortal ethereality of the Shroud of Turin to the storytelling of the exquisite Bayeux Tapestry, from iridescent Indian saris to vibrant African head wraps, fabric communicates our history and culture. It tells our stories in bridal trousseaus, christening gowns, hope chest linens, camp blankets, campaign bunting, parachute silk, mourning crapes, and funeral shrouds.

Textiles are the first thing I notice about a room: What is on the walls? How are the windows treated? Are the draperies for privacy, sun protection, or atmosphere? What types of textures and prints happily coexist?

Great fabrics can lift the room's mood every bit as much as a good curry or Daube Provençal can lift a person's. It makes me giddy to install a series of interiors with colors and textures that don't appear to go together but have a unique relationship to one another once in the same space and ultimately fill its inhabitants with joy and enthusiasm, comfort and élan. In my own surroundings,

I take risks with the interplay of prints and weaves. Having my own printshop allows me to play when developing new colorways and designs. Creating a successful room is all about the interplay and arrangement of prints, patterns, and solids on pillows, sofas, and drapes and how those textiles mingle with the artwork, the furniture, and the carpets. The right combination of all these things in a room is magic.

I am an unapologetic iconoclast when it comes to designing and employing textiles in my work, and while I know there are rules about corresponding weights and hands and complementary colors and whatnot, I just can't abide any sort of edited menu. I want a quiver stuffed full of options. My childhood souvenirs from various trips abroad were always examples of Ghanaian patchwork or Scottish tartan, Japanese watered silk or Irish linen. Seeing the pleasant jumble in my drawer taught me that you never know what delight a happy accident might yield. I love velvet at the beach and in the desert. I love silks in the snowy north and carmine-red chintz in the breakfast room and peach toile on the library walls. One should never be afraid of the implausible impulse if it strikes the right note. Trope and cliché only garnered those connotations because those solutions were tame and overused.

For me, textiles convey time, place, and even mystery, and it's all wrapped up in a sensual power punch that takes you somewhere you want to go. The layering and juxtaposition that I love is not unlike the dialogue between portions of an orchestra or between the coyote and the moon. Textiles are fantastic pieces with a myriad of disparate references and inflection points that together create moments of poetic enthusiasm, bawdy humor, or tender calm. Interior designers are not musicians, but they can knock you over with an intricately beautiful symphony of textiles.

This great room is in a former cow barn in Ojai, California, that was turned into a residence in the 1930s. White stucco walls are the perfect backdrop for a heady mix of textiles and patterns on the upholstered pieces. The chandelier is original to the house and was forged on the property.

Books

ROSE TARLOW

I am surrounded by books. When asked where, whom, or what continues to inspire and inform my aesthetic the answer invariably can be found in my treasured reference books, books which I have consciously collected throughout my life. For designers, architects, artists, and any creative persons, the vast amount of information found in books is the foundation for much that inspires us and forms our unique way of seeing.

Thankfully, many books are easily accessible to anyone with the thirst for instruction and inspiration. There is an abundance of knowledge to be gleaned through the march of design and architecture through the ages. There are new movements in architecture and furniture design throughout history. We study the works of luminaries such as Alvar Aalto, László Moholy-Nagy, Le Corbusier, William Morris, and Frank Lloyd Wright, to name just a few. If we did not have books to consult and consort with, we would have little visual or spiritual knowledge of the past. Books are the foundation with which we continue to build, form, and feed our own inventiveness—gifts to enhance our own personal creativity.

My books provide inspiration when I need it. They are also the best possible form of decoration. A room without books is a room that lacks some visual portent of intelligence. In my personal rooms books naturally and quite simply contribute to the beauty and serenity that nurtures and enhances my daily life. Here are some of my favorites.

The first book on design, *The Decoration of Houses*, by Edith Wharton and Ogden Codman, was published in 1897 and is an example of how design had begun to evolve and simplify.

Today's Parisian icon, Andrée Putman, revived the recognition of such twentieth-century talents as Eileen Grey, Mariano Fortuny, and Jean-Michel Frank, as well as others of this genre, as found in Putman Style, by Stéphane Gerschel.

In Mario Praz's extremely respected 1981 volume, *An Illustrated History of Interior Decoration*, he provides us with brilliant interiors in paintings and works of art from the Renaissance to the twentieth century.

In my library is a group of books depicting wonderfully modern interiors presented through very sophisticated watercolor renderings. Originally published by the German company Jules Hoffman in 1927, these books are unfortunately out of print and invaluable if you can find them. Most of the eight volumes are in German; a few were reprinted in English. They are called *Decoration in Color* or *Farbige Raumkunst*.

Among my other rare volumes are Percy Macquoid's *A History of English Furniture: The Age of Oak, the Age of Walnut, the Age of Mahogany, and the Age of Satinwood*, originally published between 1904 and 1908. Various out-of-print editions are available. They make an invaluable find for furniture designers.

It may still be possible to have a bookseller find the four very large volumes of *The English Interior*, by Arthur Stratton from 1920. This is an amazing source of inspiration for me.

Some of the aforementioned books are not easy to locate, so I will name a few that are still in print today, such as William Kent's 2013 work *Designing Georgian Britain*. New volumes depicting the works of Andrea Palladio are being printed and reprinted constantly. I always recommend students of interior design read Nancy Mitford's highly enjoyable biographies, *The Sun King*, *Madame de Pompadour*, and *Frederick the Great*. They are an excellent introduction to the lively courts of France and the style of living that incorporates the structure of those interiors.

An old circular staircase, found in a Paris flea market, was carefully reinforced to reach the sleeping alcove above Tarlow's studio. The skylight illuminates the polished plaster walls, which hold a collection of books in niches.

A collection of the designer's books on architecture, casually arranged on wooden shelves, stands near a window that looks out to the garden.

RIGHT: Ample morning sunlight streams through three sets of French doors in the library of Tarlow's home in Los Angeles. A desk and chair provide a spot for reading, drawing, or painting.

Bookstores everywhere are closing at an alarming pace. Will our own portfolios and books on design be available to be studied by architects and design students in the years to come? It seems very possible that one day libraries will be considered antiquated and dusty relics of the past. Sadly, this may be the natural way of evolution as the world turns. I feel it is our duty to treasure our libraries and preserve them for future generations who may never experience the rich resources that the past has to offer. It's something we take for granted because it's so easily accessible: a simple book!

Provenance

THOMAS JAYNE

The sentence "This belonged to my grand-mother" can trigger both delight and terror in my heart. Perhaps no other provenance—a fancy word for the history of ownership—conveys such power. Yet rooms without a single personal object are often soulless to my eyes, even if very beautiful.

When I am fortunate, a client's family treasure is something of great beauty. On one happy occasion, a patron proposed the use of his grandmother's Picasso. Now it hangs in his New York library on medium green strié walls with brown velvet sofas to flank it. In contrast, I have my grandmother's ungainly, if not ugly, Victorian bed. The headboard and its robust machine carving might, to most cultured eyes, tip it toward the junk heap. Still, I have used it ever since I could have a real bed, and it is always one of my greatest challenges to place it in a setting befitting my career as a New York decorator. Over the years, I have made it work by contrasting it with beautiful objects and strong colors. One of its best incarnations was when it sat in my sparsely decorated all-white loft against a big square of yellow painted on the wall. From this bed I have learned that homely objects must be of the highest sentimental value to use in an interior. Of course, ideally, possessions have both a memorable history and beauty.

Another bed I own is the perfect nexus of beauty and history: it is a daybed, French circa 1830, veneered in fruitwood and neoclassical in style. I bought it at Christie's for our New Orleans apartment. When I was at the auction viewing, my old friend and mentor Albert Hadley appeared, as much of the sale came from his longtime client Jane Engelhard. He decorated her house in preparation for a visit

from the Duke and Duchess of Windsor. I can still see him placing a hand on one of the bedstead's round finials and saying, "This is the bed the Duke used." I was already planning to bid on the daybed, so this distinguished provenance just added value for me.

Provenance can also lend credence to the historical significance of an object. The best examples in my career are a client's collection of Matisse prints, some of which were owned by Andy Warhol, and a John Singer Sargent picture that the artist kept for himself. Both have the endorsement of famous ownership or a "good" provenance.

Over the years, I have learned to be careful not to discount clients' possessions casually. I always ask if there is a sentimental reason they are keeping something that will not fit into the decoration I imagine. Early in my career, this caution was cemented when a patron asked me to use an unassuming blanket chest covered in dated chintz and yards of passementerie. We simplified the upholstery to match its basic nature by using a beautiful printed linen and simple trim, then moved it into her newly decorated room. Some time later, she made a special point to thank me for using the piece and making it worthy of her new interior, adding that her father had made it for her mother before his untimely death.

It is good to remember that a personal provenance begins with the purchase of every object of decoration. In my career, I have bought and placed hundreds of antiques and decorations. Hence, I trust one day a client will bestow some precious object I helped her select on a grandchild, and the grandchild will offer the fine provenance that it once belonged to her grandmother.

A Picasso portrait from the artist's Blue Period, inherited from the client's mother, speaks of the early twentieth century, as does the beautiful Aubusson carpet from the same period. A pair of graciously proportioned armchairs and a matching sofa are covered in a cinnamon velvet and trimmed with bullion fringe.

Sometimes it makes sense to retain a piece of furniture based on provenance, as with this quirky carved bed, originally owned by Jayne's grandmother. The yellow square assigns pride of place to this dissonant note in the loftlike bedroom.

OPPOSITE: In the sitting room of the designer's New Orleans apartment, late-nineteenth-century German wood-block prints of carnival characters hang above a daybed once slept on by the Duke of Windsor. The art deco lamp was once owned by automotive executive and fine arts connoisseur Walter Chrysler.

Craft

BRAD FORD

What gives a room soul? The people who occupy it certainly do, but there are other elements at play that contribute to the intangible feelings of quality, beauty, and personality that possess truly remarkable spaces. Handcrafted pieces carry with them the stories of the people who made them: a history of the craftsperson's skill, a record of his or her effort, and an expression of his or her creativity.

Indeed, to sit in a handmade chair—its wooden legs turned on a lathe, its leather upholstery sewn stitch by stitch—is to be enveloped in the maker's creative energy. One might think of it as a type of currency built into a piece; if a certain amount of energy is invested into it, that same amount still exists in the final product. As in physics, energy can be neither created nor destroyed, but it can change in form. For the owner of handmade pieces, appreciation builds over time as a relationship of sorts develops and new details are discovered. Imagine a room with only manufactured items; it would be undoubtedly more sterile than one with even just a single carefully crafted vase, chair, bowl, or table. The value of these pieces and the work behind them far exceeds any dollar amount.

When what started as necessity—building furniture to sit upon or sculpting vessels to hold water—became more focused on the decorative, the artistic value in these pieces was unleashed. To pick up and feel a handmade object, whether it's furniture, glassware, pottery, metalwork, or textiles, is to literally feel its quality and idiosyncrasies.

Natural materials—wood, clay, leather, wool, or plant fibers—play a sizable role in defining artisanal pieces. My work is largely influenced by nature, perhaps in part thanks to a childhood spent in Arkansas, surrounded by lakes, rivers, mountains, and forests. The earthy quality of handcrafted items feels familiar and good to the touch. These attributes are then

A sinuously curved sofa by Vladimir Kagan, a pair of vintage swivel chairs, Michael Coffey's Satan's Tongue table, and a pair of vintage André Sornay cabinets all illustrate the value of craftsmanship in this Manhattan apartment.

An illuminated vertical "vine" sculpture by Jeff Zimmerman, a vintage Dunbar sofa, Kagan's floating ottoman, and Wendell Castle's Wishbone chair all rest on an undulating rug.

bestowed upon the rooms in which the pieces are placed. Simply put, they make for warm and approachable interiors. Humans are very attuned to nature, instinctively responding to organic materials. In large cities where there is a dearth of green space, natural textures are needed even more; they ground us, make us feel comfortable and even safe, literally bridging the gap between natural and built environments.

For me, the strong belief in integrating handmade works into every interior is quite personal. I've always been drawn to the art of craft. As a small child, I scoured the encyclopedia to find things to make. When I was a little older, my father put together a woodworking shop in a barn behind our house where he would make anything from clocks to large pieces of furniture. I would watch him work, fascinated by the tools, the process, the smell of sawdust, and, of course, the final result. Watching him gave me an appreciation of the time, technique, and care that went into everything he made. Over the years, as his skills and confidence developed, his works became more complex, exemplifying the dedication and passion that goes into true craftsmanship.

But the appreciation of handcrafted pieces is wholly subjective. What resonates with one person may not with another. For me, the artisans who took bold strides and whose work has enduring impact range from furniture designers Wharton Esherick, Sam Maloof, George Nakashima, and Wendell Castle to ceramists Eva Zeisel, Gunnar Nylund, and Lucie Rie, who each took the functional aspect of his or her craft and spun it into something much more beautiful: works of art.

Craft, unfortunately, is often undervalued when compared to fine art; even the words convey a different meaning. The work of artisans is sometimes seen as more casual, lacking in the same level of finesse needed for "true art." But the attention to detail, the high level of skill, and the artistry involved, equate the two in my mind. If there is a shift in thinking, the vision for an entire room changes; when the focus on what is special or what adds personality is not limited to the artwork alone, each piece in a room, fine art or craft, offers an opportunity to add dimension and character, in essence adding meaning.

Unlike mass-produced goods, artisanal pieces express the vulnerability and humanity of the craftsperson—an imperfect beauty that's indelibly noted in the art of interior design. A layer of soul and simple luxury comes with things that are lovingly crafted by hand; this legacy continues as the piece ages, develops a history of its own, and moves forward through the generations.

The focal point of an understated bedroom in this sun-filled apartment is a vintage René-Jean Caillette credenza. The photograph hanging above it is by the postmodernist James Welling.

Alchemy

GLENN GISSLER

Alchemists have existed in every major civilization—along with great artists and artisans—all engaged in an attempt to transform base metals into gold. Similarly, a good designer possesses a knowledge of elements that when amalgamated create magic in an interior.

Two of my favorite elements are fine art and objects.

Every surface of an interior is important, but the alchemy of design comes into play when the designer introduces and orchestrates fine art and objects, humble or precious, simple or ornate. Art in the interior is the great transformer, the secret formula for achieving superlative design.

The selection and placement of art in an interior is extremely important, possibly the single most important decision a designer will make. You can arrange and rearrange things almost infinitely, creating fresh, startling design perspectives and tableaux. The talismanic power of an object is enhanced by its position and the objects adjacent to it. The whole, forged by the intuitive selection and arrangement of objects in an interior, is exponentially greater than the sum of its parts.

I often assist my clients in purchasing art—in some cases forming the nucleus of their collection—and I emphasize to them how important it is to mix things of great value with other kinds of artifacts. I encourage clients to buy the very best art and objects they are willing to afford, but caution that if everything they purchase is at the highest level, the provocative potential—the poetry— of juxtaposition is neutralized.

The quality of interior design cannot be quantified; it does not have a price tag. Art and artifacts evoke a moment in time. It doesn't matter if it is "original"; it might be a nineteenth-century plaster cast of a Roman bust or the real thing. A beautiful object possesses an aura, an energy you cannot fake.

Art and objects alone do not make the room, although they may ignite its magic. The culmination of all the endless design decisions can be the most perfectly understated background, giving the illusion that nothing, neither heavy-handed nor weak, was done. The designer must learn to distribute resources to create design alchemy, a process which need not be enormously costly, but may pay great dividends to the client in the future in terms of increased value. Yet this is merely a fringe benefit: the presence of art creates an added value. Clients of relatively modest circumstances may be willing to spend a surprising proportion of their money on art and objects simply because they perceive their incalculable aesthetic—and even spiritual value—in the interior.

Seeking visual relationships between artifacts of different eras and places is important to the alchemical process. A gifted photographer will uncover an affinity between two things that may have escaped me, see something I haven't yet seen, as in the white, curving swathe in the middle of Richard Avedon's photograph of Dovima and the elephants and the adjacent tall, white, curving vase on the mantelpiece. Sometimes between like and unlike, there is a hidden correspondence, as in a "fancy" gilded X-legged Regency stool that is nevertheless clean and modern in its lines, which might be felicitously juxtaposed, say, with a modern gold-leafed Carlo Scarpa vase. Although sometimes I transmit my own sensibility to my clients, I am always open to the inspired object, be it Bauhaus or Baroque. The fascination of form is to be found in all eras— all styles—but there is one caveat: eclecticism in the wrong hands is permission for chaos.

Everyone seeks rooms that are inviting and pleasurable, designed for living life in

Pared-back silhouettes, tactile surfaces, and an artful ensemble— including Richard Avedon's iconic portrait of Dovima, primitive pottery, and an African mask— create an aura of magic in this Brooklyn Heights dining room.

all its complexity and depth. Art and objects may cause a visitor to pause; they may, at the same time, prompt an inhabitant to see a new visual relationship, previously undiscovered, a dense web of relationships and resemblances, an interior world endlessly enriched and enriching. And the result is pure gold, brought forth by design alchemy.

Marking the transition between the living room and dining room of this Upper West Side apartment in Manhattan is Frank Gehry's Wiggle chair, which echoes the curves of the Danish rosewood pedestal table. Hervé Van der Straeten's Tornade lamp and a vintage Italian armchair by Guglielmo Ulrich speak to the Austrian midcentury chairs in the dining room.

Art

BRIAN J. McCARTHY

The Venetian plaster patterned sand and ivory walls of this house in Florida draw inspiration from African Kuba cloth textiles; they serve as an architectural background for seminal works by Adolph Gottlieb (left) and Helen Frankenthaler. The Jean Royere coffee table is topped with travertine. The pair of modern lamps (the client's own) feature wavy brass and brown enamel stripes.

Several years ago, I was engaged to design the interiors for a David Adler–inspired house in California, one with a clean-lined classicism overlaid with 1930s-style glamour. The residence featured a long central hallway with a sweeping staircase on axis with a library, and I wanted to place an element beneath the stair that would serve as a focal point. Initially, I had an eighteenth-century Italian center table there, but it did little more than occupy space and act as decoration for the sake of decoration. Then, inspired by my clients—avid collectors of modern and contemporary art—we replaced the table with a 4,000-pound stainless steel egg by artist Jeff Koons. The effect was transformative. The wittily surreal object contrasting with its traditional surroundings created a magnetic moment that defined and vitalized the space, while capturing the character of my clients and their passion for collecting. In so many ways, that simple, telling gesture connected the dots.

In the prewar years, forward-thinking designers viewed interiors as holistic environments in which the integration of art, architecture, and decoration produced a single aesthetic idea—for example, the Fifth Avenue apartment that Jean-Michel Frank designed for Nelson Rockefeller, balancing the architecture of Wallace K. Harrison, decorative objects by Diego Giacometti and Christian Bérard, and Rockefeller's exceptional art collection. In the 1960s and 70s, the relationship between art and interior design began to balkanize—typically, once the decoration was completed, the art would be hung where it looked best. And as my Koons experience revealed, if a decorator considers art to be as central to a project's success as the fabrics, finishes, and furniture, the outcome can be something that goes beyond conventional decoration. Happily, many of my clients today are knowledgeable collectors

for whom art remains a central component of their lives. Their receptivity to letting artwork inform, or even drive, the pattern, color, texture, and scale of their homes is having a transformative impact on contemporary design, both reaching back to an earlier period and pointing the way to the future.

In fact, art can help solve challenges that might resist the usual design gambits, as was the case in a house I decorated in Florida. The size of the living room—thirty feet square, with a twenty-six-foot-high ceiling—made it intimidating, and we were searching for ways to create an alternate scale, through decoration and furnishings, that would humanize it. My clients had purchased one of Picasso's cubist canvases, which we planned to install above the fireplace, and it compelled me to consider that particular moment in art history and cubism's aesthetic underpinnings, African tribal art in particular. I wanted to create a two-dimensional panel effect on the walls, and I began developing a layered design based on a Kuba cloth that played off the period of the Picasso. The result introduced an exotic, casual pattern that made the room much friendlier to inhabit and more interesting in terms of finish.

Many of my clients are enthusiastic about working directly with artists, a process that can invigorate interiors while making them unique and very personal. There are a number of individuals I greatly admire, and with whom I frequently collaborate: Philippe Anthonioz, Louis Cane, Saint Clair Cemin, Patrice Dangel, Miriam Ellner, Claude Lalanne, Helene de Saint Leger, and Bill Sullivan, on everything from furniture, lighting, and sculpture to doors and staircases, and the experience is invariably revelatory. A creative interpretation of a functional element blurs the boundaries between fine art, architecture, and design, of course, but it can equally transform the artist's

own sensibility, pushing it in unexpected directions that are then channeled into more personal work. With all of us—artist, decorator, and clients—influencing one another, the outcome is an aesthetic tree branching in multiple directions.

Integrating art into the interior design process can be beneficial in multiple ways. When I have clients who are more traditional, an infusion of contemporary art can give a heartbeat to a home that keeps it current. Frankly, it keeps me on my toes. I am often called upon by clients to offer a second opinion regarding art purchases, and I've learned to look beyond overt art-historical references (even if well done) and nose out creators who speak in an original voice. Above all, bringing art into design—which means looking and looking, with curiosity and without judgment—enables me to keep an open mind, not get stuck in a particular style or period or pigeonhole, and learn from things that might not conform to my taste. I have a client who collects sporting art, and although the work isn't what I'd choose to live with, I have enjoyed immensely seeing how it has enriched his interiors and his sensibility. In turn, his collection has enabled him to appreciate my personal taste: whereas he used to crucify me unmercifully for a lack of culture, he now comes to my home and marvels at how the art transforms the spaces. It's not his thing, but he genuinely enjoys the experience.

That critical leap from "I hate that" to "I appreciate that" is a game changer for which art is an excellent vehicle—in collecting, interior design, and life.

In a living room on Long Island, New York, a painting by Sophie von Hellermann titled *Please Don't Forget to Tip the Waiter* holds court above the sofa. On the old-fashioned easel is *Untitled, 2009,* by Josh Smith. The room's pale blue–and-ivory palette was inspired by the art.

Sourcing

 EMILY SUMMERS

Peter Lanyon's *Blue Round Corner* hangs in the living room of this penthouse in Dallas. The pale periwinkle of the cushions on the T. H. Robsjohn-Gibbings Klismos chairs pick up colors in the canvas, while the warm tones of the sofa, throw pillows, and carpet provide a counterpoint.

My designs are on the spare side. I embrace the modernist anthem that less is more, meaning less clutter and pretension and, instead, more open space surrounding carefully selected furniture and decorative arts. The result is a certain balance and serenity when each piece is in sync with the space and volume of a room. Spare designs, therefore, must be assembled thoughtfully.

As a fine-arts major in college, collage was my favorite technique. Today, that translates to my interiors. I think of each room as a collage with every object having a function, not only in how it is utilized but also in how its shape, scale, tone, and texture contribute to the overall conversation within a space.

Sourcing the building blocks of these collages has introduced me to some of the most skilled artists and designers of the twentieth and twenty-first centuries. It is clear that the creative mind knows no boundaries when design and function meet.

Methods for navigating the world of unique furniture and decorative arts have grown exponentially since the advent of the Internet. For me, however, it always begins with my collection of books about design, art, and architecture; my library is a major resource for every project.

Before the Internet, furniture selection included frequent trips to local antiques shops as well as showrooms in Dallas's Decorative Center and manufacturers' catalogs. As an ardent follower of the Bauhaus, the Knoll and Herman Miller catalogs were my bibles.

Travel greatly expands search possibilities. Exploring museums, period homes, flea markets, and antiques and design stores are all part of my practice. Trips to Vienna, Glasgow, London, and—especially—New York and Paris have introduced me

to the most knowledgeable decorative-arts dealers in the world. There is no better training ground for a student of design than the shops along the Left Bank in Paris. No online search or catalog can offer the same experience as being able to actually touch, for example, a straw marquetry screen by Jean-Michel Frank or an eggshell mosaic table by Jean Dunand. I love the thrill of the hunt. I once discovered the dismembered discarded prototype of a 1966 Bernard Rancillac "Elephant" chair in a dark and dingy basement in New York.

With fairs and exhibitions more numerous than ever, an interior designer can be exposed to dozens of dealers in just one weekend. Annual modernism shows have become mainstays for me, and such events have popped up in nearly every major city in the United States. The Palm Springs Modernism Show now brings more than 100,000 people to the California desert each year, and Design Miami has been added to South Florida's ever-growing art fair, Art Basel, indicating that patrons want their furniture and decorative arts to keep pace with their fine-art collections.

The International Contemporary Furniture Fair in New York is a command performance as well. On display each May are the latest in contemporary design, emerging technology, and the pure potential of the creative mind. At the 2005 ICFF, I was dazzled by the "Cinderella Table" prototype by Jeroen Verhoeven. His virtual design sliced 741 layers of plywood 57 times, turning a lowbrow industrial material into an exquisite eighteenth-century form. Today, that table is in the permanent collection of New York's Museum of Modern Art, London's Victoria and Albert Museum, and Paris' Centre Pompidou. I still agonize over not buying that table the moment I saw it.

Technology now helps the consumer as much as the creator. The current online marketplaces offer the designer unprecedented access to auctions and other sales around the world. The addition of design categories to sales at major auction houses like Sotheby's and Christie's points to this increasing interest in furniture and decorative arts for collectors' homes. As the line between art and design becomes more blurred, auction houses like Phillips are incorporating fine art and design in a single sale: a Donald Judd wall-mounted stack is now sold alongside a Judd side table.

No matter the myriad exciting ways to source innovative design, sophisticated interiors still need to be assembled quite carefully. That is why I always return to the ideals of twentieth-century designer John Dickinson, who maintained that a room is finished when you can no longer take something away without it being missed.

In this expansive Dallas home, the view of the garden is as exciting as the room one can view it from. A Swedish rug informs the room's palette, and a pair of leather armchairs by Josef Hoffmann harmonize with two white leather-topped side tables by Jacques Adnet.

Color

MARIO BUATTA

Every color is potentially beautiful, provided one uses it in a fitting context and harmonious combination. The colors of the houses and apartments I've lived in and designed comprise an adventure into the myriad moods a full, bold spectrum has to offer. Color should be an expression of happiness.

While growing up, the only color I vividly remember was white—tinted with a dab of color—in every room of my parents' house. The living room had a hint of pink; the dining room a tinge of tan, and on and on. My bedroom had a hint of blue and a Mondrian-inspired rug in browns, tan, and cream that was there until my sixteenth birthday, when I was allowed to decorate the room to my liking. Rebellious as I had become at that point, I envisioned the interior of a barn, with dark brown walls, a cream ceiling, and the interior of my closet cherry red. The painter looked at my mother and said, "It will look like the inside of a barn."

She agreed with him but let me do it anyway.

Grounding my bedroom with wall-to-wall carpeting in hunter green and typical maple-wood furniture, I went on to furnish it with early American antiques, lighting, and objects. By the start of my twenties, I had filled my parents' attic and basement with more of my finds. Eventually, I would get a grown-up apartment in New York City and experiment with many color and pattern combinations.

Looking back, my parents' art-deco style was not my taste. Their living room, tinted pink, had a chartreuse silk mohair velvet–covered chesterfield sofa with tan silk bullion fringe and two dark brown satin-covered square pillows in each corner. Tan and brown upholstered chairs sat on a rust-colored plush velvet carpet. The curtains, in a gold-and-brown Deco leaf weave, hung from steel poles with mirrored finials.

At age ten, I remember being wowed by the combination of blue, white, and yellow in my Aunt Lily's kitchen. I asked my mother why we didn't have those colors in our house, and she whispered, "Too Irish."

Well, Irish or not, I've had that combination in my last two apartments.

The real turning point in my life happened when I was a student in Paris with the Parsons School of Design under the tutelage of Professor Stanley Barrows. During our earlier visits to the postimpressionist painting galleries at the Musée d'Art Moderne in 1961, he exclaimed that if we didn't understand the use of color as Henri Matisse, Pierre Bonnard, and Édouard Vuillard did, we would never make good decorators.

I am grateful that I took the advice of Professor Barrows that day; it changed my outlook on using color in my career. I never forgot that lesson, and in later decades Color Field painters like Mark Rothko, Kenneth Noland, and so many others have carried the torch of using color in new and exciting ways.

My first apartment was an L-shaped sitting room–bedroom. I painted it all eggplant, right down to the crown moldings. The fabric at the windows was an English floral chintz I used in four later apartments against walls in banana yellow, silver tea paper, pistachio green, and pale blue. As it was windowless, I painted the kitchen off-white with a pale blue ceiling to bring in the sky, and the bathroom dark blue with a blue-and-white shower curtain featuring a zebra print and citron Turkish towels. The effect was a happy mix of nature's colors.

In interior decoration, colors set the mood of a house and therefore require deep thought. I always advise clients to think of setting the entry in a color from nature, for example, pale blue for sky, pale green for a park vista, tans for the beach, or yellow for sunshine. Bringing

Cheerful sherbet colors abound in this Manhattan apartment owned by a financier and his wife. A pewter-colored barrel-vaulted ceiling caps the space, which is decorated with Buatta's signature floral chintzes, stylized leaf prints, and geometrics.

the outdoors in can be a great success in city environs, whereas in the country, neutrals like grays or tans give relief to the bright mix of color in your garden.

Using these prescriptions, you then start moving from room to room applying different colors—none to be repeated!—making sure that they correspond to the way each room in the house or apartment is used. For example, paint a library or den a dark color such as brown, red, or hunter green to create a cozy setting. The same applies to a family room or upstairs sitting room. Make sure that colors proceed from nature's neutrals to mood-changing tones that suit the various spaces.

There isn't a shade or color I've ever seen that I haven't liked. Sometimes I think I was born under a rainbow, but with no illusions of finding the proverbial pot of gold. Then again, the inspired and thoughtful interior designer, one who is willing to immerse him- or herself in the miraculous world of color, may find gold in a pot of paint.

Salmon pink, cinnabar red, the palest blue, and a dash of cheetah print meld to create an unexpected and slightly exotic room in this apartment, which was once owned by American design legend Sister Parish. The silver tea paper that lines the walls acts to ground an otherwise riotous mix of color.

271

Gray

LAURA BOHN

When it comes to interior design, gray, like any color, goes in and out of fashion. But from the beginning of my career gray, in all its guises, has been the color—or, more correctly, noncolor—I'm most passionate about and the one I've probably used the most. It's an unfailing classic that, for me, is always in style.

My love affair with the design possibilities of gray started when I was a young child in postwar Texas, where my super-stylish mother installed dark gray carpet and a pink sofa in our living room—a scheme that raised many suburban Houston eyebrows. A few years later, when I was applying to be a couture house model at Christian Dior in Paris, I'm not sure what I found more dazzling: the fact that I was interviewed by Marc Bohan himself or the Avenue Montaigne salon's impossibly chic and enduringly famous pale-gray-and-white decor. Often dubbed Dior gray, the pearly shade is actually *gris Trianon*, named for the exquisite little eighteenth-century château at Versailles where it was used extensively; the couturier adopted it as an exemplar of Louis XVI style, which he adored.

Those early impressionistic lessons were superseded by formal instruction at the Pratt Institute, where I studied in the late 1970s under the legendary designer Joe D'Urso, famed for his iconic high-tech interiors. Of course, his achromatic spaces, with their glossy white walls, black leather and chrome furniture, charcoal carpeting, and gunmetal industrial accoutrements, were an inspiration—a master giving permission to a novice to splash her favorite noncolor around. But more importantly, under D'Urso's demanding tutelage, I learned how to think about color architecturally, as an integral part of the design rather than mere decorative embellishment.

I was taught to approach every project as a fundamental question of space—how to create it, control it, organize it, expand it,

shrink it, energize it, tame it, make it bend to our will. Clearly, color is an extraordinarily powerful means of achieving those ends. But I noticed almost immediately that gray was a very potent player in the game of manipulating space and that, unlike some brighter hues, it never got loud, aggressive, or abrasive. No matter what shade—wispy and pale or dark and brooding, cool and aloof or warm and welcoming—gray always remains soft-spoken, tranquil, and restful. Despite its name and associations, even battleship gray is peaceful, not belligerent; storm clouds may be ominous and threatening, but their color is soft, calm, and deep.

Gray's conquering-lamb quality was really brought home to me when, as a student, I began to visit jobsites with walls of unfinished Sheetrock. Even covered in tape and Spackle, the material proved to be a perfect shade of gray—one that recedes so far into the background it is almost invisible, yet it often defines the space with more authority than the final paint color does. I found a similar quiet power in the raw concrete walls and floors that I saw not only on construction sites, but also in the trendsetting projects of the era's leading high-tech designers.

By the time I set up my own design practice, the vogue was for mostly white environments. While I've done white interiors, as well as used other colors, I've always been drawn back to gray as the predominant tonality in my spaces. I think the best way to describe how I use gray is to compare it to shadows on the facade of a building. No matter how dramatic or subtle, the play of daylight over a structure always seems perfectly integral to the surfaces, volumes, and voids it illuminates or leaves in darkness. Because they are a totally natural and expected phenomenon, shadows can do their work of articulating a piece of architecture—bringing it

Under spotlights, Sherwin-Williams's Repose Gray assumes a crisp character that complements the den's angular architecture and black-and-white photographs by Gordon Parks. Matte porcelain floor tiles and a pair of iconic anodized-aluminum Tolomeo wall lamps contribute to the tailored look.

to thrilling life or, in their absence, leaving it flat and listless—without drawing attention to themselves.

For me, gray works the same way. Like shadows, it's a noncolor that usually doesn't draw attention to itself. It can be anonymous without being faceless. There's nothing wrong with wanting the color of an interior to be assertive and memorable, to paint it deep crimson and call it the Red Room. That's a traditional and legitimate way to think about decorating, but it's not what I'm interested in. I want you to experience and remember the integrated space—the full ensemble of furniture and art arranged within a pleasingly defined, easily navigated volume—not to notice the striking shade of its walls.

Many designers use pure white for the same reasons, but I find it too stark and unrelenting—almost like being under a desert sun with no shade in sight. Gray, on the other hand, is a wonderful chameleon that always seems to be changing its skin tone in order to blend in with its surroundings better. When the light hits certain grays, they can go completely white; others turn black when the lamps are low. In fact, grays are so affected by illumination, either turning cool (blue, green, violet) or warm (orange, yellow, red), that each shade needs to be tested under different light sources. My handful of favorite grays have been put through this sort of analysis a thousand times—by now, I know instinctively which tint will work where. But like Dior, I'm always seeking the same gray: the one that provides a perfect background for the business of living.

The walls in this living room are painted in Sherwin-Williams's Dorian Gray; the color is animated by the changing light but quiet enough to set off an Antonio Murado canvas perfectly. The painting's impressionistic layering is echoed in polished-concrete floors, brown mohair and taupe leather upholstery, and textured throw pillows.

White

DARRYL CARTER

What constitutes a good interior is, of course, highly subjective; beauty lies in the eye of the beholder, or in this instance, the home dweller. In my opinion, what distinguishes a great interior is continuity of vocabulary, and how each space harmoniously gives way to another; hence, my penchant for neutral palettes. I do not choose these as a default, but rather as an ideal backdrop for populating a space that serenely supports all of the design elements. When approaching my work, I place tremendous emphasis on person, lifestyle, sense of place—drilling down to art, fine art, and antiquities, all in the context of the architecture. Shades of white create natural silhouettes emphasizing the sculptural qualities of all of the aforementioned. And with a varying tonality of white, architecture is crisply articulated.

As a lover of art, it is my natural inclination to create spaces that do not compete with the art itself. I imagine this is why most gallery spaces are uniformly white. People often ask if I use color. The answer is, of course, yes, depending upon the client's wants and the space. Where I generally like to see color is on a canvas, or a rug. I often use antique rugs on their reverse as the color palettes become highly muted, and once more defer to the larger composition of a room. Generally, if I am using any color I will take the faintest hue in the rug and try to create a nuanced white of that shade. I dare say I would never use art to inform wall color.

I am very prone to bold gestures, huge canvases, and large overscaled antique pieces placed singularly on a wall, as the white space surrounding makes all of these objects far more outstanding. The punctuation of a burled-walnut or ebonized antique set against a white backdrop creates a natural landing spot for one's eye at the end of a hallway for instance. These punctuation marks appear when thoughtfully adapted to a space much like the punctuation within the body of a sentence.

A white architectural envelope sets the stage for a dramatic sweeping staircase, accentuated by a dark brown banister and treads. The antique carpet has been installed with the reverse side facing up in an act of deference to the stairs.

White is a profound color, and it is unforgiving in spaces that are simply adorned, so one must choose whites carefully. I find myself the subject of much grief in my office when neutral palettes are presented to me for review. Invariably, I will say they are too pink, green, or yellow, and begin to surgically excise the offending hues.

I am highly sensitive to the varying undertones that are an innate quality of any paint compound, particularly the color white. Tonality plays a vital role as one selects textiles that will discretely and harmoniously outfit the home. There is a popular misconception that all whites and neutrals can live together with ease. Whites and neutrals can be more challenging to work with, as there should be an organic color story told. In this context texture plays a very important role in creating a sense of contrast.

When working with textiles this is often achieved by bringing white or neutral linens, velvets, flannels, and leather or suede together in one space. If the assembled palette is well edited and unified, an initial scan across such a space will provide an uninterrupted landscape, with the overall topography being the sum of the parts. The secondary effect will be the drawing of the eye toward the individual pieces, whereupon the deeper layer is revealed, and one sees how each unique texture contributes to the larger assembly.

When working with a continuous palette of white as the core of a space, the experience is that of a unified and meandering sight line, uninterrupted by abrupt changes in color or pattern. The resulting response is always one of calm.

In this Washington, D.C., home, a pair of Renaissance Revival armchairs flank the ornately carved mantel. The tight-backed sofas are custom designs and covered in a neutral, slubby linen. The antique French daybed has bolsters in a muted stripe that echoes the strict linear pattern of the white boiserie walls.

Red

ALESSANDRA BRANCA

I'm not sure when my love for red began, but I was born and raised in Rome, a culture saturated with color in all its incarnations, from the Pompeian reds and cerulean blues of Italian Renaissance paintings to yellow stucco walls dripping with emerald ivy. Red seeped into my consciousness right from the beginning; I found it in the mesmerizing work of masters like Raphael and Titian, the bright red tomatoes in Campo de' Fiori, and even the red earth of Tuscany that's been baked in the sun for centuries. These were all strong influences and became part of me, not unlike my mother tongue or biographical map.

While I love every color of the spectrum, my compass is often redirected to red in all its variations. There is an exuberance about red that makes me happy. To me, red symbolizes passion—passion for history, culture, traditions, family, and even excellence. Many people find red exciting, but I actually find it calming. Some scientists think it's the first color perceived in the womb after black and white, but red is not a single hue. There's sang de boeuf, Chinese red, flag red, alizarin, crimson, coral, and hundreds of pigments in between.

I'm not suggesting bathing an entire room in red, although that's exactly what the great *Vogue* editor Diana Vreeland did. She collaborated with design genius Billy Baldwin in the 1950s to create the "garden in hell," her all-red living room that became one of the most iconic rooms in decorating history. Vreeland once said, "All my life I've pursued the perfect red. I can never get painters to mix it for me. It's exactly as if I'd said, 'I want rococo with a spot of Gothic in it and a bit of Buddhist temple'—they have no idea what I'm talking about. About the best red is to copy the color of a child's cap in any Renaissance portrait."

Historically, red is full of symbolism. It has been known to have protective powers, and warriors painted their faces with red paint to protect them against evil spirits. The red rose symbolizes enduring love and fidelity. Red is the most revered color in China and signifies good luck in much of Asia. Red is festive, red celebrates life, and red is strong. In America, indelible cultural references abound as well. Who can forget the image of Dorothy in *The Wizard of Oz* intently clicking her heels in her ruby-red slippers, or the mysterious Rosebud memorialized in the epic film *Citizen Kane*? We can't help but connect with iconic Radio Flyer tricycles, red cardinals in spring, classic red lipstick, or a shiny red apple.

Red's richness varies immensely depending on the effect of light, context, and material. Blue-based reds and yellow-based reds are worlds apart, and yet they can be mixed with great success in interiors. Paints soak up red pigment like a sponge, and that changes their intensity. Upholster red felt or fabric on a wall, and that same color commands greater attention and depth. Light changes red too, causing it to read differently in every region of the world and in every season. Terra cotta–red walls in a living room in Rome look vastly different from the coral red in the Bahamas, the rugged reds of the American West, and the refined red of a New York City apartment. Texture gets in on the game as well, from the luscious red of mohair velvet to the luster of the lacquer on a japanned screen to the warmth of red fibers in an antique Turkish rug.

To those of you who are dyed-in-the-wool "neutralists," consider a dash of red. This makes a statement even when it's a supporting player in the design—on lampshades, pillows, book covers, porcelain, or a piece of furniture. Think of red like a spice—use it wisely and in good measure, and it will bring zip to your life.

A fantastic grisaille wallpaper from Zuber establishes a cool tone for welcoming guests in the entryway of this penthouse in Chicago. An 1820s English Regency rosewood breakfast table, a pair of Louis XVI–inspired painted benches covered in red velvet, and a collection of midcentury Italian Empoli glass pitchers and vases complete the setting.

Neutrals

MARIETTE HIMES GOMEZ *and* BROOKE GOMEZ

Neutral need never be boring, but neutrals can, in fact, be a bit dull if they aren't used in a proper fashion. The great secret for the effective use of neutrals is subtle layering and variation. We are often regarded as proponents of neutrals, and while there is a history of our love affair with muted tones, our rooms do indeed have colors—they just don't scream at the eye.

The rules for neutrals change according to the room you are using them in. Neutral bedrooms are calming. This use of neutrals carries throughout the entire space, from the wall color to the rug to the upholstery and drapery. We start with the rug and work our way from there, preferring a tone-on-tone plush wall-to-wall carpet as opposed to an area rug, something that meanders through dressing rooms and closets and feels very luxurious.

Neutrals can and should be layered and not matched to add depth to a room. And one must be mindful of using neutrals that aren't too cold. White can feel sterile rather than warm and inviting. Using wood-framed furniture imparts warmth, from a chair to a bedside table. Coupling a wood frame with neutral textured upholstery adds yet another level of layering to the room. Like furniture, lighting can bring color and energy into a space. Carry the color from an antique glass lamp onto throw pillows, bedding, or even leather desk accessories. Using a version of the pale green from a lamp translates well into a shagreen blotter or pencil cup.

Living rooms need light, neutral, and soothing tones, as opposed to the deeper, richer tones of a library or dining room. Libraries call for wood paneling, and dining rooms invite wall colors that add excitement and perhaps a little shimmer for candlelight. In a living room, the layering of neutral tones achieves calm and depth; pairing these tones with varying textures elevates the sophistication of the palette. Again, sprinkling in a color isn't off-limits. Living room accent colors may be a bit more vibrant with these calm colors and should express the homeowner's personality. A shot of Hermès orange or Tiffany blue is relevant and often appropriate. The use of neutrals does not prohibit or prevent the use of color, but we wouldn't necessarily throw a hot pink pillow into an otherwise neutral space. Instead, we would employ a pale blue or celadon, reserving more spirited colors for a powder room, foyer, or kitchen.

A word about white: there are, in fact, a million different whites, and selecting the perfect shade for walls is imperative, for wall color dictates the overall impression of a room. Bathrooms call for a crisp white, yet art collectors may prefer a warmer white wall; art affords an opportunity that needs to be respected and is best presented against a neutral background.

Accessories present a further opportunity for neutral additions, and collections of ceramic vases, glass vessels, or antique boxes will add flavor to any interior. The task here is to highlight such inclusions while maintaining their subtlety. This isn't to say that there can't be a star in the room—for example, a large-scale overhead light fixture paired with a neutral backdrop.

All in all, a neutral palette results in a tailored, cohesive space in which there is much more than meets the eye. Such rooms are appreciated on many levels, as there is always something new to discover. Our challenge as designers is to elevate neutral rooms while imparting an element of surprise and a new, disciplined way of thinking about and using color . . . or the lack thereof.

Cream-colored walls in the entryway of this Park Avenue apartment are the foil for a contemporary stone-and-iron console table that draws its inspiration from the art-deco period. The small bronze figures echo the figure in the work by Lucien Freud.

The living room walls of this duplex on Manhattan's Fifth Avenue hold a surprise: the paneling is actually a trompe l'oeil finish that was original to the apartment. The designers tracked down the artist who originally painted it in Paris and commissioned him to do the refurbishment. Balance is found in neutral sofas, lavishly trimmed with a deep bullion fringe.

Black

KARA MANN

Black is substantial. It is both graphic and intriguingly varied. It straddles the old and the new; it is the link between the traditional and the modern. And above all, it is always deeply glamorous.

Black is not uniform. There are variations that can resonate with warmth or conjure the austere or the luxurious. There are soft blacks, warm blacks, green-blacks, and brown-blacks. From bare matte to velvet, black's textures are equally wide-ranging. Its many variations create warm layers that provide depth and visual intrigue without compromising clean sophistication.

Black's different incarnations provide the intersection where classic elegance can meet a modern edge. In my apartment in Chicago, for example, I used a special mixture of black and brown on Beaux-Arts moldings. This set off the more traditional backdrop and allowed a blend of modern pieces by Christian Liaigre and Hermès to exist comfortably in the same space—an effortless bridge between the old and the new.

While black can make a space recede, it can also highlight its architecture. The clean, graphic lines created by painting certain features of an interior black infuse the space with a heightened sense of drama. At the Chelsea Hotel in New York, I painted the walls lining the grand iron staircase a deep green-black, creating a dramatic passage across twelve winding floors.

Black furniture pieces take on a solid, sculptural mass within lighter surroundings, clearly announcing their presence inside a room. And any black piece of furniture instantly has sculptural mass, a silhouette, and presence. Furniture that is ebonized as opposed to being stained a traditional brown

may work as a kind of three-dimensional calligraphy against light walls. Timeless designs defined in the arresting clarity of clean black lines are another way in which the color brings an edge to the classic.

For a bachelor's New York duplex loft in SoHo, I used deep black liberally to evoke toughness. Deep charcoal Caithness stone on the kitchen floor, a rope-wrapped island by Christian Astuguevieille, and black-lacquer vanities in the bathroom established strength and masculinity.

The next room I want to do for myself emphasizes a color relationship inspired by one of Robert Heinecken's photographic images of a naked woman in a darkened room. It makes me think about black's nuanced relationship with white: against pure white, black becomes too perky and too poppy. I'm more interested in the moody black and white of film noir. A murky purple, a toned-down amber gold, and deep, slightly metallic blue and green all act as handsome accents.

Black rooms have an impeccable pedigree. Think of Mark Hampton's iconic 1971 room: brown-black walls, ivory moldings, and persimmon silk sofas. For fashion designers, from the severe chic of Coco Chanel to the audacious beauty of Alexander McQueen, black is perennially the last word in style. Fashion moves faster than interior design, giving designers an opportunity to draw inspiration from fashion: Balenciaga, Givenchy, Céline. I love taking classic fashion materials and tailoring reinterpretations for today.

Black is synonymous with luxury and mystery. Whether as an accent or dominant color, it transmits a powerful message of art and style in any room.

Wall-to-wall sisal unifies this almost-open-to-the-outdoors room in a brick home in Chicago, while a vintage Khotan rug establishes a seating area near the windows. A tailored slipcovered chair is placed next to a bronze-and-glass coffee table that provides an edge. Black accents include a cabinet by Jean de Merry, granite shelving, and a Sputnik-style ceiling fixture.

Rarity

ERNEST DE LA TORRE

The scarcity of an object has long been the motivation for people to travel great distances, endure hardships, and even go to war over. Whether it was spices, rubies, or scrolls, man's obsession with the rarities of this world is well documented.

In design, the scarcity of an object has been the measure both rulers and religions have used to raise themselves above their peers or define a divine presence. Fabergé eggs are still associated today with the Russian czars, as much as porphyry marble is with the Romans, and, subsequently, with the Pope. Many of these treasures outlasted their patrons, and subsequent generations used them as measures of success and fulfillment.

Through the ages, the great masters like Robert Adam, Emile-Jacques Ruhlmann, and Renzo Mongardino who created timeless interiors certainly used rare finishes and objects but what all of their masterpieces have in common is that they are the creation of a single artist's vision, brought to life with myriad artisans controlled by the precision of a conductor directing his orchestra. While designers may populate their interiors with rare objects, I believe it is the designers' skill and knowledge that creates true rarities.

When I was studying French art deco design at the Sotheby's Institute in London, I learned that those working in the style designed every aspect of their interiors, from lighting to furniture to carpets to textiles, and that was truly how they created a rare and perfectly tailored environment for the client. In today's world, where thousands of chair, rug, and textile selections are a click away, such effort is a lost art.

Using expensive materials is not a measure of rarity. A rare interior is one that is crafted exactly to the wishes of the clients and suits their every desire to perfection while also integrating rare materials and objects. This takes great thought and skill to achieve. I find one

A custom woven-leather-and-linen panel on the wall, with a hand-loomed bedspread to match, contrasts with a Mira Nakashima bed in this stylish bedroom. A pair of Mathieu Matégot reading lights and a pair of coral stone lamps illuminate the room at night.

A large painting by Eric Freeman hangs behind a custom silk sofa, inspired by a Jean-Michel Frank design, in this Palm Beach, Florida, home. The coffee table is surrounded by four chairs in the manner of Émile-Jacques Ruhlmann, and the drum table is covered in shagreen and features a Macassar ebony top.

way to make an interior special is with rare finishes—rare in the fact that only a handful of artisans now know how to execute them perfectly. Subtle at first, they slowly intoxicate owner and guest alike.

Straw marquetry paneling is one such finish. Though special straw reeds are sought out by artisans, it is their skill, not the material, that is rare. Straw marquetry is an art form that has been practiced for centuries; Renaissance artists used it to make precise pictures with very thin pieces. Jean-Michel Frank then brought the art form into the twentieth century. Very few architect-designers possess the wherewithal to work out the details with the few artisans who still exist today. It's not just the application but the fact that it takes very precise drawings and execution. The end result is a strikingly unique room few will ever be lucky enough to appreciate.

There are other examples of custom applications that may make clients feel special and give them a room all their own: hand-plastered walls, custom embroidery, delicate hand-painted or embroidered wallpapers, and carved and gilded glass. Some clients respond to more lasting elements, like hand-forged bronze metalwork or custom-designed micro-mosaic marble floors. Whatever the elements used—precious or humble—the owner of such a home feels a special tie to his or her environment that reflects his or her individuality.

Today, true rarity resides in the creation and possession of an architectural and decorative environment that has been orchestrated and executed using artistic vision and artisanal precision. Such an environment is greater than the sum of its parts; its aesthetic unity transcends the rarity or value of any one object or artifact it may contain.

INSPIRATION

Inspiration

No element of the design process is more important to me than finding true inspiration. In all the years I have been a creator of interiors and furnishings, I have developed my own eye for seeking out those special moments of inspiration that lead to a space, a table, or a color palette.

The world is an endless source of inspiration; all you need to do is take the time to experience it. However, inspiration is *not* imitation. It is not simply re-creating something you have seen; it is about taking something you have experienced and allowing it to filter through your own aesthetic sensibilities so that when it emerges, it comes out new.

A good example would be the discovery of a beautiful antique chair in a Parisian gallery. Taking a photo of the chair and sending it to a workroom to be reproduced is just that, reproduction. Now, there is nothing wrong with having an eye for objects worthy of reproduction. There are plenty of talented designers who have built careers on a discriminating eye. On the other hand, to be *inspired* is to study this chair and really look to see what makes it so special. Is it the proportions, the finish, or the details that capture your eye? Now take the elements you find interesting and use this understanding to create a chair that is new but has a vital connection to the source of inspiration.

Inspiration can come from anywhere. I think too often we are trapped inside the walls of our own surroundings, too busy to discover what's going on right outside our front door. Getting outside is the best tool any creative person can give him- or herself. Over time, you will find that your eye is quick to discover those things that help motivate and inspire you.

As a designer known for simplicity in furnishings and palette, I find that each project is its own unique canvas, and the process of designing should begin with a clear vision and direction. Having said that, not every project presents wonderful elements to inspire or build upon. In fact, some of the most exciting houses I have worked on have come with a need for thoughtful review of what is worth keeping and what needs to be removed.

A good example of this is a project I completed in Southampton, New York. The house was 100 years old, and the classical Shingle Style exterior was brilliant. The problem was that the interior of the house had suffered from years of multiple owners performing renovations unsympathetic to the handsome architectural style of the exterior. As I looked to renovate the interior using the existing architecture as my foundation, I felt that I needed something extra to inspire the interiors.

While walking the spectacular grounds of the house, I was struck by the beauty found within the gardens. I decided to make the gardens my inspiration for detailing the interior. Within the vocabulary of classical style, I brought various garden elements into the interior architecture and furnishings. Floral ceiling details in white plaster and wall panels in treillage patterns infiltrated the traditional aesthetic of the house. Carpets and decorative wall treatments quietly introduced elements residing just outside the windows.

There are certainly many projects that do not arrive with existing sources to inspire your design direction. A very special client presented me with a large amount of raw square footage that was contained by two slabs of concrete. When I arrived at the new site, the only element I had to work with—other than lots of space—was a series of large windows with breathtaking views of Manhattan's Central Park.

I needed to generate an idea, an inspired vision of what this empty space could be. I immediately imagined the Hollywood films of

The dining room of this Southampton, New York, home was designed to evoke a gazebo adjoining the renowned gardens. The ceiling was inspired by the white dogwood trees just outside the windows and features a delicately meandering branch of blossoms realized in plaster.

ART + ARCHITECTURE OLSON SUNDBERG KUNDIG ALLEN ARCHITECTS

the 1940s that presented glamorous New York apartments with large windows looking out to beautiful skylines. I used that imagery as a tool in designing a serene, modern oasis elevated high above the city. Taking cues from the sleek, idealistic interiors of midcentury Hollywood designers such as William Haines, I began to build an interior that was inspired by those old films but remained true to my contemporary vocabulary of simplicity.

There are endless stories of using inspiration to ignite designs. The most important thing to remember is that each of us views the world through our own unique lens. The key is to find your way of interpreting the things that surround you and knowing where to plant your focus. If imitation is the sincerest form of flattery, then inspiration fashions mere influence into the seed—the flowering—of creation.

Inspired by the Hollywood films of the 1940s, this grand-scaled and glamorously modern apartment on Central Park South has commanding views of the park and the upper half of Manhattan. It houses the clients' modern art collection, which includes the sculpture by Isamu Noguchi on the pedestal at right.

Jazz

SANDRA NUNNERLEY

If you were sitting with me in the living room of my New York apartment, here are a few of the things you would see: a 1930s Jean-Michel Frank chair, a twentieth-century black lacquered Royal table by Maison Jansen, an Ethiopian chief's chair, a Richard Serra painting, a Louis XIV console stripped of its gilding so you focus on the beautifully carved wood, a 1970s Italian acrylic side table, a pillow made of hand-loomed silk fabric from a trip to Burma, and a sculpture made out of sardine tins that I picked up on the side of the road when I was in South Africa.

There is no logical reason why these objects should be together—other than the fact that I love them all. But if I had to explain how I designed this room, I think the simplest, most vivid way to describe it is *jazz*.

While studying architecture in Sydney, I worked at an art gallery owned by Kym Bonython, a remarkable man with a passion for jazz. He arranged concerts and brought all the greats to Australia to perform. I remember Duke Ellington kissing my hand and Thelonious Monk playing the piano on one of Kym's rollicking harbor cruises. My eyes and ears opened wide to art and music, thanks to Kym.

There's a freedom in jazz that's completely exhilarating. It's about improvisation and the ability to react spontaneously, to invent and explore. I like to think I've applied the same freedom to design. I draw my inspiration from cultures around the globe and free-associate among things from all sorts of places and periods.

Yet just as a piece of music starts with a score, I start with the architecture of a house. You have to get the bones right first before you can play off them, just as a jazz musician riffs

on the written notes. In my own apartment, I had to gut the place, combining two adjacent units on the fifth floor of a turn-of-the-century Carrère & Hastings townhouse. The front apartment had exceptionally high ceilings, and I couldn't wait to take down the walls so I could create a large, square, classically proportioned living room, to which I added classical details such as custom-made crown moldings and baseboards. In order to get the fireplace to work, I had to rebuild it with a low firebox. A large classical mantel would not have worked since the opening was so short and squat. Instead, I designed a minimal bronze surround and hung a tall, rectangular mirror above it to give the whole composition the proper scale. I designed a long, low sofa that can seat six easily and built it into a niche. And then I began to play, arranging my eclectic collection of chairs and objects, placing a Maori war club next to a Kenneth Noland painting. That kind of juxtaposition is what jazz is all about.

I knew I didn't want to give up any space to a formal dining room—that's not my style. When friends come over, it's much more fun to dine anywhere we like. The Jansen table usually lives by the front windows, piled with books, but I'll often roll it into the center of the room for a dinner party. That way, we can stay right by the fire on a cold, wintry night. I love that kind of flexibility. It's an idea of change and movement that comes straight out of jazz.

When jazz musicians are jamming, you don't have any idea where they're going to end up, but that's half the fun. Dream and then decorate. Be spontaneous. When you're on a roll, it's a great feeling . . . and a great ride.

A myriad of furnishings and art establish a riff of cross-cultural fusion in the designer's Manhattan home and include a painting by Richard Serra, a Louis XIV console, and Italian Lucite tables from the 1970s.

Classical Music

MICHAEL SIMON

Two art forms often complement and correspond to one another in parallel fashion. I discovered this in a most personal way.

Long before my work in interior design, my formal education was in music composition. Consequently, my design process mirrors that of a composer. Since music exists in both real time and psychological time, composers must create a vocabulary that enables listeners to comprehend their "language" and remain invested in that expression of emotion for the duration of the piece, whether it's solo, chamber, symphonic, or operatic.

Composers frequently limit themselves to a handful of ideas, small cells that can be characterized as leitmotifs and are easily recognizable to the ear. If the cells are well developed, the listener perceives the sound world that the composer has invented. Consider Beethoven's famous four-note theme in his Fifth Symphony. His illustrious refrain is continually repeated, expanded upon, disguised and embellished through musical variation. Beethoven's deceptively simple four notes inform an entire sound universe that carries the listener through a series of sensations from beginning to end. Each movement builds upon the themes and multiplies exponentially into a cohesive entity, where the whole is greater than the sum of its parts.

These same theories apply to the design of a home. In my own practice, I likewise confine myself to a handful of ideas or cells—two-dimensional and three-dimensional—that are systematically manipulated and realized in the form of textiles, carpets, furnishings, objects, and a myriad of other components. Cells are created by developing distinctive markers that inform the entire design. I restrict myself to an economy of thinking because too many ideas can clutter the strategy and undermine the purity of the interior. These cells can be inspired by almost anything: a pattern, a texture, a quality, a shape, or a color.

Three decorative elements—stone, plaid, and corrugation—inspired a recent project in Arizona. I explored the potential for variation that lay dormant in these components to create a visual atmosphere based solely on these ingredients. In analyzing just the stone, I chose six different qualities of limestone—pitted, sand-like, fossilized, etc.—and installed them in a series of horizontal courses on exterior and interior walls. Then, when using glass for the facing of a chimney breast, I found six varieties that shared the qualities found in the stone. The limestone was dense and flat; the glass—luminous and reflective—created an almost orchestral counterpoint to the stone. I had the reverse sides of the glass treated with palladium leaf, gold leaf, moon gold, mica powders, Japan paints, and other precious materials that served to enhance the sensibility of the stone without directly mimicking it. For the pattern of a tone-on-tone rug, I simulated the swirling tessellations of the sandy stone and then adapted the rug design for the eglomise decoration of the breakfast room wall. The stone derivatives continue to appear throughout the residence in subtle repetition.

My clients are remarkable for consenting to journey with me as we identify the voice for their dwellings. Since many of the components must be created, time is spent sampling and fabricating keynotes, or fundamental constructs that proliferate while the project unfolds. Once the voice has been established, the process gains momentum and develops unique rhythm. For one client, the keynote was a hummingbird-and-fret detail on a Chinese Chippendale handrail. We developed these symbols in a variety of media, expressed in numerous configurations and at times unrecognizable from their precursors.

Much like a piece of classical music, this residence in Arizona features variations on a theme. The chimney-breast eglomise and the rug design are derived from six different types of limestone that inspired the creation of varying leitmotifs throughout.

The journey was inspiring and carried great meaning for the clients, since two of their favorite features from a previous residence now formed the decorative underpinnings for their new home.

Just as human cells break off and multiply through mitosis, so, too, can the various elements in an interior. The tiny cells—of form, texture, or color—beget new entities that inform every design decision. To implement a cellular, economic approach, start by identifying details that have meaning for you. The possibilities are endless. In the end, like a powerful piece of music where all the notes are in place, the architecture and decoration seamlessly integrate, and the elements "sing" in chorus. The advantage of this approach is that it is not driven by any particular style or period but stands on its own because of its fundamental simplicity— indeed, its universality.

The family room of this Minneapolis residence employs tricks of scale on a system of grids. Shades of the palest blue and celadon green on the upholstery and walls are grounded by the cream references throughout.

Paris

PENNY DRUE BAIRD

The rooms in this prewar building on Manhattan's Upper East Side, which was designed by Rosario Candela, are voluminous in proportion. The clients, contemporary art collectors, were looking for a classical interior with a bit of an edge: To that end, the ceiling in the center room is filled in with gold-leaf tea paper.

Paris is not just a city; it is also an idea that cannot be defined. Arguably the most visited city in the world–for its beauty, its history, its food, its luxury, and its cultural perfection– Paris, like an intricate dish, has a secret ingredient: its intangible joie de vivre.

For hundreds of years, Paris has been the world's style capital. Parisian design has always influenced architecture, interiors, gardens, fashion, perfume, art, cuisine, literature, sculpture, furniture, and fabrics. Even when the French don't actually invent something, they manage to dominate, as they did with the Venetian mirror industry in the seventeenth century, when they bribed Murano artisans to come to France and teach their trade.

Any student of design knows that Paris has had a profound influence. And yet the most impressive aspect of this influence is that it changes throughout epochs and geography.

When one looks back at the past 300 years, one finds that Paris was a bizarre epicenter. Ornate architecture as seen on buildings and bridges was clearly evident, but the city was an unpleasant place to be. For all its glory, Paris positively stank. However, that did not stop kings from living there, as well as in fabulous country palaces or hunting lodges outside the city walls. The royals were intensely involved in the design of their residences, and they surrounded themselves with the finest craftsmen and professionals of the day, such as Jean-Henri Riesener and Georges Jacob. The royal design became the style of the day, and all the courtiers copied the dictates to the best of their budget. No client was more influential than Joséphine Bonaparte, who worked closely with her architects Charles Percier and Pierre François Léonard Fontaine to forge the Empire style, which abides to this day as the dernier cri in rich simplicity.

This cycle repeated itself until the second half of the nineteenth century, when social and technical changes impacted design in a different way. The monarchy had given way to the Republic, and the advent of machinery transformed the types of domestic furnishings that were now available to the masses.

With the dawn of the twentieth century, social conditions seriously impacted design as well. Women went to work in World War I, and by the 1920s, Parisians had turned toward what was thoroughly modern in design and fashion: the worlds of Coco Chanel and Paul Poiret, Émile-Jacques Ruhlmann and Jean-Michel Frank, Le Corbusier, and Pierre Chareau. This was a time of particularly rich design innovation, which resulted in thoroughly modern lines of furniture and objects using the finest materials.

Unfortunately, this fertile period was cut short by World War II; when the dust finally settled in the 1960s, it was back to the traditional Parisian hôtel particulier, until the 1970s hippie era, which rebelled against almost everything, especially the look of one's parents' home.

Then in the 1980s, haute traditional came racing back, with every Louis in sight. While a few more swings brought us into the twenty-first century, the message remained the same: Parisian decor keeps influencing design, no matter the trend.

There are other cities rich in design whose artistic influences shape what we produce today, but Paris and its je ne sais quoi imbue our world with thoughts, ideas, and feelings all garnered from its history, whether by being there, reading about it, or dreaming about it.

It is impossible to summarize which particular aspect of Parisian life, ideas, and design influence today's designer at any given time or in any given project. For myself, I know that my relationship with Paris affects all that I do, design, create, and value.

A French chair from the 1920s vies for attention with several important works of art amassed by the clients in this off-white room in New York City. On the left is a large-scale painting by Damien Hirst, and a black-and-white work by Hiroshi Sugimoto hangs to the right of the fireplace.

America

JEFFREY BILHUBER

American interior design is not about Federal houses or Colonial furniture, but about a vision marked by clarity and optimism, one that reflects the directness of our society as a whole. To define yourself as an American designer is to do what we do best: to sample, to imbibe cross-cultural influences, to put them together with an optimistic, intellectual, bright approach. American design is not nostalgic, but very much of this moment, of the twenty-first century. My clients want to be current; they don't yearn for another time or place, and as such, American luxury is what's ahead of us, not what's behind us.

American design is grounded in function and based on necessity. One thinks of rooms that work well—form following function—before one even reaches the decorative level of color, pattern, and style. The way we move through space, navigating through society and the world, is mirrored in the fluidity of our rooms, which are about comfort and hospitality more than culture.

In contrast to French houses, where the goal is the constant evolution and enhancement of an unchanging plan, American interiors cull freely from the influences that surround us, orchestrating them in a fresh way. Japanese interiors are based not on function, but on an orderly, admirable placement of objects meant, above all, to please the eye. English interiors are about an immersion in history; it helps that they have four times as much of it as is available to us. And it is near impossible to think of English designers without reference to their brazen competence with color. American interiors, whether Shaker house or SoHo art gallery, in contrast, often have a white background—even when it's not white. We seek clarity and purity.

We are still a very young nation. When we look back to the interiors created by Washington and Jefferson, it is obvious

Dominating a wall in this Manhattan living room is a grid of framed etchings by artist Thomas Schütte. A turquoise ceramic lamp, topped with an emerald-green coolie shade, stands between a Bridgewater club chair and a sofa with contrasting tiger velvet cushions.

OVERLEAF: A vibrant chartreuse tiger velvet covers the armchair and matching tufted ottoman in the library of the same home. Dark, atmospheric walls serve as a counterpoint to the ethereal textile on the Roman shade.

that they drew upon all the sources that the first inklings of world travel afforded them. Monticello, far from being Colonial, is a repository of furniture from France, England, and Ireland as well as significant collections of Native American artifacts and Roman antiquities. There are French wines at an Irish table and English classics in the library: these statesmen went somewhere and brought things back, orchestrating rooms that could only happen in America, that wouldn't exist anywhere but here.

I once asked the esteemed couturier, Hubert de Givenchy, whose apartment and atelier I designed, what the difference was between French and American design. "French design is about refinement; American is sportif. You can't find it elsewhere," he said.

In the future, American design will continue to be up-to-the-moment and responsibly modern as our past moves further away. We work diligently to define ourselves as a forward-thinking culture. One of my very high-profile clients, who owns houses in Paris, Rome, New York City, and other magnificent places, told me he always returns to New York because "it is the city the twentieth century gave us." New York is not a city meant to be beautiful or meticulous—it's belching and smoky, with boxy dwellings—but it's also filled with boundless energy and optimism, with forward movement. New York is the microcosm of America, the reason people come here: to shed the layers, to partake of its energy, to reinvent themselves.

An interviewer once asked the photographer Man Ray how he stayed so ahead of the curve. Man Ray replied, "No I'm not, I'm of my time!" He responded only to the time he lived in. Americans are good at that. We have to create what we want rather than borrowing it. In this country, we have no option but to be modern, of our time. This will become increasingly more important. To be an American designer, you needn't align yourself with the Colonial perspective. We have always been allowed to take from what surrounds us and put it together, with boundless enthusiasm, in new and surprising ways. In the twenty-first century, we will give the world American design.

Automobiles

JOE NAHEM

"We declare that the world's wonder has been enriched by a fresh beauty: the beauty of speed. A racing car [that] . . . is more beautiful than the Victory of Samothrace.*"*

—THE MANIFESTO OF FUTURISM, 1909

For the interior designer consumed with beauty of form and excellence of fabrication, automobile design provides visual inspiration and unsurpassed practical resources. My own interest in cars permeates my interiors, an indirect yet poignant connection.

As a teenager growing up in Brooklyn, I dreamt about buying a new car. Photographs of Rolls-Royces lined my bedroom walls. I worked every day after school and all summer to save up for an automobile, and my first new car was a two-door navy blue Mercedes coupe, 1978 or 1979, with a tan leather interior. I bought it before I even had my own apartment.

I am inspired by the car designs of the 1960s and 70s, especially Cadillacs, Oldsmobiles, and Chevrolets. I am also attracted to the extravagant shapes, forms, and colors—aqua blue, pink—of the 50s. Car finishes enthrall me, as they are beautiful sheaths of seamless, shiny paint. For one of my earliest projects with my late business partner, Tom Fox, we went to Mercedes and bought their paint to use on screens as a silver, metallic finish. At that stage, we weren't thinking about durability—another advantage of car paint—only of the superlative quality of the finish achieved.

Car designers used to mold the fantastically curved, angled, and faceted shapes out of clay long before the advent of computers; determination of the form was essentially a sculptural task. Now we have the ability to make 3D printouts when designing furniture. We create a maquette of a table secured underneath the floor with steel plates so that the curved base can be very slender and minimal. The process of creating stability for an attenuated base is very similar to designing an automobile body; both involve forging a structure that functions while fulfilling an aesthetic imperative. While such design can be dramatic, it is also intensely practical. Just as automobile shape and finish must stand up to years of abuse from snow, rain, and traffic, so must our industrial-inspired furniture designs resist aging and damage.

In another project, we used bronze and resin fused together into an interestingly corroded finish for a set of doors, which reference the metal of cars and the denting that happens to them over time. The result is rugged yet elegant, a combination often evinced by cars. We have also designed screens that are perforated all over, reminiscent of screens by Eileen Grey, and finished them in car paint. I once borrowed the bright lime green of my family's early Cutlass Supreme for the color and finish of a bar. In another interior, we used fluted walnut paneling, echoing the fluting seen on some 1950s cars, to create architectural interest in a space that began as a Sheetrock box.

An appreciation of durable, rugged materials borrowed from industrial design can profoundly inform an approach to rooms and furniture. From the creativity of architects, designers, artisans, and artists working in fields not necessarily part of your own, you can draw upon talent, ingenuity, and verve. As the information age we inhabit leads to a dematerialization of experience, the longing for real, substantial things will be increasingly served by industrial design, whether we find it in a classic Avanti or the long, low lines of a sleek electric car.

Fashioned from stainless steel, this stylish bar in a house in Southampton, New York, is punctuated by a horizontal band of high-gloss green lacquer that mimics the finish of a freshly waxed car. Brightly colored stemware evokes the palette of vintage automobiles.

A quintessentially modern room in this TriBeCa apartment is anchored by a vintage coffee table by American design legend Joe D'Urso; the austere shape has a machinist feel. The Fox-Nahem-designed custom column surround is made of thermoformed Corian with amorphous cutouts.

Fashion

ROBERT COUTURIER

Received wisdom proclaims that what was fashionable yesterday will be fashionable again tomorrow—that fashion proceeds in an endless circle.

In considering the fate of fashions in decoration, for example, eighteenth-century furniture and what happened a few years back to the Biedermeier style—its rapid rediscovery and decline—I am not sure there is any truth to this opinion.

The truth is that in the eighteenth century, when a well-to-do young couple established themselves, they did not use their grandparents' furniture. They simply had built a contemporary house (or what was then contemporary), something clear and brightly lit, with huge windows and full of comfortably upholstered furniture. When their grandparents died, that furniture was relegated to the attic of their townhouse, or it furnished the less elegant dwellings of poor country relatives.

Fashion dominates and dictates which things become fashionable, then less fashionable, and then go into hiding. At the end of the nineteenth century, most bourgeois fashions dictated that one had to have a Henry II dining room, a Louis XIV entry hall, a library with a scattering of sixteenth-century elements, a Louis XV living room, and a Louis XVI bedroom. Contemporary styles still flourished, but a real sign of wealth was the use of antiques. That was the new fashion, a way for the nouveau riche to get a bit of class.

The robber barons built Renaissance-inspired townhouses, filling them with "haute epoque" furniture and covering their walls with verdure tapestries. William Randolph Hearst pillaged and looted Europe, dismantling entire buildings—moving and shipping paneling, coffered ceilings, mantels, and other decorative elements to furnish his newly built castle.

The same elements, and the elegant furniture produced alongside them, today sell for a fraction of what they would have then, and truly for a trifle compared to what the gentleman that ordered them in the sixteenth century paid. There is little chance that anyone today, or in the near future, will decide to furnish his or her house with sixteenth-century decorative elements. These fashions have expired, unlikely to be revived. Such furniture—except in a museum—is destined to gather dust in some forsaken storage bin and eventually disappear.

Some say that in dress, fashions come back. But who has seen, of late, a crinoline make its way down a city avenue? It is the same in decoration. Fashions evolve; they don't repeat.

There has to be a relationship in time between the object and the person who buys it. When I was growing up, there was a lady in Paris who was able to say that her grandfather had sat on Louis XV's lap, so for my parents to buy eighteenth-century furniture was normal. We had always lived with it, known it, sat on it. We had a physical and emotional relationship with it, a familiarity. However, the comfort that our great-grandparents had with sixteenth- and seventeenth-century furniture—which was as remote in time for them as the eighteenth century was for us—was no longer. We could not relate to all the coffers, benches, straight-backed chairs and stools, or enormous buffets. Slowly these pieces were forgotten, put away, discarded. Today there is no market for them, except for the very exceptional ones with a provenance, a history—and these only as witnesses of the past rather than elements of decoration.

As for the eighteenth-century furniture I have bought, loved, coveted, and cherished for so long, it seems to be going the way of the sixteenth-century cassone, (a large decorated chest so unusual today that we have to define it here). It does not matter to me because I am not planning on selling it, but the

Parquet de Versailles floors give this apartment on New York's Fifth Avenue an immediate sense of history, while a contemporary bronze-and-crystal chandelier by Hervé Van der Straeten alludes to a more modern time. A Croco console by Claude Lalanne is tucked beneath a mirror and flanked by custom-embroidered curtains.

received idea that it is safe to buy antiques
as an investment is foolish. Antiques should
be purchased instead for the pleasure
they may bring to us, with their look, or their
personal connection to history.

Ultimately, fashions change as the world
changes. Not only are we ourselves different—
physically bigger and taller—but our lives
are profoundly different as well. Our aesthetics
have become global, and style is shared
instantly around the world at the click of
a button. It's hard to say these days what is
specifically American, or French. But that
only means a broadening of horizons when
it comes to the fashions we choose to share
our lives with.

A sinuous *Golden Ribbon* light
fixture by Ingo Maurer glides along
the ceiling of the library of a house
nestled in the English countryside.
A playful mix of silhouettes
provides a counterpoint to the
stately architecture; the marble
columns and plasterwork at the
hearth are original to the house.

Food

 CARL D'AQUINO *and* FRANCINE MONACO

Shopping on Bleecker Street in Manhattan for New Year's Eve dinner is our ritual. There's no plan or preselected menu. We shape the meal by going to the various Italian specialty shops to buy what is fresh. In this way, cooking is very much like design. How you edit, select, compose, and ultimately serve the ingredients is the creative process.

When we first decided to work together, it seemed simple—shouldn't the interior and the exterior of a structure have a fluid dialogue? Both of us possess disciplines and interests that overlap. Carl, who trained as an architect, found his passion lives within the decorative. Francine is an architect and educator whose interest in the details and materiality of the Italian modernists led her to teach interior design. Our dialogue is much richer than a strict division of decorator and architect. Our two disciplines interweave, and both are subject to reason and intuition.

Our common Italian-American heritage forges other bonds that are hard to break; food is one of them. Yes, there are the cultural landmarks of St. Joseph's Day pastries, Easter bread, and an addiction to pignoli cookies. Our collaboration in the office is similar to the way we cook together: beginning from traditions—learned or inherited—and allowing intuition and originality to influence and enhance the process.

Carl reads about food constantly, devouring cookbooks as though they were novels, but he relies on a couple of tested recipes when asked to prepare a dinner, whereas Francine starts with techniques she learned from her grandmother that have become second nature or works from recipes handwritten by her mother in a small black book.

An underlying understanding and appreciation of tradition imparts a sense of timelessness to any endeavor. Whether you are following a recipe or decorating a room, you must understand the rules thoroughly before you can bend them. Take curtains, for example. When hooked together, handblown Venetian glass links can become a "fabric" that creates a gently swaying ethereal surface brushed with light.

In our work, we may start a project with an underlying ideal, yet never a hard-and-fast one. Like cooks, designers allow their ideas to evolve as they work. There is absolutely an element of chance to both pursuits. For a chef, the discovery of a particularly wonderful, seasonal ingredient from the farmers' market may inspire an entire menu. The designer, like the chef, must be consumed by the beauty of materials, found or invented, "raw" or "cooked," analogous to the ingredients in a recipe. Imagine hand-hewn walnut columns with slender patinated-steel shelves as an element in a library.

The cook shops the market for the freshest and the best available at that time. The decisions are then made as to the menu. So it is with the design of a room. Mock-ups, drawings, and models are "tastings," places to explore novel ingredients and to provide the client with a preview of how a space will feel. A designer spends a great deal of time searching, viewing new and old, improvising with unexpected special finds, and locating the pieces that make a room unique. The perfect lighting fixtures, the texture of the rug, the size and proportion of the objects, and the proportion of the space are what make the recipe complete.

Design, like cooking, evolves and improves over years of experience. It is when one is most familiar with a preparation that one can take creative liberties. A designer's work becomes special when he or she begins to improvise.

This inviting bay window area reveals the story of the house. The stylized motif and colors of the custom coffee table and carpet are the key ingredients repeated throughout the public and private spaces of this townhouse.

Poetry

ANN PYNE, McMILLEN, INC.

"We'll build in sonnets pretty rooms" —JOHN DONNE

I like to think of a room as a poem.

Is the room composed in silvers and silvery whites? If so, it would remind me of lines from Walter de la Mare's poem "Silver": "slowly, silently now the moon, walks the night in its silver shoon." Or is it neoclassical and elegiac, like Matthew Arnold's "Dover Beach," in which case I picture long curtain panels holding their form like the fluting on columns, or a pair of Adam Weisweiler commodes caught in candlelight. Is the room spunky and funny, like an Ogden Nash poem? Or is it arch and odd, like a poem by Emily Dickinson?

Then comes the notion of structure.

Is the room "matchy-matchy," a term some use to deride a room that is conspicuously well-coordinated, like a poem with an obvious rhyme scheme. I love rooms like this, particularly guest rooms and country sitting rooms.

And as to meter, is the meter of the room clipped and obvious? Or is it more casual and conversational, like Walt Whitman's "Song of Myself," suggesting a large, airy room, very democratically arranged with no authoritarian seating groups and lots of room for lolling and meditation.

To take the other extreme, can a room be like a sonnet, strictly organized and formal, with an argument? Here I think of Robert Frost's "Design," the title of which is no coincidence. In the octave Frost describes a design that is entirely white—a white spider, a white flower, a white moth. In the sextet he asks, is this a design of evil? Or is it benign? Can a room ask questions too? I contend it can and should.

"The Canonization" by John Donne is a poem of structural layering, with images that morph from tears into hymns and half-acre tombs. A room, too, can be layered—a layer that is visual (what a beautiful table),

a layer that is practical (what is that table doing there?), a layer that is academic (what is the table's history?), a layer that is sentimental (that table was my grandmother's . . .). Interest in a room is created by the interplay between one layer and another. In "The Canonization," images that initially seem contradictory resolve into something larger than those the poet started with. The tears and moths become "counties, towns, courts"—a virtual empire. So too with the layers of a room—they threaten disruption, but their unity, when achieved, gives the room its power.

As to a room as metaphor, I reference Mrs. Eleanor Stockstrom McMillen Brown, McMillen's founder, and her large drawing room at the Four Fountains in Southampton, New York, which was originally a theater. The room is dominated by a large Dufy tapestry *Circus Horses*—a printed fabric, not valuable— and the poem that occurs to me in relation to this circus metaphor is William Butler Yeats' "The Circus Animals' Desertion."

In short order, the theme assembles its minions: a painting of a clown playing an accordion, isolated on a large wall; an androgynous plaster-work figure positioned on the mantel, hands raised, as if to start a routine; the layout of the room, with circles of activity (library, dining, seating groups); the fact that the room itself had been built as a space for performance. The center table, the Venetian chandelier, the center carpet—all keep the arenas for the room's performers at a distance from one another.

Did Mrs. Brown know this Yeats poem to which I refer?

Whatever the case, to anyone who knew her, there were no alternatives acceptable to Mrs. Brown other than "circus," with "circus" meaning an insistence on elegance, refinement, performance, program, distance, and irony—the opposite of the "foul

This bedroom takes *A Midsummer Night's Dream* for its theme. This bed is the bed of Titania and Oberon, Theseus and Hippolyta, Lysander and Hermia—not to mention Puck. For in dream, we all exchange places, and a happy bower is what we all wish for, and all deserve.

rag-and-bone shop of the heart," the final words of Yeats' poem. Indeed, to anyone who came to the Four Fountains for Mrs. Brown's lunches or small dinner parties, there was nothing more dignified or sophisticated or challenging to the visitor than this space. It demanded to be remembered.

So, what does poetry tell us about a room?

A room, like a poem, offers ways of looking. It provides windows.

A room, like a poem, is also a way of excluding the world, of being private.

A room, like a poem, has authority. Its rhythm, its rhyme, its metaphor system, its tone—these are elements with which a visitor cannot argue.

A room, like a poem, must be understood in time—the time it takes to read the poem from beginning to end, the time it takes to look around the room. To re-read; to re-look. Sometimes, after many years, to return.

A room, like a poem, is an argument against the expectations of the person entering. It forces the visitor to ask, "If this is *you*, who am *I*?"

A room and a poem present the same question. Within the immensity of the universe surrounding us, do our feelings matter, do our constructions matter?

This is a room's greatness, its argument against mortality.

This drawing room is about a love of classical civilization that does not fear the questions such a landscape raises, or the rebukes and misgivings it opens us to. On the parchment top of a small table Pyne copied W. H. Auden's poem "In Praise of Limestone."

Japonisme

 ELLIE CULLMAN

My love affair with the Far East is long-standing, and stems from the two years I spent in Tokyo as a newlywed. Those years were a pivotal step in the development of my aesthetic vision and an important influence on my future career as an interior designer. An entire new world, foreign and exotic, was opened up to me, and I reveled in the education I received.

Of course, the Western world had been awakened to Japan's aesthetic tradition from the moment Commodore Perry's black ships sailed into Yokohama harbor in 1854. And Japonisme has had a profound influence on Western thought and culture, from ceramics to gardens, fashion to food—and especially on architecture and design.

Perhaps the most important arena has been painting. Ukiyo-e prints, which depicted the courtesans of the "floating world," were introduced to the West as wrapping paper on the cargoes coming from Japan. The fragmentation and flattening of perspective and the occasional absence of background of these colorful illustrations were perhaps the single greatest influences in the development of Impressionist composition. During the modern period, the gestural brushstrokes of Japanese ink painting and calligraphy have provided the main influence for Abstract Expressionists.

The Japanese impact on Western architecture is well known. Early visitors to Japan such as Frank Lloyd Wright were much influenced by the rectilinear, undecorated style of Japanese buildings. This, in turn, spread to the Bauhaus, which rejected overdecoration and espoused the Mies van der Rohe philosophy of "Less is more." Likewise, in interior design, the spare interiors of a traditional Japanese tearoom had a huge influence on the new postwar minimalism.

I am hardly a minimalist, yet the three cornerstones of Japanese design—*kazari, wabi-sabi,* and *shibui*—are everywhere in my

This Hamptons dining room epitomizes the subdued beauty expressed by *shibui*. The palette is monochromatic, but details abound. The subtle shading of the silk-and-wool carpet and the muted tones of the whitewashed boarded ceiling are an understated envelope for a painting by contemporary Japanese artist Yayoi Kusama.

work. Striking a balance between these concepts is my ultimate goal.

Kazari is a philosophy of decoration that calls attention to every surface through embellishment and articulation. This concept is made manifest in my firm's work when we highlight and articulate details, particularly with paint and embroidery. With paint, we can lacquer the rails of a bed to add a reflective focal point to a bedroom, gold-leaf the walls to add a layer of light, or plaster-coat and rough-finish a ceiling to add texture and depth. When we embroider the edges of a curtain, we are highlighting the scale of the window and adding subtle shadows to the fabric's texture.

While *kazari* helps me realize opportunities to embellish, *wabi-sabi* asks us to look for perfection and beauty in the imperfect and minor details of everyday objects—to find beauty in what is inconspicuous or overlooked, in what is rustic, humble, and simple. As such, I celebrate the honest signs of wear in antique furniture that speak to the history of objects and the stories they tell about our lives. For example, I would prefer a blanket chest with worn paint rather than a newly veneered one. This is why I won't refinish furniture unless it is really falling apart, and then only with the utmost care.

Finally, the term *shibui* refers to beauty that is subdued, unassuming, and refined. This is not a minimalist statement. I see this as a goal for all of my firm's work, whether a room is filled with antiques and art or just a few strong, sculptural pieces. Even a monochromatic room has subtleties of texture and tone. A room filled with antiques of different periods and origins has restraint and an underlying logic. The stories that every room tells about the people who live there reveal themselves slowly and only with time.

Over the years, I have returned more than once to Japan. Several years ago, on a shopping trip to Kyoto, my husband and I received a rare—but most welcome— invitation for an intimate dinner at the home of a lacquer artisan. As we sat on simple tatami mats, his lovely wife served an elaborate ten-course meal of exotic foods, each one presented in one of his lacquer vessels. We not only had the chance to see how the lacquer is used, but we

also had the exquisite experience of seeing the empty cinnabar and black vessels laid out on the mats as we slowly completed the meal. As I sat on the simple mat, awash in the afterglow of the warm sake and the delicious meal, I became acutely aware of the accidental arrangement of the richly colored pieces, many with gold decoration, in the dimly lit room. This moment was a profound aesthetic experience for me, as I finally understood that the Japanese passion for tradition and craftsmanship elevates all aspects of daily life. This unique Japanese sensibility has, over the years, enriched my life, as I am sure it has for others around the world.

Rather than restoring the worn surface of a nineteenth-century French farm table, we embraced the concept of *wabi-sabi* and celebrated the imperfections of the piece.

OPPOSITE: Parisian master Bernard Dunand appropriated the crane, a Japanese symbol of good fortune and longevity, for this 1940s six-panel cinnabar lacquer screen.

Literature

MAUREEN FOOTER

As a child, I read everything. Books transported me to marvelous and unfamiliar places. The first interior I drew in my mind's eye was Bemelmans's Parisian school, with its twelve little beds in two straight lines; a few years later, it was the Conestoga wagon that transported Laura Ingalls to the Dakota Territory. At ten, I heard Harriet the Spy's footsteps on the parquet floor of her townhouse. In college, I languished in Tolstoy's sitting rooms strewn with half-consumed cups of chocolate and neglected silk shawls, glided through Mrs. Dalloway's drawing room with yellow curtains floating at the windows, and admired the worldly Paris townhouse with "spare sallow gilt" in Henry James's *The Ambassadors*. Inevitably, I conjured dorm rooms and, even more seductively, future grown-up apartments that would mirror these magical interiors. Reading had trained me to visualize spaces, the essential task of a designer.

But novels and biographies offered something else: a catapult into ambiguities, desires, subtleties of character, and vagaries of life beyond one's own experience. Reading augments perspective. It sketches multiple visions of how life may best be lived. And where do we live more meaningfully than in our own houses? George Eliot is a virtuoso on this topic.

Despite its broad canvas and 700-plus pages, Eliot's *Middlemarch* is an intimate study of interior life. While charting the course of young people in search of relevance and passion, Eliot whispers truths about houses. When bohemian Will Ladislaw notes the transformative power of private happiness on the world at large, the author implicitly raises the home from basic need to societal force. Home is the haven that enables our best selves and best efforts. Further, bare-bones domiciles will not suffice. By Eliot's logic, one's house must be aesthetically fulfilling, for beauty is a spiritual need—one so compelling that even a high-minded heroine cannot resist its power.

When sparkling emeralds mesmerize ascetic Dorothea, she realizes that worldly beauty can nourish the soul.

Even with its well-appointed bourgeois homes and stately manors, inherited jewels and expensive horses, *Middlemarch* emphasizes balance, moderation, and scale. In Eliot's universe, like that of Sister Parish and Bunny Mellon, understatement confers distinction. To this, Eliot adds a useful caveat: just as her pedantic Casaubon stifles vitality with rigid dogma, an over-studied room is suffocatingly inhuman. Casual accumulation of ideas as well as objects—what editors call "layering" today—is the natural by-product of curiosity and a well-lived life. And as we also know, but sometimes forget, copying even the most captivating fashion is never to be confused with style: taste, like character, is a personal hallmark and must be earned. While painting on the Grand Tour, Ladislaw refuses to copy the masterpieces of Rome verbatim, signaling his individuality and independence. (So it is no coincidence that by novel's end, he wins the best girl.)

Middlemarch embraces imperfection (even the graceful vicar Farebrother has a weakness for the gambling table, after all) while encouraging dreams and aspirations. Although this makes *Middlemarch* a ravishingly romantic novel, Eliot also quietly endorses equanimity, interaction, and purpose as keys to fulfillment, a classical attitude that gently checks Baroque excess. With its transcendent point of view, *Middlemarch* reminds me what a house must be at its essence: a personal sanctuary.

When Dorothea, at an emotional crossroad, gazes out of her window, she finds solace in the pearly light, in watching the early morning activity in the fields, in the perception of her existence as part of a larger whole. It is the beauty of nature, the richness of experience, and the breadth of human endeavor that counts; our interiors, after all, merely set the stage.

The unabashed prettiness of a shimmering mirrored tent, a Mongolian lamb's-wool rug, eighteenth-century and art deco pieces, Baguès lighting, and sensuous upholstery pays tribute to George Eliot's view that a room is a sanctuary for the soul and the senses.

Travel

MATTHEW PATRICK SMYTH

I have always loved to travel, but I first began to realize how important travel was for an interior designer while I was working for David Easton. David's knowledge of architectural history and the decorative arts is famously encyclopedic—and one of the primary reasons I wanted to work for him in the first place. He has a noteworthy library, but he believes passionately in seeing things firsthand. He's an avid, adventurous traveler.

When I started to explore the world as a young designer, my eye began to evolve in unexpected ways. My first trips to France, England, and Ireland were revelatory. From Gothic to medieval, from Renaissance to Reformation to Enlightenment, the human capacity for creating beauty as I then understood it (like so many young people, I actually thought I knew it well from books and photographs) became much more complex and rich through the face-to-facade encounter. It struck me then that for every designer, the Grand Tour—or any sort of tour, for that matter—is a necessity, not a luxury (though clearly it's that, too).

A formal design education gives us an academic familiarity with the continuum of styles and the essentials of architecture, interiors, and the decorative arts: the everyday tools of design that include proportion, scale, form, floor plans, ornament, materials, and color. To comprehend in any real way how we can transform them into rooms and homes that are greater than the sum of their parts, I think we need to see up close and personal how our predecessors around the world, legendary and anonymous alike, accomplished the same at the highest levels. For me, that has meant visiting historic sites, cities, landscapes, houses, and rooms to witness the extraordinary and ongoing tradition of design. The more I have seen and learned from experience and research, the more I have been able to offer my clients. A city, an architectural marvel, a remarkable work of

A tranquil neutral palette is offset by the rich brown velvet of the club chairs, the zebra-print carpeting, and the blue and coral throw pillows in this apartment on Manhattan's Park Avenue. A pair of haunting lithographs by Lin Tianmiao hang above the sofa.

art, a specific countryside: how can we know, really know, what it is without being there to experience it to the tips of our fingers?

As a designer, the learning never stops. After a career full of extensive travel, I finally went to Athens. As I stood and looked out at the Acropolis from my hotel room that first night—the Parthenon's classical perfection was brilliantly lit in the moonlight—I asked myself why on earth I had waited so long to go there. Contemplating that heart-stopping view and anticipating the days of exploration ahead, it seemed so odd to me that I'd seen so much of the world but not yet experienced the real ground zero of Western design and culture. I love Paris, where boredom is out of the question. New York is my hometown, so I've experienced the city and its influence on design and culture my entire life. But Athens? To be in the city that gave us democracy, the classical orders and perfect forms that we designers continue to reinterpret to this day, the blueprints for drama and opera and politics and warfare, the evidence of a millennia of human activity everywhere around—a city that has itself been a crossroads of East and West, a city where the Byzantine and the eighteenth century exist side by side with the prehistoric and the twenty-first century— there's no place quite like it. Whether or not you're intrigued by today's Athens, you should put it on your itinerary now.

When I create rooms and houses, I sometimes know precisely where the spark comes from for a particular detail. Other times, though, I don't, although it feels right. That's the essence of design. What I am aware of, however, is that my choices come from a collective memory of things I've seen and places I've experienced in person. Whether at home or overseas, travel is my ultimate source of inspiration.

A work by Pierre Marie Brisson hangs above a button-tufted sofa in this New York apartment and informs the room's palette.

OPPOSITE: Curios from travels on this bedside table include a Parisian clock, several tortoiseshell boxes, and an ivory elephant from India.

Couture

CHARLOTTE MOSS

*"We live in clothes the way we live in rooms,
hoping for security, delight and design
that will not age overnight."*

— HUBERT DE GIVENCHY

When the late, great department store innovator Stanley Marcus published *Quest for the Best*, his epilogue featured his "best things" list, which included Chateau Petrus '53, Galanos dresses, *The New Yorker* magazine, London cabs, felt-tip pens, and the linen sheets at Claridge's. The red threads of commonality here are quality, comfort, invention, and convenience; all items describe necessities and luxuries, some that are one and the same. What they also have in common is our desire for the best, our desire to be discriminating and to lead a life where everything is on a par with couture level quality.

Architecture and interior design must also be considered part of this lifestyle equation. The backdrop of our lives, our home should be easy on the eyes, comfortable, luxurious, and inviting. In this context, the role of an interior designer is to deliver a couture ambiance via quality and detail. As a couturier requires multiple fittings and the taking of meticulous measurements, so it goes that a designer could never begin the shopping, searching, selection, and design process for a client without a dossier of information.

The natural and inevitable evolution of our tastes guides us through life. In our search for beauty and our quest for a more dignified approach to daily living, each of us will turn to our own individual methods in creating a curated and couture lifestyle that suits us.

Our homes are our havens, so why shouldn't every aspect be addressed with a

couturier's eye? When an interior designer is involved, it is the close and often intimate collaboration with the client that produces the most authentic results.

The famous decorating partnership of Nancy Lancaster and John Fowler of Colefax and Fowler set a new standard in the client–decorator relationship. They encouraged dialogue at the onset of the project, and both felt that the best interiors were the result of an exchange that included what they called "the minutiae of life." The most beautiful, elegant, authentic, and luxurious interiors could be created only when a client subjected him- or herself to the pair's interrogation. Understanding where someone read his morning paper, ate her breakfast, how often he entertained, how many ball gowns she owned, and where he liked to sit to write letters or read books was essential information that was critical to a successful result.

Dig to discern and question to understand, so that as the designer, you are capable of what Miles Davis believed when he said, "Don't play what's there, play what's not there." That will provide you with an opportunity to create magic.

Matching atelier for atelier, couture and interior design cater to those who demand customization, personalization, and bespoke from stem to stern. In our ever more globalized, democratized, and homogenized world, the demand for this high level of detail and design has only strengthened. There is not a designer alive today who could function without the ateliers and workrooms that produce his or her designs, execute the vision, and collaborate as true partners.

My dear friend the couturier Ralph Rucci speaks poetically and eloquently about his métier: "Couture is the marriage of a designer with his atelier. One cannot exist without the other." I couldn't agree more.

The curtain fabric inspired the wall pattern, which was hand-stenciled by James Alan Smith. The design is a backdrop for the gallery-style arrangement of fashion photographs by Henri Cartier-Bresson, Cecil Beaton, and Lillian Bassman of such women as Babe Paley, Claire McCardell, Coco Chanel, and Elsie de Wolfe.

Dressing a room is like dressing yourself: first is the planning and scheming, then the accessorizing, layering, and attention to detail. Knowing when enough is enough and when to quit is of utmost importance.

Feng Shui

BRUCE BIERMAN

Fire, earth, metal, water, and wood: these primal elements, even in the twenty-first century, compose our world. Feng shui, the ancient Chinese philosophy, is a spiritual science, the study of how to balance these five elements in the rooms, buildings, and landscapes we inhabit. Feng shui teaches us to enhance our daily lives through spatial harmony: the position of a building in a landscape, the design of the building itself, and the placement of furniture and objects in an interior. Through the complementary principles of yin and yang, feng shui strives to create harmony and a sense of well-being that subtly influences our health, wealth, career, and relationships. The philosophy dates back to at least the eighth century and the Tang dynasty, and while a full exploration of feng shui's complexities can take a lifetime of study, everyone can benefit from its basic principles.

The gut renovation of a large Palm Beach apartment provided a perfect opportunity to put into practice the spatial principles of feng shui. On the thirtieth floor of a modern building, the previous tenant had placed a wall directly in front of the entrance, blocking the energy flow—and also a spectacular view of the ocean. I had this wall pushed back by only two feet, but the effect was momentous. Not only did the energy flow improve, but you could also now see from one end of the apartment to the other, encompassing an ocean view and a city view. A wall dividing the kitchen/dining area and the living room was eliminated, creating a single large space now unified by a two-sided fireplace, which brought the element of fire into the center of the home.

We also rearranged the furniture according to the principles of feng shui. The library desk, for instance, was situated in the power position, giving the client an oblique view of the room's entrance, balanced by the view out of an adjacent window. The bedroom was

The harmonious placement of a large color photograph softens the strong lines of the dining room in this Miami apartment, preventing the flow of potentially harmful *sha chi*. The vases of flowers have a similar effect.

OVERLEAF: This colorful room, which faces the Atlantic Ocean in Palm Beach, Florida, is a case study in balancing the primal elements of fire, earth, metal, water, and wood. A large mirror, itself an element of water, reflects the expansive ocean views.

organized along similar principles, with the bed positioned along a wall to the left of the entrance. All clutter was eliminated, which helped clarify thought patterns and allowed the free flow of energy, or what is known in Eastern philosophies as chi.

Feng shui teaches that the world is influenced by energy lines around the globe, which affect one's life for better or worse. When designing a home, one must augment the flow of positive chi, also known as *sheng chi*, in order to bring good fortune and harmony, rather than discord. Harmful chi, also known as *sha chi*, may be caused by too many straight lines in a room, making energy flow too quickly. This is remedied by the harmonious placement of objects or the use of leafy plants that filter and slow the energy flow.

Color in feng shui is a richly energetic factor. Fire is balanced by earth, metal, water, and wood, with each element corresponding to one or more colors. An excess of one element or color creates an unbalanced, disharmonious effect. White is linked to metal; brown to wood; blue or black to water; and taupe to earth.

Another principle of feng shui is to design a space based on the personality and astrological chart of the client. A large Palm Beach house was designed in a traditional vein and featured furniture and fabrics chosen to create a calm oasis for the client. Mirrors, representing the element of water, were used to enhance views and redirect the flow of energy, or chi, in a positive way. Mirrors can also redirect negative energy away from the home. One of the most pleasing rooms was the family room, with French doors on three sides. The room was grounded by taupe furniture and a green patterned rug, symbolic of the earth element, and any potential negative chi was softened by the use of large leafy plants and curtains.

Whatever the project, the basic principles of feng shui cultivate many aspects of our clients' lives and well-being. Even the smallest project benefits from feng shui principles of balance and harmony. The correct positioning of a bed or a desk, of artwork or lighting, may dramatically change the way a room is experienced. The rich, complex tradition of feng shui, implemented for centuries, continues as a major force today.

Cross-Culturalism

JIUN HO

Cross-culturalism, while trendy in literary and cultural studies in the last decades of the twentieth century, is by no means new. This interchange between nations, continents, and cultures has had an inestimable impact on interiors, architecture, and decorative and applied arts.

Homer and Hesiod wrote about the existence of trade in ancient Greece, where pottery, precious metals, and luxury goods were exchanged with Egypt, Asia, and Asia Minor. Connecting the East and West, the Silk Road was central to the trade of textiles and access to China, India, and the Mediterranean Sea. It was also a network of economic and cultural transmission, sparking ideas of unimagined exotic places and peoples. Later, in the fifteenth and sixteenth centuries, newly discovered sea routes directly connected Europe to the rest of the world and propelled the creation of the first global trading community. With each passing century, further geographical advances linked cultures with the past and present in a conflagration of styles (Orientalism and Japonism), manias (Egyptomania, chinoiserie, and Turquerie), movements (Arts and Crafts), and revivals (Greek, Gothic, and Renaissance).

In *Legendary Decorators of the Twentieth Century,* Mark Hampton wrote that prior to the twentieth century, great American rooms (now called "period rooms") were usually designed to reflect an exact moment in history. The twentieth century saw the rise of the importance of personal preferences, a mix and blending as, Hampton says, "style gave way to styles." An anything-goes spirit took hold and has not since loosened its grip.

Materials newly invented or mined from places far and near are also a part of the cross-cultural lexicon and there are endless examples of inspired references. Architects Greene and Greene looked toward the East with joints, pegs, and complex woodwork inspired by

Japanese houses. Historic precedents captured and realized with modern sensibilities have also inspired enduring designs. Who can forget the klismos chair by T. H. Robsjohn-Gibbings, an homage to the grandeur of ancient Greece, or Philippe Starck's Ghost Chair, a sly reinvention of a Louis XVI armchair?

Cross-culturalism is best ingested experientially, though one can easily go to Shanghai, Mesopotamia, ancient Rome, or seventeenth-century France with just an iPhone. Books and catalogs, architecture and design magazines, the theatrical arts, galleries and art museums, and the Internet all provide endless ideas.

Travel is the freedom to discover and to look at things firsthand, and at its best, it should be totally immersive and a little impulsive: give yourself permission to make detours, reroute, and reboot your plans. It is also a chance to live for a while in other worlds and eras and to understand that life and beauty can be malleable. I was born in Malaysia, and childhood trips throughout Asia with my family ignited my interest in design. I have now crossed the globe several times and visited a total of 108 countries. New places and experiences are a great clarifier, revealing unimaginable beauty, which I believe has kept my work fresh, vibrant, and relevant. When I took a bike trip through the Loire Valley in France, panoramic views of Château de Chenonceau and Château de Chambord offered a fairy-tale confection of lanterns, gables, dormer windows, columns, chimneys, and turrets that provided me with the inspiration for furniture designs. Travel has also allowed me the freedom to imagine, innovate, and try out not just new designs, but also new materials, new technologies, and new methods of manufacture. Crossing boundaries has given me the opportunity to study the language of design, for in design the cultural world is one country without borders.

In the living room of this home in San Francisco, a sofa designed by Ho mixes casually with a pair of vintage leather Eames chairs. On the wall is a framed portfolio of lithographs by Spanish artist Antoni Tàpies. The blue-and-white porcelain vase on the study table is Qing dynasty.

Film

STEPHEN SHADLEY

I started working in the movies before I began designing interiors. I grew up in Southern California, where everyday life was touched by the magic of the motion-picture industry. Hollywood and Vine, Grauman's Chinese Theatre, and the acres of movie studios were all part of my daily scenery, and the movies I watched, some over and over, shaped my artistic vision.

My first job was as a scenic artist at 20th Century Fox. One of my very first assignments was to help trace and paint the Manhattan skyline on a massive movie backdrop for *On a Clear Day You Can See Forever*. I spent months learning to paint in precise detail on a grand scale, and I got to see my efforts on the big screen later with friends. A painterly approach to color, texture, and composition still underscores my work today. I don't have a specific style or signature approach to interior design. Rather, my work is an expression of a story.

I often find myself drawing inspiration from the production designs of my favorite films, whether fantastical, as in Wes Anderson's *The Grand Budapest Hotel*, or more literal and contemporary, as in Tom Ford's *A Single Man*. I was drawn to the vibrant and unexpected combinations of color in *The Grand Budapest Hotel*, and its cartoonish characters and lavish sets reminded me of my days at the studios. While watching *A Single Man*, I could almost inhabit the meticulous interior of a still-relevant house from 1949 by noted architect John Lautner.

I love the films of Alfred Hitchcock with their stylish interiors and attention to detail. Cary Grant's stone villa on the French Riviera in *To Catch a Thief* features traditional European furniture and just the right mix of modern to suggest eclecticism. James Stewart's tiny, disheveled bachelor pad in *Rear Window* looks out onto the densely layered,

theater-like set of Greenwich Village, painting an urban existence that is inseparable from the New York experience. And, perched above Mount Rushmore in *North by Northwest*, a mountainside house is portrayed by Hitchcock with a deliberate nod to Frank Lloyd Wright. Though the exteriors were merely a series of hand-painted matte shots, the interiors were carefully constructed, detailed, and beautifully appointed in classic midcentury style. That film was a wealth of inspiration when I did the interiors of a massive timber-and-glass hillside home in rural Pennsylvania designed by architect Peter Bohlin.

A lifetime's worth of James Bond films never failed to set the bar for outlandish and gadget-infused interiors. A continuing catalog spanning more than fifty years, these films are a barometer of tastes and styles. In a more practical way, Diane Keaton's character's Hamptons beach cottage in Nancy Meyers's *Something's Gotta Give* was decked out with an envious open floor plan and perfect kitchen. Though it was just a set on a soundstage, it was featured in *Architectural Digest* and helped define today's standard of an enviable modern, casual lifestyle.

Through my work, I've met inspirational people in the film industry, people with an inherently keen vision of interiors and design. As we placed furnishings and art, Woody Allen would stand and direct from one spot in each room as if he were behind the camera. Jennifer Aniston and I fashioned a serene and intricately detailed home as a refuge from the spotlight. The late Robert Altman used a vintage collection of photographic images silk-screened on towering glass panels to overlap interior vistas, much like his singular style of overlapping dialogue in *M*A*S*H* and other films. Diane Keaton and I have done many homes together, and she is willing to experiment endlessly with an idea until it's

Robert Motherwell's *Throw of Dice #17* features prominently on an intricately paneled wall in the living room of television and film star Jennifer Aniston. A blond baby grand piano provides a counterpoint to the saturated colors of the furnishings, which include a pair of aubergine chairs and a nail head-trimmed console.

right. On one project, a Spanish colonial, hundreds of carefully chosen new tiles were tossed aside in favor of vintage replacements that we spent months accumulating.

Production design in film is a part of our common experience and our visual lexicon. A window on the world, a reflection of so many cultures and eras, real and imagined, cinema can affect how we see the world around us and, sometimes, how we actually want to live in it. Films come and go each year, and yet the stories they tell and the places they portray live on in our heads and spark our imaginations.

The kitchen, dining, and family room are all in one space in this Los Angeles house, at the time the home of film icon Diane Keaton. Vintage 1940s Monterey style furniture sets a mission-like tone. The "California" sign is one of many such pieces Keaton owns; a native of the area, she has always paid homage to the early history of Los Angeles and California. The fireplace was custom designed.

Index

Page numbers in *italics* refer to photographs.

Abstract Expressionism, 68, *324*
Adam, Robert, 22, *132*, 288
Adler, David, *176*, *179*, 260
aesthetics, 18, 25, 222–23
    function and, 35, 82, 130, 136, 170, 310
America, design influence and inspiration of, 6, 22, 25,
    135, 164, 172, 228, 236, 268, 280, 306–9, 342
Angus, Martha, 236
antiques, 126, 154, 222, 230–31
    collecting and stewardship of, *316*, 228–29
    combining modern elements and, 96, *108*, 224
    as design element, *152*, *168*, *229*, 232–35, 327
Apfel, Iris, *172*
architecture, and design, 22, 32–35, 40, 42, 50, 92–95,
    102, 108, 144, *192*, 204, 260, 292, 296
art, *255*, 256
    collecting and curation of, 236–37, 248
    as design element, 35, 68, 150, *152*, 154, 236–37,
        260–63, *264*, 267, 268, 276, 288, 324
    sources of, 264–67
Art Deco style, *250*, 268, *282*, 288, 328
artists, 16, 216–17, 236, 260
Artist's Way, The (Cameron), 66
Asia, design influence of, 154, 164, 230, 342
aspiration, 68–71, 112
Asplund, Erik Gunnar, *95*
authenticity, 10, 12–15, 76, 124, *135*, 140, 198, 230, *230*
automobiles, design influence of, 310–13
Avedon, Richard, 256, *256*

Baird, Penny Drue, 302
balance, 21, 76, 82, 90, 118, 120, 140, 148, 184, 196,
    222, 224, 230, *328*, 338, *338*
Baldwin, Billy, 6, 68, 146, 164, 280
Baratta, Anthony, 144–46
Barrows, Stanley, 268
Barry, Barbara, 18–21
Bauhaus Manifesto (Gropius), 32, 35
Bauhaus style, 28, 256, 324
Beaton, Cecil, 68, *334*
Beaux-Arts style, 40, 214, 286
Bemelmans, Ludwig, *175*, *328*
Bennett, Ward, 6, 58
Beuys, Joseph, 144
Bierman, Bruce, 338–41
Bilhuber, Jeffrey, 306–8
black, as design element, 26, 286–87, *286*
Bohan, Marc, 272
Bohlin, Peter, 344
Bohn, Laura, 272–75
Bonython, Kym, 296
books, 244–47, *246*, 264
Braithwaite, Nancy, 228–29
Branca, Alessandra, 280
Brown, Eleanor Stockstrom McMillen, 6, *320*, 322
Brown, Timothy, 196

Buatta, Mario, 268–71, *268*
Bullard, Martyn Lawrence, 180–82

California, design in, 18, *52*, *136*, 146, 164, *166*, 180,
    236, 242, 260, 347
calmness, 16, 56, 96, 152, 210, 213, 222, 264, 272, 278,
    280, 282, 292
Carrier, Jesse, 140–43
Carter, Darryl, 276–78
Castaing, Madeleine, *175*
Castle, Wendell, 254, *255*
Chanel, Coco, 122, 182, 286, 302, *334*
childhood:
    influence of, 10, 25, 68, 108, 118, 152, 168, 202, 242,
        252, 254, 268, 272, 328
    personalization for, 95, 150
China, design influence of, 338–41, 342, *342*
classical style, 22, *132*, 164, *322*, *333*
clients, 294
    addressing needs and goals of, 26, 35, 40, 46, 50,
        64, 70, 108, 112, 122, 124, 140, 160, 206, 214–15, 241,
        260, 263, 276, 288
    designer's interaction with *see* designer-client
        relationship
    personalization for, 31, 46–49, *135*, 168, 170, 192, 222,
        282, 290, 341
    personal provenance in possessions of, 248–51
Cochran, Anthony, 208
Codman, Ogden, Jr., 6, 25, 244
Coffinier, Etienne, 80
Cohler, Eric, 118–20
Colefax, Sibyl, 222
Colefax and Fowler, 146, 168, 334
collecting, collections, 126, 224, 236–37, 244, 246, 248,
    256, 260
    as design element, 68, 112, 228–29
color, 242, 310, 341
    as design element, 15, 20–21, 74, *132*, 136, 144, 146,
        148, 152, 159, 180, 182, 184, 196, 208, 210, 212,
        268–71, *271*, 306, 330
    light and, 202–3, 280
    see also specific colors
comfort, 22, 110, 146, 156, 168–71, 222
    style and, 168–71
commissions, artists, 216–17
communication, 96–97, 132, 148
    between designer and client, 194, 214
    design for, 170, 221
computer technology, limits of, 89, 98, 221
confidence, 36–39, 130
contrast, 40, 76, 130, 152, 156, 158, 196, 198, 224,
    226, 248, 320
Cooper, Celeste, 194
Corrigan, Timothy, 156–58
couture, design influence of, 334–37
Couturier, Robert, 314–16

craft, craftsmanship, 218, 221, 230, 232, 252–55, 327
cross-culturalism, 28, 31, 82, 306, 342–43
Cullman, Ellie, 324–27
Cunningham, Mark, 76
curation, 236–37
curiosity, *136*, 172, *179*, 228–29, 263

D'Aquino, Carl, 318
de Beistegui, Carlos, 144
Decoration in Color (*Farbige Raumkunst*), 244
Decoration of Houses, The (Wharton and Codman), 6,
    25, 102, 244
de la Torre, Ernest, 288–90
Dellatore, Carl, 6
designer-client relationship, 10, 42–43, 125, 204–7,
    214, 256
    collaboration in, 54, 66, 68, 80, 116, 122, 124, 265,
        298, 301, 334
    personalization in, 31, 46–49, 54, 168, 206, 290
    trust in, 192–93, 208
Designing Georgian Britain (W. Kent), 244
destinations, flow and, 114–17
de Wolfe, Elsie, 6, 164, *176*, 232, *334*
Dickinson, John, 267
Dixon, Barry, 204–6
Draper, Dorothy, 6, 144, 176
Drysdale, Mary Douglas, 102–5
Dunand, Jean, 264
Dunham, Arthur, 22–25
Duquette, Tony, *172*, 172
D'Urso, Joseph, 6, 98, *272*, 313

Easton, David, 28–31, *28*, 328
Eastridge, Katie, 16
eclecticism, 28, 64, *135*, 194, 224, 256, 344
ecological consciousness, 86, 184, 187, 224
editing, 28, 222–23, 232
Eleish, Rhonda, 184–87
Eliot, George, *328*, 328
Elkins, Frances, 6, 164
Engelhard, Jane, 248
England, design influence of, 22, 168, 222, 232,
    306, 328
English Interior, The (Stratton), 244
ethnic influence, 180, *201*, 256, 296, 328
Europe, design influence of, *129*, 224, 342
exuberance, 144–47, 280

Fantasy, style and, 95, 139, 160, 180, 188–90
fashion, 164
    in decoration, 314–17
    design compared to, 54, 122, 124, 182, 334–37, *337*
    design influence of, *179*, 286
feng shui, 339–41
Fiell, Charlotte and Peter, *73*
film, design influence of, 280, 295, *295*, 344–47

flea markets, 139, 232, 244
floor plans, 35, 80–81, 118, 152, 194, 330
    open, 31, 96, 148
Florida, design in, 140, 160, 221, 260, 260, 290, 338
flow, 80, 96, 114–17, 160, 222, 338, 341
Footer, Maureen, 328
Ford, Brad, 252–55
form, function and, 32, 80, 114, 306
Four Books of Architecture, The (Palladio), 118
Four Fountains, 320, 322
Fowler, John, 334
Fox, Tom, 310
framing, 82–85, 98–101
France, design influence of, 22, 28, 132, 154, 175, 224, 232,
    244, 272, 280, 288, 296, 296, 308, 314, 328, 342
Frank, Jean-Michel, 92, 106, 164, 224, 244, 264, 290, 290,
    296, 302
Frank, Michael, 259
function, 28, 132, 184, 221
    beauty and, 35, 90, 130, 139, 140, 145, 170, 310
    form and, 32, 80, 114, 306
furniture, 184
    arrangement of, 118, 146, 160, 338, 341
    restoration and renovation of, 218, 232, 327
    selection of, 152, 156, 264

Gambrel, Steven, 12–15, 15
gardens, 15, 267, 271, 292
geometry, in design structure, 118–20
Georgis, William T., 40
Gerschel, Stephanie, 244
Giacometti, Diego, 224
Gissler, Glenn, 256–59
Givenchy, Hubert de, 308, 334
glamour, style and, 136–39, 286
glass, as design element, 184, 187, 238, 298
"glass box" house, 130
golden ratio, 118
Gomez, Brooke, 282
Gomez, Mariette Himes, 282
Goralnick, Barry, 42–45
gray, as design element, 272–75, 272, 275
Grey, Eileen, 244, 310
Gropius, Walter, 32
Groves, S. Russell, 32–35

Hadley, Albert, 6, 28, 50, 64, 106, 164, 175, 176,
    228–29, 248
Hagan, Victoria, 202–3, 208
Hampton, Alexa, 132–35
Hampton, Mark, 6, 132, 286, 342
harmony, 18, 32–35, 64, 82, 95, 130, 154, 222, 224,
    338, 341
Harrington, Meredith, 192
Hayes, Thad, 218–21
Hays, Tyler, 216
Heinecken, Robert, 286
Heissmann, Harry, 172–75
Hicks, David, 146
Hill, Malcolm, 216
History of English Furniture, A (Macquoid), 244
Ho, Jiun, 342
Hollywood Regency style, 136, 144, 146
"home couture," 206

House in Good Taste, The (de Wolfe), 6, 232
humor, style and, 26, 90, 106, 172–75, 172, 175, 179,
    260, 320
Hunziker, Terry, 198–201

*Illustrated History of Interior Decoration,
    An* (Praz), 244
imitation, 176–79, 292, 295, 328
improvisation, 26, 296, 318
industrial style, 12, 42, 310
informality, 28, 31, 139, 156, 344
innovation, 25, 39, 164, 188, 292
inspiration, 176–79, 202–3, 292–95
instinct, 26, 64, 96, 136, 192
Institute of British Decoration, 22
integration, 32–35, 40, 154
integrity, 56–59
interior decoration, 28, 35, 70, 72
    interior design vs., 102–5
interior design:
    art and science of, 106, 226
    elements of, 227–90
    evolution and history of, 6–7, 22–25, 28
    historical perspective of, 22–25, 86, 102, 105, 118, 126,
        129, 130, 132–35, 139, 176, 184, 216, 222, 228–29, 228,
        230, 232, 242, 302–5, 314, 330, 342, 347
    inspiration for, 291–347
    licensing requirements for, 102
    process of, 152, 168, 188, 191–226
    structure of, 75–120
    style in, 121–90
    theory of, 9–74
    triumvirate of relationships in, 204–7
International Contemporary Furniture Fair (ICCF), 264
International Style, 132
Internet, 6, 28, 216, 221, 264, 342
intimacy, 108–11, 116
intuition, 26–27, 66, 228–29, 256
Ireland, design influence of, 15, 328
Ireland, Kathryn M., 242
Italy, design influence of, 15, 22, 26, 28, 132, 175, 232, 234,
    280, 296, 296, 302, 318

Jacob, Georges, 302
Jacobsen, Hugh Newell, 68
James, Charles, 68
Japan, Japonisme, design influence of, 306, 324–27, 342
Jayne, Thomas, 248–51
jazz, design influence of, 296–97
Jeanneret, Pierre, 232
Jefferson, Thomas, 222, 306, 308
Judd, Donald, 267
juxtaposition, 16, 106–7, 175, 194, 202, 256, 296

Kasler, Suzanne, 122–24
kazari, 324, 327
Keaton, Diane, 344, 347, 347
Kent, William, 22, 132, 168, 224, 244
Kips Bay Decorator Show Houses, 92, 146, 210
Kleinberg, David, 62–64
Ku, Ed, 80

Lalanne, Claude, 172, 175, 260, 313
Lalanne, François-Xavier, 172, 175
Lancaster, Nancy, 146, 168, 334

Larosa, Salvatore, 98–101
Lau, Amy, 216
Lautner, John, 90, 344
layering, 146, 180, 184, 224–26, 275, 282, 320, 328
Le Corbusier, 32, 92, 112, 144, 244, 302
Legendary Decorators of the Twentieth Century
    (Hampton), 342
Liaigre, Christian, 10, 286
lifestyle, 28, 72–73, 96, 130, 145, 222
    authentic style derived from, 12–13
    of client, 26, 156, 164, 168, 170, 214, 334
light, use of, 90, 110, 184, 184, 194, 202–3, 202,
    275, 280
lighting, as design element, 116, 136, 154, 156, 180, 187,
    196, 238–41, 238, 282
Lindores, Kevin, 112
literature, design influence of, 328–29
    see also books; poetry
luxury, style and, 145, 158, 160–63, 226, 286, 334

McAlpine, Bobby, 108–10
McCann, Colum, 76
McCarthy, Brian J., 260–63
McMillan, Inc., 320–22
Macquoid, Percy, 244
Manifesto of Futurism, The, 310
Mann, David, 46
Mann, Kara, 286
Man Ray, 308
Marcus, Stanley, 334
mass production, 302
    craft vs., 218, 221, 252, 255
materials, 198–201, 252, 310, 330
Matisse, Henri, 144, 188, 248, 268
Mellon, Bunny, 328
memory, 52, 140, 188
    collective, 126, 176, 333
    emotional, 26, 96, 112, 116, 168, 230
Messel, Oliver, 15
Michaels, Jayne and Joan, 90
Mies van der Rohe, Ludwig, 32, 112, 324
Miller, Mara, 140–43
minimalism, 56, 130, 140, 144, 184, 324
Minter, Marilyn, 236
mirrors, 238, 241, 341
Mishaan, Richard, 82
modernism, 28, 112, 126, 144, 163, 196, 216,
    264, 313
    classicism and, 106–7, 122, 224
modernity, 130–31, 164, 302, 310
    future of, 306, 308
    glamour and, 139
    in New York style, 21, 126, 308
    traditional style combined with, 122, 126, 256,
        263, 286
Monaco, Francine, 318
Mongiardino, Renzo, 175, 288
Montoya, Juan, 92–95
mood, 180, 232, 268, 271
Morris, William, 222, 244
Moss, Charlotte, 334–37
museums, 228, 264, 268
music, design influence of, 296–97, 298–301
Muybridge, Eadweard, 98, 100
Myers, Timothy Paul, 90

Nahem, Joe, 310
nature, design influence of, 21, 86, 101, 136, 139,
        184, 187, 198, 230, 268, 271, 292, 328
negative space, 16–17, 89, 90
Neutra, Richard, 90
neutral colors, as design element, 280, 282–85,
        282, 285
New York, N.Y.:
    modernity in, 21, 66, 126, 130, 308
    style and design in, 15, 26, 31, 32, 40, 44, 60, 79, 84,
        90, 92, 112, 130, 132, 135, 148, 175, 194, 202, 210, 214,
        218, 224, 224, 234, 248, 259, 259, 268, 292, 295, 295,
        306, 313, 333, 344
Nisbet, Amanda, 26
Noland, Kenneth, 268, 296
nuance, 21, 152–55, 182, 202, 224
Nunnerley, Sandra, 296
Nykvist, Sven, 202

O'Brien, Thomas, 126–29
observation, 18–21, 60, 172
1000 Chairs (C. and P. Fiell), 72
Ortiz, Benjamin Noriega, 72–74

Palladio, Andrea, 15, 22, 118, 222, 244
Papachristidis, Alex, 224–26
Paris:
    design in, 76, 144, 236, 268, 272
    design influence and inspiration of, 132, 232, 244,
        302–5, 302, 304, 328, 333
Parish-Hadley, 28
Parish, Sister, 6, 28, 64, 168, 175, 271, 328
Passal, Robert, 66
passion, 66–67
patina, as design element, 154, 222, 230–31, 232,
        327, 327
pattern, 146, 210–15
Peretti, Elsa, 175
Perez, Enoc, 144
"period rooms", period decor, 135, 342
personalization, in interior design, 46–49, 54, 58,
        66, 95, 122, 168, 170, 176, 182, 204–7, 226, 248,
        282, 288, 341, 342
Personnage en Buste (Picasso), 10
perspective, 72–74, 86–89
Petit, Philippe, 76
Pheasant, Thomas, 292–95
Picasso, Pablo, 10, 176, 248, 248, 260
Picasso, Paloma, 180
Pinsent, Cecil, 15
planes, 112–13
Platt, Campion, 86–89
poetry, design influence of, 320–23
Pollack, Jackson, 66
portals, 82–85, 98, 114, 198
Praz, Mario, 244
primal elements, 338, 338, 341
problem solving, 194–95
proportion, 21, 86–89, 90, 120, 156, 222, 228, 232, 302, 330
    scale and, 92, 95, 146, 148, 204
provenance, 248–51, 250, 314
psychology, in interior design theory, 42–45,
        50–53, 68, 156
Putman, Andrée, 244
Pyne, Ann, 320–22

Quality, 252, 334–37
    value of, 10, 218–21, 232, 256
Quest for the Best (Marcus), 334

Radhakrishnan, Raji, 188–90
Rancillac, Bernard, 264
Ratia, Armi, 184
recycling, 165, 172, 224
red, as design element, 280–81, 280
Redd, Miles, 175–79
Reflection (Houshiary), 10
Regency style, 132, 234, 256, 280
reinvention, style and, 176–79
reproductions, 292
restoration, 218, 232, 327
restraint, 10–11, 25, 28–29, 56, 160, 222, 327
reveal, in design process, 194, 208–9
Rheinstein, Suzanne, 152–54, 212
rhythm, 90, 99, 101, 101
Richter, Gerhard, 196
Riesener, Jean-Henri, 302
Roberts, Markham, 210–15
Robinson, Eve, 148–50
Robsjohn-Gibbings, T. H., 18, 264, 342
Rosselli, John, 66
Rucci, Ralph, 334
Ruhlmann, Émile-Jacques, 288, 290, 302

Sachs, Daniel, 112
Saladino, John, 194, 208
Salvator, Scott, 54
Sargent, John Singer, 248
Saunders, Lauren, 216
scale, 6, 6, 85, 90, 92–95, 98, 146, 148, 156, 196, 204,
        208, 210, 222, 228, 260, 301, 328, 330
Scandinavian style, 74, 158, 184–87, 184, 187
Scheerer, Tom, 160–63
Schrager, Ian, 74
Schwab, Jane, 222–23
Scott, Kathryn, 230
Seandel, Silas, 216
senses, effect of design on, 39, 158, 202, 221, 228
Serra, Richard, 296, 296
Sévigny, Charles, 68
sex, style and, 180–83
Shadley, Stephen, 344–47
sha chi, 338, 341
sheng chi, 341
shibui, 324, 324, 327
Showers, Jan, 238–41
silhouette, 74, 90–91, 316
Sills, Paul, 26
Sills, Stephen, 68–70
Simon, Michael, 298–301
simplicity, 28, 31, 95, 139, 140–43, 164, 182, 184, 222,
        292, 301, 302, 327
Siskin, Paul, 214
Smith, Cindy, 222–23
Smith, Henry Holmes, 16
Smith, Windsor, 96
Smyth, Matthew Patrick, 330–32
sourcing, of design elements, 264–67
spaces, 80, 148, 264, 292
    transitional, 114–17, 192, 198, 259
    welcoming, 156–59, 168, 170

squint test, 86
Starck, Philippe, 74, 342
Stilin, Robert, 36–39
Stratton, Arthur, 244
Stuart, Madeline, 6, 164–66
Summers, Emily, 264–67
symmetry, 76–79, 135

Tanksley, Alan, 114–16
Tarlow, Rose, 244–46
taste, 26, 62–65, 70, 180–83
    personal evolution of, 25, 328, 334
Taylor, Michael, 6, 50, 146
technology, 25, 264, 267, 302, 310
textiles, 156, 160
    as design element, 152, 210, 216, 242–43, 278
texture, use of, 110, 196–97, 198, 223, 242, 280
timelessness, 164, 166, 203, 226, 318
tradition, 40, 132–35, 224, 302, 318, 327
travel, design influence of, 12, 15, 16, 60, 168, 188, 230,
        242, 264, 288, 330–33, 333, 342
trends, style and, 164–67, 314, 316
Tucker, Suzanne, 50–52

Utility, function and, 140, 145

Van Breems, Edie, 184–87
Van der Straeten, Hervé, 46
Vardy, John, 232
Verhoeven, Jeroen, 264
Vermeer, Johannes, 90, 98, 202
Villard Houses, 92, 210
vintage, 18, 126, 136, 140, 164, 165, 166, 168, 310, 310, 347
vintage modern style, 126–29
Vitali, Massimo, 84
Vitruvius, 118, 194
Volpe, Steven, 10
Vreeland, Diana, 64, 68, 116, 280

Wabi-sabi, 230, 324, 327
"walk-in still life," 194
Wanzenberg, Alan, 130
Warhol, Andy, 112, 248
Washington, George, 306, 308
Wearstler, Kelly, 136–39
Webb, Frank, 106–7
welcoming spaces, 156–59, 168, 170
Wharton, Edith, 6, 25, 102, 244
Whealon, Timothy, 232
whimsy, 26, 118, 204, 316
white, as design element, 76, 184, 272, 275, 276–79,
        276, 278, 282, 286, 306, 320
White, Matthew, 106–7
White, Stanford, 106, 107, 210
Williams, Bunny, 168–70
Wolf, Vicente, 60
Wormley, Edward, 28
Wright, Frank Lloyd, 32, 112, 132, 244, 324, 344

Photography Credits

Page 2: Thomas Loof

Page 7: Victoria Pearson

Pages 8, 11: Simon Upton/
The Interior Archive

Pagez 12-13: Eric Piasecki/Otto Archive

Page 14: Eric Piasecki

Page 17: Joshua McHugh

Pages 18-19, 20-21: David Meredith

Pages 23, 24-25: Nick Johnson

Page 27: Roger Davies/Trunk Archive

Page 29: © 2009 Durston Saylor

Pages 30-31: © 2007 Durston Saylor

Pages 32-33, 35: Anastassios Mentis

Page 34: Eric Piasecki

Pages 36-37: Joshua McHugh

Pages 38-39: Manolo Yllera

Page 41: T. Whitney Cox

Pages 43, 44-45: Hector Manuel Sanchez

Pages 47, 48-49: Nikolas Koenig for
Architectural Digest

Page 51: Edward Addeo

Pages 52-53: Photo by Matthew Millman

Page 55: Christian Garibaldi

Page 57: Steve Freihon

Pages 58-59: William Waldron

Pages 60, 61: Vicente Wolf

Pages 62-63, 64-65: Pieter Estersohn

Page 67: Maura McEvoy

Pages 69, 70-71: Photography by
Francois Halard

Pages 72-73, 74: Antoine Bootz

Page 77: Pieter Estersohn

Pages 78-79: Dana Meilijson

Page 81: Bruce Buck

Page 83: Photography by Roger Davies

Pages 84-85: Photography by George Ross

Page 87: Scott Frances/Otto Archive

Pages 88-89: Eric Striffler Photography

Page 91: Eric Laignel

Pages 92-93, 94-95: Eric Piasecki

Page 97: Luca Trovato

Pages 99, 100-101: Scott Frances/
Otto Archive

Page 103: Peter Vitale

Page 104: Angie Seckinger

Page 105: Ron Blunt

Page 107: Antoine Bootz

Pages 108-109, 110-111: Mick Hales

Page 113: Inez and Vinoodh

Pages 115, 116: Peter and Kelly Gibeon

Pages 117: William Abranowicz

Pages 119: William Waldron

Pages 120: Courtesy Kohler

Pages 123: Erica George Dines

Pages 124-125: Simon Upton

Page 127: Durston Saylor for
Architectural Digest

Pages 128-129: Laura Resen

Page 131: Michelle Rose

Pages 133, 134-135: Steve Freihon

Pages 136-137, 138-139: Grey Crawford

Pages 141: Brantley Photography

Pages 142-143: Jesse Carrier

Pages 144-145: George Ross Photographs

Pages 146-147: Mark Roskams

Page 149: Scott Frances

Pages 150-151: Peter Margonelli

Pages 153, 154-155: Pieter Estersohn

Pages 157, 158-159: Eric Piasecki/
Otto Archive

Pages 161, 162-163: Photos by
Francesco Lagnese

Page 165: Simon Upton for
Architectural Digest

Pages 166-167: Max Kim-Bee

Pages 168-169: Ricardo Labougle

Page 170-171: Courtesy Bunny Williams

Pages 172-173: Russ Gera

Pages 174-175: Peter Murdock

Pages 176-177: Thomas Loof for
Architectural Digest

Page 178: James Merrell

Page 179: Roger Davies for
Architectural Digest

Pages 180-181: Douglas Friedman

Pages 182-183: Douglas Friedman/
Trunk Archive

Page 185: Neil A. Landino, Jr.

Pages 186-187: Simon Upton/
The Interior Archive

Pages 188-189, 190: Photography by
Rikki Snyder

Page 193: © James McDonald

Page 195: © 2013 Richard Mandelkorn

Page 197: © Marco Ricca

Pages 199, 200-201: Photo by Aaron Leitz

Page 203: Scott Frances/Otto Archive

Page 205: Edward Addeo

Pages 206-207: Photograph: Erik Kvalsvik

Page 209: Eric Piasecki/Otto Archive

Page 211: Nelson Hancock

Pages 212-213: Thomas Loof

Page 215: Eric Laignel

Page 217: Bjorn Wallander

Pages 218-219, 220-221: Scott Frances/
Otto Archive

Pages 222, 223: Laura Resen for The
Welcoming House

Page 226: Tria Giovan

Page 227: Photograph: Philip Ennis

Pages 228, 229: Simon Upton

Page 229: Simon Upton

Page 231: Ellen McDermott Interior
Photography

Page 233: Max Kim-Bee

Pages 234-235: Joshua McHugh

Page 237: R Brad Knipstein

Pages 239, 240-241: Courtesy Jan Showers

Page 243: Victoria Pearson

Pages 245, 246, 247: Tim Street-Porter

Page 249: Pieter Estersohn

Page 250: William Waldron

Page 251: William Waldron

Pages 252, 253, 254: Scott Frances/
Otto Archive

Page 257: Thomas Loof

Pages 258-259: Gross & Daley

Pages 261, 262-263: Photo by
Fritz von der Schulenburg

Page 265: Scott Frances for
Architectural Digest

Pages 266-267: Casey Dunn

Pages 269, 270-271: Scott Frances for
Architectural Digest

Pages 273, 274-275: Garrett Rowland

Pages 276-277: Max Kim-Bee

Pages 278-279: William Waldron for
Architectural Digest

Page 281: Courtesy Douglas Friedman

Pages 283, 284-285
Scott Frances/Otto Archive

Page 287: Nick Johnson

Pages 288-289: Peter Murdock

Page 290: Photo: Carlos Domenech,
Miami, FL

Page 293: © 2013 Durston Saylor

Pages 294-295: © 2014 Durston Saylor

Page 297: Photography by Giorgio Baroni

Page 299: Christiaan Blok

Pages 300-301: Gwynne Johnson

Page 303: Francis Hammond

Pages 304-305: © 2013 Durston Saylor

Pages 306-307, 308-309: William Waldron
for Architectural Digest

Page 311: Peter Murdock

Pages 312-313: Peter Murdock

Pages 315, 316-317: Tim Street-Porter

Page 319: Michael J Lee

Pages 321, 322-323: Bjorn Wallander/
Otto Archive

Pages 324-325: William Waldron

Page 326: Eric Piasecki/Otto Archive

Page 327: David O. Marlow

Page 329: Photo © Laurie Lambrecht, 2010

Pages 330-331, 332, 333: John Gruen

Pages 335, 336-337: Pieter Estersohn

Pages 338-339: © Dan Forer

Pages 340-341: © Kim Sargent

Page 343: Photo by Matthew Millman

Page 345: Scott Frances for
Architectural Digest

Pages 346-347: David Glomb

Acknowledgments

Without the support and encouragement I received from the interior design community, I could have never realized my vision for this book. I will be forever grateful.

I would like to thank my friends Glenn Gissler, Alexa Hampton, and John Des Lauriers, who first saw the merit in this project and championed my efforts; as well as Robert Couturier and Matthew Patrick Smyth for their generosity of time and spirit at the start.

I would like to thank my literary agent William Clark, for representing me with patience and direction; my editor Kathleen Jayes, for her talent and kindness; my astute copyeditor, Jen Milne; and the book's designer, Susi Oberhelman, who brought its pages to life so beautifully.

I would like to thank Justin Hambrecht, a young man with an old soul, whose enthusiasm for life is infectious.

And finally, I would like to thank Abby Kaufmann, Frank Quinn, Jimmy O'Brien, Patrick Key, Shalita Davis, Erin Larkin, Brian Gorman, and Lisa Zeiger, along with so many others, who by their example cleared a path for me on the road to reinvention.

First published in the United States of America in 2016
by Rizzoli International Publications, Inc.
300 Park Avenue South | New York, NY 10010 | www.rizzoliusa.com

Interior Design Master Class © 2016 Carl Dellatore | Individual essays © 2016 their authors

2017 2018 2019 / 10 9 8 7 6 5 4 3 2

Distributed in the U.S. trade by Random House, New York

Book design: Susi Oberhelman

Printed in China | ISBN-13: 978-0-8478-48904 | Library of Congress Catalog Control Number: 2016938943

PAGE 2: A hanging lantern by Gilbert Poillerat in the entryway of this Manhattan townhouse designed by David Kleinberg illuminates the elegant furnishings, including a French carved marble urn that stands on an English Regency mahogany pedestal. The metal rail was based on a French eighteenth-century iron railing and was custom made for the project.